Poetics of Emergence

*Contemporary
North American
Poetry Series*

Alan Golding
Lynn Keller
Adalaide Morris
series editors

P oetics *of Emergence*

....

Affect

and

History

in

Postwar

Experimental

Poetry

Benjamin Lee

University
of Iowa Press
Iowa City

University of Iowa Press, Iowa City 52242
Copyright © 2020 by the University of Iowa Press
www.uipress.uiowa.edu
Printed in the United States of America

Design by Omega Clay

Printed on acid-free paper

Library of Congress Cataloging-in-Publication Data
Names: Lee, Benjamin
Title: Poetics of emergence: affect and history in postwar experimental
    poetry / Benjamin Lee.
Other titles: Affect and history in postwar experimental poetry
Description: Iowa City: University of Iowa Press, [2020] | Series:
    Contemporary North American poetry series | Includes bibliographical
    references and index.
Identifiers: LCCN 2019047732 (print) | LCCN 2019047733 (ebook) | ISBN
    9781609386979 (paperback) | ISBN 9781609386986 (ebook)
Subjects: LCSH: American poetry—20th century—History and criticism. |
    Experimental poetry, American—History and criticism. | Affect
    (Psychology) in literature. | Radicalism in literature. | Social change
    in literature. | Literature and society—United States—History—20th
    century.
Classification: LCC PS325.J46 2008 (print) | LCC PS325 (ebook) | DDC
    005.8—dc23
LC record available at https://lccn.loc.gov/2019047732
LC ebook record available at https://lccn.loc.gov/2019047733

For Lisi

Contents

Contents

ACKNOWLEDGMENTS

This book began as a dissertation at the University of Virginia, where it benefited from the wisdom, good humor, and encouragement of Eric Lott, Jahan Ramazani, and Jonathan Flatley. Lessons I learned from them then, as I handed them first and second drafts of the chapters in this book, guide me to this day. It would not be here now, as a book, without the patience and continually perceptive editorial responses of Alan Golding, Lynn Keller, and Dee Morris. I will always be grateful to them, as I will be to Meredith Stabel and Susan Hill Newton at University of Iowa Press.

Between dissertation and book lie all the optimism and discouragement of revision, during which countless friends and colleagues reminded me, sometimes without realizing they were doing so, why I cared so much about the arguments I was making. At the University of Tennessee, Chuck Maland, Stan Garner, and Allen Dunn supported my work in myriad ways, not just as department heads but as models of intellectual generosity and calm. Amy Elias read more project descriptions than I care to remember and never failed to improve them. Anthony Welch, Alan Rutenberg, Gregor Kalas, and Alexis Boylan all read sections of the manuscript; their comments made me wish I shared my work more often. Colleagues in the English Department Theory Group, the Americanist Reading Group, and the Contemporary Arts and Society Reading Group let me work out ideas in conversation that made their way into *Poetics of Emergence*. Colleagues in the UCW-CWA and the UTK chapter of AAUP reminded me why these ideas mattered, as did the countless hours I spent discussing poems with Marilyn Kallet, Joy Harjo, Amy Billone, and Art Smith. Colleagues with a knack for hosting parties or inviting me for a drink just when I needed one include Bill Hardwig, Michael Knight, Urmila Seshagiri, Chris Hebert, Margaret Lazarus Dean, Michelle Commander, Mary Papke, Heather Hirschfeld, Tom Haddox, Jeff Ringer, Dawn Coleman, Martin Griffin, Katy Chiles, Misty Anderson, and Gerard Cohen-Vrignaud.

Funding for archival research from both the University of Virginia and the University of Tennessee improved this book immeasurably, as did the exceptional librarians at the University of Virginia Library's Special Collections, the New York Public Library's Berg Collection, and the Ransom Center at the University of Texas at Austin, where I was a fellow from 2009 to 2010. My students at Tennessee, Oberlin College, and New College of Florida improved this book even more. They are the reason I read poems every day, the interlocutors with whom I most often discuss them. My graduate students at the University of Tennessee deserve special thanks; they sat with me for hours at a time, discussing the poems I quote in the pages that follow, offering insight and enthusiasm that echoed and transformed what I already knew.

Friends I made as I was writing this book, and whose own scholarship and encouraging responses to mine helped me along the way, include Andrew Epstein, Brian Glavey, Jonathan Eburne, Hester Blum, Bill Albertini, James Kim, Ana Mitric, Derek Nystrom, Mike Millner, Sam Turner, Ken Parille, Danny Siegel, Karlyn Crowley, Brenna Munro, Scott Cohen, Scott Saul, Bryan Wagner, and Heather Love. Poetry scholars whose intellectual companionship and generosity I came to depend on include David Caplan, Susan Rosenbaum, Mark Silverberg, Ellen Levy, Walt Hunter, Lindsay Turner, Omaar Hena, Robert Zamsky, Marit MacArthur, Maria Damon, Chris Nealon, Aldon Nielsen, Billy Joe Harris, Kathy Lou Schultz, Meta Jones, Jean-Philippe Marcoux, Lyn Hejinian, Barrett Watten, Tan Lin, and Tyrone Williams. Aaron Jaffe, Fran McDonald, Kristi Maxwell, and Merinda Simmons made me celebrate. Ken Taylor and Pete Moore invited me to contribute to the little magazines of the future. Tim Gray read the full manuscript for University of Iowa Press and offered friendship and advice. His comments on the manuscript, as well as those of an anonymous reader, improved it substantially, as did Karin Horler's careful edits. A discussion I once had with Chip Tucker, over lunch in Charlottesville, changed my arguments about anaphora in "Howl"; Rita Felski's comments on an earlier version of my chapter on di Prima made an enormous difference. Brian Glavey, Andrew Epstein, Bryan Wagner, and Jonathan Flatley, already mentioned, deserve special thanks: for always asking me about my work, offering to read it, and urging me on.

Lisi Schoenbach read it all, in multiple drafts, and so much more besides. There is not an idea in this book she has not discussed with me, helped me better understand, illuminated with her kindness. Time spent writing this book has been time spent with her; nothing could be luckier. David and Judy Lee were my first bit of luck. That it has never failed me is only one of their gifts. Josh Lee, Seema Desai, Jay Fisher, Carole Handler, Lani Schoenbach, Peter Schoenbach, and Anne Tobey have been the very best family I could imagine. Sol, Julius, and Clara, who I could never have imagined when I started this book, have made every word mean something new.

CREDITS AND PERMISSIONS

An earlier version of chapter 3 appeared as "Avant-Garde Poetry as Subcultural Practice: Mailer and Di Prima's Hipsters." *New Literary History*, Vol. 41:4, Autumn 2010, 775–794. Copyright © 2010 *New Literary History*, The University of Virginia. Published with permission by Johns Hopkins University Press.

"Howl and Other Poems: Is There Old Left in These New Beats?" was originally published in *American Literature*, Vol. 76:2, 367–389. Copyright © 2004 Duke University Press. Republished by permission dukeupress.edu.

"Kenyatta Listening to Mozart," from *Black Magic* by Amiri Baraka. Permission by Chris Calhoun Agency © Estate of Amiri Baraka.

"Song for Baby-O, Unborn" and excerpts from "Thirteen Nightmares," "More or Less Love Poems," "Three Laments," "April Fool Birthday Poem for Grandpa," and "Magick in Theory and Practice" from *Pieces of a Song: Selected Poems*. Copyright © 2014 Diane di Prima. Reprinted with the permission of The Permissions Company, LLC on behalf of City Lights Books, citylights.com.

"In Memory of My Feelings," "Joe's Jacket," "October," and "Present" from *The Collected Poems of Frank O'Hara* by Frank O'Hara. Copyright © 1971 Maureen Granville-Smith, Administratrix of the Estate of Frank O'Hara, copyright renewed 1999 by Maureen O'Hara Granville-Smith and Donald Allen. Used by permission of Alfred A. Knopf, an imprint of the Knopf Doubleday Publishing Group, a division of Penguin Random House LLC. All rights reserved.

"A Poem for Neutrals" by Amiri Baraka, from *S.O.S Poems 1961–2013*. Copyright © 2014 The Estate of Amiri Baraka. Used by permission of Grove/Atlantic, Inc. Any third-party use of this material, outside of this publication, is prohibited.

"For James Dean" by Frank O'Hara, from *Meditations in an Emergency*. Copyright © 1957 Frank O'Hara. Used by permission of Grove/Atlantic, Inc. Any third-party use of this material, outside of this publication, is prohibited.

Poetics of Emergence

Introduction

Affect and History in Postwar Experimental Poetry

> I could not change it into history
> and so remember it,
>   and I have lost what is always and everywhere
> present, the scene of my selves, the occasion of these ruses[.]
> —Frank O'Hara, "In Memory of My Feelings"
>
> His work cannot be categorized merely as historical, like anyone else's,
> but it intended to be so and understood itself as such.
> —Walter Benjamin, "On Some Motifs in Baudelaire"

....

The story of experimental poetry in the United States in the two de-
cades following World War II is a complicated one, marked by ambitious
claims for the literary and cultural influence of poems like Allen Ginsberg's
"Howl" (1956), often hailed as the most important poem since *The Waste
Land* (1922), but also by the opinion that such claims have been exaggerated.
The New American Poetry, as the experimental poetry of the era is sometimes
called in tribute to Donald Allen's influential anthology of that name, helped
propel readers beyond the staid, self-referential forms endorsed by the New
Critics. It opened U.S. poetry to a range of innovative formal approaches and
to content—sexual, political, psychological, spiritual, pop cultural, antisocial,
absurdist—largely discouraged by both the influential literary journals of the
day and a repressive and deeply conservative culture. Getting its start among
close friends, at underground readings, in little magazines, it generated a kind
of countercultural force and momentum to which subsequent literary move-
ments have aspired. It altered the course of English-language poetry and even
managed to affect the culture at large, a rare feat for poets.[1]

This story has always attracted skeptics, even among partisans. The "fabled
'opening of the field,'" the influential critic Marjorie Perloff has written, was
in fact "less revolution than restoration: a carrying on, in somewhat diluted
form, of the avant-garde project that had been at the very heart of early mod-
ernism."[2] The "expressive," improvisatory, transparently autobiographical po-
ems favored by midcentury experimentalists have in the long run proven less
radically transformative than the concrete experiments with sound and word,

or the conceptual and multimedia techniques, of predecessors and successors. The real revolution, Perloff insists, took place in the first and final decades of the twentieth century, in the materialist poetics of Gertrude Stein and Velimir Khlebnikov, Lyn Hejinian and Susan Howe. Nor is Perloff the only critic to make such a case. Similar arguments have been advanced by a range of poets and critics invested in downplaying New American innovations so as to direct our attention elsewhere: to Objectivism, Language poetry, or the movement poetries of the late 1960s and 1970s.

This rhetoric of deflation, or of lowered estimation in the realm of literary history and aesthetics, gets echoed in recent political assessments of U.S. experimental poets of the 1950s and 1960s. Poets once celebrated for their queer subversions are now read as meditating on their own guilt-inducing entrapment in the spectacular expansion of capital after World War II.[3] Poems thought to have insisted, actively and at some significant risk, on expanding lyric territory to encompass the everyday racial, sexual, or class politics of the era are now overheard channeling the market or preparing the ground for the advertising strategies of Nike and Coca-Cola.[4] How, recent criticism asks us to consider, could postwar experimental poets have failed to resist or criticize more explicitly structural and economic transformations whose consequences now seem so dire? Perhaps the subcultural poetics of the era, one version of which I consider in chapter 3, were never as resistant as its practitioners liked to think. Perhaps the New American Poetry, like abstract expressionism or cool jazz, was only providing accompaniment for the expansion of markets abroad, the intensification of consumerism at home, the consolidation of corporate privilege.[5] As contemporary poet and critic Juliana Spahr has observed, raising questions about Allen's anthology if not the myriad scenes it purported to represent, *The New American Poetry* once seemed "progressive" and "resistant," a gateway to "autonomous" literary forms. It now seems apolitical, hostile to diversity, "amenable to literary nationalism."[6]

Though I tend to be more celebratory than skeptical in the pages that follow, both readings of postwar experimental poetry have influenced my approach. Moreover, both seem inevitable features of our attempts to describe an almost mythically transitional period in U.S. history, and in global histories as they helped frame and were framed by U.S. interests. Moving on after the Great Depression and World War II and into the Cold War, Americans made bold claims for social equality and civil rights while yielding ever greater authority to finance capital and conglomerates. Through the 1950s and 1960s, increasingly radical politics and aesthetics coincided with the legendary complacency of the postwar middle class: with suburbs, automobiles, and television sets. Abroad, the struggle for self-determination in Cuba, Ghana, and elsewhere overlapped with the cynicism of U.S. involvement in Vietnam, or of Cold War diplomacy in general, conducted to the rhythm of military-industrial development and nuclear threat. It seems unlikely, then, that the most ambitious poems of the era wouldn't speak to us of both its radical possibilities and eventual dissipation into a culture and economy that have yet to be sufficiently transformed. Our sense of the past, as I argue in chapter 4, is shaped inevitably by the pull of the future. And we have arrived now at a future of such desperate contradictions—spectacular luxury and care shadowed by precarity and the low hum of impending catastrophe—that it would seem difficult to look back on the poems of preceding generations without seeing predictions there of our current situation.

And yet what if we tried to read poems of the 1950s and 1960s without feeling the need to offer definitive literary-historical judgments or to assess them in relation to the crises of the present? What if the value of these poems is greater to us as a model of lyric engagement with their own contemporaneous circumstances?[7] As much as possible—knowing that it is never possible to reinhabit the past or to set aside present concerns—*Poetics of Emergence* tries to return to the historical imagination of the poems themselves, or at least to what Jonathan Culler describes as their "evocation of a present."[8] How do postwar poets like Ginsberg, Amiri Baraka (then LeRoi Jones), Frank O'Hara, and Diane di Prima orient themselves, historically and aesthetically, in relation to events whose significance is not yet clear, or in order to register their fears and disappointments, the pleasures they take, the things to which they had grown attached? Whom do they address?

The answers to these questions, I argue, are embedded in a particular kind of postmodern lyric, a fluid and adaptable sort of free-verse poem—what Charles Olson called "open form"—able to accommodate historical juxtapositions and structures of feeling that very often remain preliminary or unresolved, sites of potential rather than completed transactions.[9] The painter Grace Hartigan, to whom O'Hara dedicated "In Memory of My Feelings," his great poem from the mid-1950s, wrote that it was about "how to be *open* but not violated, how *not to panic*."[10] O'Hara's poem tries not to panic in the face of both the demands of the past and the continued threats of the present, echoing the cool mode of engagement I examine in di Prima's writings in chapter 3 and yet adopting a slightly different tone, more camp than hip, more exuberant than detached. It looks forward to O'Hara's most famous poems of the late 1950s and 1960s, which gesture constantly toward the things he likes or wants to love, a broad field of subjects, objects, and environments to which he is attuned and which solicit in him what Jonathan Flatley describes as "a readiness to pay attention to something and to be affected by it."[11]

The concluding lines of "In Memory of My Feelings," quoted in my first epigraph, imagine a precarious balance of history, memory, art, and experience. They call to mind the source of my second epigraph, Walter Benjamin's famous essay on Charles Baudelaire. In Benjamin's reading, the nineteenth-century French poet manages to keep lyric poetry alive during an era in which "the conditions for [its] reception . . . have become increasingly unfavorable."[12] New readers need to be addressed, and the poet can make his work historical only by indicating how, with the previous rituals of collective life disrupted by modernity—by industrialization, mechanization, mass culture, the overwhelming surge of the crowd—individual experiences might still be recorded and offered to readers as collective. "This is the nature of the immediate experience," Benjamin writes, "to which Baudelaire has given the weight of long experience,"[13] an attempt echoed in the concepts O'Hara strains to set in relation at the conclusion to "In Memory of My Feelings." "I could not change it into history / and so remember it," O'Hara writes, suggesting that history is something we both experience and remember, a process art participates in by capturing experience in forms to which we can return.[14] Though the terms shift perceptibly between Benjamin's essay on Baudelaire and O'Hara's great self-elegy, the processes they strain to represent are similar. How can poetry help us manage loss, shock, or psychological or bodily threat, thus letting us retain something that feels like experience, or what O'Hara elsewhere describes simply as "what is happening to me"?[15] For it is experience O'Hara seems to point to with his closing references to memory and to that which is "always and everywhere / present." Nor is it just immediate or individual experience that O'Hara seeks out in this and in other poems, or that di Prima, Ginsberg, and Baraka are after, but rather collective or historical experience, that "long experience" Benjamin refers to that might connect us to others whose experiences resemble our own, even if they are not identical.

"In Memory of My Feelings" attempts to thematize the circuits of affect and aesthetics that in most of the poems I read closely in the chapters that follow—Baraka's lyrics of bourgeois dissatisfaction, for instance, or di Prima's hipster sketches—assume more spontaneous, haphazard, uncertain forms. The serpent that appears throughout "In Memory of My Feelings" and lives on at the conclusion of the poem is a formal, even ornamental totem. It will give way in the "I do this I do that" poems O'Hara writes in the months and years that follow to more literal good luck charms (to a jacket or a coin or some other bit of metal) and to more site-specific images of O'Hara's movements through a particular street or store at a particular date and time. These are some of the "scenes" of O'Hara's selves or "occasions" that O'Hara can contemplate once others—less productive, more damaging or distracting—have been deflected.

The serpent is also an important figure in O'Hara's poems for affect, for the feeling of feeling or the thinking about feeling that I return to throughout *Poetics of Emergence*. The serpent is "coiled around the central figure, / the heart / that bubbles with red ghosts," O'Hara writes in a passage that shifts suddenly to apostrophe, as if the speaker's interior meditations were addressed all along to the snake, so like him and yet different. "I am not quite you, but almost," he remarks, "the opposite of visionary" (*CP*, 256). Neither serpent nor poet claims to see what others can't but rather to register what so many know already yet haven't managed to articulate. They encircle the heart to feel it bubbling or stay close to the ground to feel their own movements and the movements of those who pass by, "watching the ripple of their loss disappear / along the shore, underneath ferns." "When you turn your head / can you feel your heels, undulating?" O'Hara asks, adding "that's what it is / to be a serpent" (*CP*, 256). And he should know, since his poems are full of circuits of affect he constructs in order to register them for himself and for readers. These circuits connect internally but leap as well from subject to object or from person to person, in a constant interaction among internal and external environments and stimuli. So reading D. H. Lawrence's "The Ship of Death" in the middle of the night in "Joe's Jacket," to offer just one example, leads O'Hara to "lie back again and begin slowly to drift and then to sink / a somnolent envy of inertia makes me rise naked and go to the window / where the car horn mysteriously starts to honk" (*CP*, 330).

* * *

In the work of the literary theorists who most influence my approach, affect is always already a form of historical knowledge. We are always trying to gauge the historicity of our own moods, to assess our connections with those who feel similarly, to relate our own sense of optimism or frustration about recent events to long-standing historical patterns. The present, as Lauren Berlant has argued, is "not at first an object but a mediated affect . . . sensed and under constant revision, a temporal genre whose conventions emerge from the personal and public filtering of the situations and events that are happening in an extended now whose very parameters . . . are . . . there for debate."[16] It is rarely clear at the moment events occur how meaningful they will be, or whether they represent breaks or continuities. As we absorb changes in our own daily lives or react to the news, our experience of the present consists to a significant extent of trying to measure how we feel about what has just happened, what happened in the past we are called upon to remember, what is going to happen about which we feel anxious or excited. This is the ongoing process Flatley has described as "affective mapping," the "aesthetic technology," "in the older, more basic sense of *techne*," that allows us to represent to ourselves "the historicity of . . . affective experience" and to engage with and try to make interesting even those things—from our own personal failures to structural problems like economic and gender inequality—that depress us most.[17] We ask ourselves continually, whether aloud or by way of subconscious murmuring, what the "affective atmospheres" are which might enable solidarities or constitute something like "shared *historical* time."[18]

Art remains one important way we access affect's historical meanings. Conditions change, and we watch to see how artists respond. Our tastes change, and we ask ourselves why a book or record that once seemed only mildly interesting now inspires such devotion, while one we once loved now feels embarrassing. New genres appear, styles shift perceptibly, individual poets drift in and out of favor, and we read these changes closely in an effort to elaborate historical hypotheses. We pay particular attention when texts or aesthetic approaches seem to articulate for us our own intuitions about the present. If affective mapping happens continually and in response to a diverse set of stimuli—people, objects, the built environment, natural landscapes, news, advertisements, social media, changing qualities of light and sound, and so forth—art has a special capacity to represent our emotional lives back to us, in forms different enough from lived experience to allow us to contemplate it anew. In "moments of rapid social change or upheaval," Flatley argues, when "[o]ur affective maps are . . . especially in need of revision, repair, or invention," aesthetic practice becomes a primary resource, a means of developing some clearer understanding of why historical conditions are making us feel the way we do and how "[t]hings might work differently."[19] In eras of Bartlebyan ambivalence about political action, Sianne Ngai emphasizes, art's uncertainty about its own social role leaves it ideally positioned to explore the "predicament of suspended or curtailed agency" and the "minor affective idioms" it produces.[20]

Such arguments build on Raymond Williams's remarkably generative account of "structures of feeling," which I return to in the chapters that follow but want to discuss here, if only briefly, as a way of further clarifying my own sense of affect theory's galvanizing integration of aesthetics and historicism. For it was Williams who first articulated something like the *poetics of emergence* I take as my title and discover in poems like O'Hara's "Rhapsody," di Prima's "More or Less Love Poems," or Baraka's "Kenyatta Listening to Mozart." These are poems I read as capturing, in their formal strategies as well as their content, "social experience[s] . . . still in process, often indeed not yet recognized as social but taken to be private." The concept of the "structure of feeling," Williams argues, "has special relevance to art and literature, where . . . social content" is often "of this present and affective kind," distinct from "belief-systems, institutions, or explicit general relationships, though it may include all of these." The analysis he hopes to make possible thus hovers continually between explicit ideologies and "social consciousness" as an active process, suffused by shifting moods and emotional responses to everyday relationships and tasks.[21] Daydreaming or doodling at work, reading the newspaper, or walking down the street: all have the potential to involve us in what Berlant describes as "the activity of being reflexive about a contemporary historicity as one lives it."[22]

The concept of the "structure of feeling," Williams is quick to point out, is itself a "cultural hypothesis," a sort of methodological improvisation intended to focus our attention on social transformations still in process yet visible enough in their basic outlines and effects. "We are talking about characteristic elements of impulse, restraint, and tone," he elaborates, "specifically affective elements of consciousness and relationship: not feeling against thought but thought as felt and feeling as thought: practical consciousness of a present kind, in a living and interrelating continuity." These are never, however, instances of "mere flux" without shape or social consequence. Rather, Williams hopes to describe affective elements "as a 'structure,'" collectively experienced and possessing specific and recognizable "internal relations, at once interlocking and in tension."[23] As Ngai observes, feelings in Williams's account are "as fundamentally 'social' as the institutions and collective practices that have been the more traditional objects of historicist criticism."[24] And though the concept of structures of feeling, Flatley argues, was originally "a supplementary term that emphasized the fleeting and nascent qualit[ies] . . . that . . . might later harden into ideologies," it has since become something more like "a full-fledged parallel to ideology."[25]

The continued importance of Williams's hypothesis for affect theory thus resides in his emphasis on mediation, or on those qualities of gesture and tone that allow us to shuttle between aesthetics and politics or between ground-level social experiences and larger historical frames. "If the function of an ideology," Flatley writes, "is to narrate our relation to a social order so as to make our daily experience of that order meaningful and manageable, then *structure of feeling* would be the term to describe the mediating structure . . . that facilitates and shapes our affective attachment to different objects in the social order."[26] Affect in this account helps get at the social valences of our attachments to aesthetic and subcultural styles; to people, places, and texts; to ideologies themselves as they strike us as more or less useful or problematic. Why is it that we retain such deep emotional investments in accounts of the world that come to seem less and less convincing over time, or more and more detrimental to our own well-being?[27] How is it that certain aesthetic approaches or performance styles seem to shape the present so forcefully, articulating for artists and audiences alike its characteristic moods and modes of sociability?

In my readings of U.S. experimental poetry after World War II, poets gravitate to a range of fluid but identifiable structures of feeling as a way of giving shape to the lived contradictions of U.S. Cold War culture, with its distinctive clash of optimism and disillusionment; economic opportunity and anxiety; bohemian swagger and grinding, teeth-gritting dissatisfaction with existing social relations. During an era in which great poems, the New Critics insisted, were supposed to develop timeless themes, the poets in my study gravitated toward spontaneous or process-oriented approaches as a way of capturing the specific accents of everyday life, the push and pull of collectivity, the feeling of their own definite if often inscrutable relationship to larger forces.

* * *

Key to these attempts, I argue, is the technique of pivoting between specific subcultures and structures of feeling—street-level and quotidian—and more distant, increasingly inaccessible historical frames. The frames I have in mind remain distinct from the officially sanctioned narratives of the postwar moment, depictions of U.S. strength and moral superiority infused with the demand that Americans devote themselves unreservedly to the coordinated efforts to keep democracy safe from Soviet communism. As has been documented by other commentators, these efforts were cultural as well as economic, as quick to police sex lives as politics. The poets I take up here went persistently in search of alternative perspectives: images of revolution, new forms of collectivity, examples of what C. Wright Mills called "the sociological imagination," literary or musicological theories of history's sudden reapplication to the present.[28] At times these perspectives take the form of speculative or celestial endorsements, points of view from which fear might recede and courage be taken. "[W]e do it for / the stars over the Bronx / that they may look on earth / and not be ashamed," di Prima writes in "April Fool Birthday Poem for Grandpa," zooming out suddenly from intimate talk of revolution and from memories of her grandfather's "anarchist wisdom" to gaze down from the heavens.[29] "[W]here is the summit where all aims are clear," O'Hara asks in "Rhapsody," "the pin-point light upon a fear of lust" (*CP*, 326). The poems I survey throughout *Poetics of Emergence* move from close-ups to long shots; they alternate between views from above and ground-level performances of creativity and dissent.

O'Hara, who manipulates these pivots as deftly as anyone, writes poems remarkably attuned to the particulars of workaday life and friendship but also suddenly expansive, dashing from the local to the global, or from the concrete detail (a specific building, a meal he's just eaten, a movie he's just seen) to abstract considerations of "the 20th Century" or historical "precedent" (*CP*, 337, 393). His poems gesture continually toward global frames, or toward what Baraka calls "some possible image / of what we shall call history."[30] While meditating on the emotional textures and micropolitical tensions of daily life in Manhattan, they pivot suddenly to imagine temporally or geographically distant influences, from the Russian Revolution to the Great Depression, from the postures of the European avant-garde to postcolonial independence movements in Africa. They set everyday life in relation to historical and geopolitical horizons that seem to exert influence and promise explanation, even if that explanation never materializes.

I read these sudden shifts and framing gestures as confronting a pressing and intractable political problem, that of snapping the ceaseless, contingent murmuring of the present into place within a newly expansive, potentially transformative perspective. They remain generic markers as well, connected to a long history of poetic forms: dense, rhythmic structures whose tendency to fuse sonic and material effects (rhyme, meter, phoneme, line break, typography) and metaphorical layering with the movements of voice or rhetoric have long allowed poetry, instead of telling stories, to capture rhythmic enunciations and register sudden shifts in tone or perspective. Poems by O'Hara, di Prima, Ginsberg, and Baraka swing on hinges between the past and the present; between one location and another; between the immediate textures of urban life and memory for a single speaker and the suddenly collective, explicitly historicizing perspective. These pivots retain a distant though not insignificant relation to the turn or volta in sonnets from the Renaissance forward, including such well-known examples as John Donne's "Holy Sonnet VII," which redirects our attention abruptly from the "cosmic . . . scale" of God's judgment to the speaker's own intimate meditations on repentance, "here on this lowly ground."[31] Closer to home, they strive to reestablish experimental poetry in the second half of the twentieth century, reimagining modernism's full array of pivots—from surrealist non sequiturs to the juxtaposition of historical fragments in Ezra Pound's *Cantos*—as part of a new poetics of immanence and spontaneity.

In an essay on what New York School poets like O'Hara, John Ashbery, and

Barbara Guest learned from surrealism and abstract expressionism in paint-
ing, Charles Altieri emphasizes these poets' ability to "elaborate[e] an ongoing
process of decisions" taken over the course of the poem, "the adjustments they
necessitate in tracking the self's energies."[32] In poems by Ashbery, O'Hara,
and Guest, "the imagination finds itself literally dwelling in sites of being that
intensify strange conjunctions and states," a dwelling and continual intensi-
fication the poem records on the level of the poetic line, the level of "scale,"
and, in O'Hara's case, in "his willingness to lay himself on the line so that
each line seems to exhaust what is happening in his present and to position
himself on the verge of another investment that may go off on a tangent."[33]
Here Altieri provides a kind of formalist echo of Hartigan's line about "In
Memory of My Feelings," arguing for an openness in O'Hara's compositional
energies that he manages to sustain even to the edge of panic.

One hears echoes as well between what Altieri discovers in specifically
twentieth-century formal techniques and Culler's recent theorizations of
the lyric across time. Culler proposes as a defining feature of the lyric, from
ancient Greece to late-capitalist America, its investment in sound patterns
designed to reinforce the reader's experience of a present of enunciation, a
moment of lyric address to a "you" who may or may not be identified but
who nonetheless structures our experience of "the poem itself as an event."[34]
Even the longest poem I consider in *Poetics of Emergence*, Ginsberg's "Howl,"
the poem perhaps least likely to be read as lyric, contains a moment during
which it gets reshaped suddenly through apostrophe, and where its recount-
ing of past events gets reconstituted as an urgent and immediate address to
the present. Like Adalaide Morris's galvanizing readings of the modernist poet
H.D., Culler's approach allows us to consider the lyric "I" in relation to the
biographical, even intimate, experiences of the poet without pretending to
have access to the poet's private feelings and thoughts. The poem itself is the
event, an ongoing performance of thinking about feeling and feeling about
thought that takes shape line by line, engaging us aesthetically while also
doing what Morris calls "cultural work" and proposing, as Culler argues, "no
one form of social efficacy for the lyric" but rather a range of them.[35]

* * *

Some examples might be helpful at this point. Consider, first, the casual uto-
pianism of the twenty-first of di Prima's "More or Less Love Poems," where
the defining pivot occurs in the first two lines:

The day I kissed you the last roach died.
The UN abolished prisons, and the Pope

appointed Jean Genet to the College of Cardinals.
The Ford Foundation
at huge expense
rebuilt the city of Athens.

The day we made it Pan returned;
Ike gave up golf;
The A&P sold pot[.][36]

Di Prima's catalog of global transformations unleashed by bohemian eros is
at once playful and a little sad. Is the lover she addresses still present, or do
we overhear her talking to herself? Redescribing the sudden plunge of sexual
intimacy as political utopianism, di Prima's speaker imagines transforming
both the quotidian activities of bohemian life and the geopolitical status quo.
Reading, writing, cooking, shopping, and hanging out with friends, all the
while trying to scare up enough money to buy groceries and keep the power
on: the daily routines she captures in other poems are swept magically aside.
"The day you padded here / The bombs dissolved," the poem concludes, pun-
ning on the bare feet and cheap apartments of hipsters as if they were the
answer to nuclear anxiety.

Di Prima's intention is not, of course, to offer policy solutions: practical
steps that might lead, for example, to the abolition of prisons or the atomic
bomb. Instead, she invokes a magical, utopian potential in the world (some
combination of love, poetry, and irony) that might motivate her in the face
of both more familiar struggles (disappointment, lack of funds) and more
distant, intractable ones. Endearingly goofy, this approach has the advantage
of engaging in cultural politics without adopting the somber, post-Eliotic
mode so common among midcentury poets. Instead of dwelling in heavily
symbolic language on the poet's alienation and its cause—the degradations
and lost connections of the modern world—di Prima gives us a utopianism
that refuses to take itself too seriously as long as it can tell us what it prefers:
marijuana over golf, Jean Genet over the traditional authority of the Catholic
Church. Nor does the humor of her straightforward assertions of bohemian
allegiance and taste disguise the geopolitical and economic truths they con-
vey. Cities were indeed being rebuilt at great expense in the 1950s and 1960s,
undeveloped countries were modernizing, and authority was shifting in ways
that were difficult to understand.

The single, concentrated pivot we encounter in di Prima's love poem is
perhaps less common among postwar experimental poems than are more
widely dispersed or disjunctive shifts. Among the poems I read closely in the
chapters that follow, pivots between everyday life and historical incitement

are often subtler, more tentative, even intentionally disguised. Consider, for example, the closing movements of James Schuyler's "Freely Espousing":

> Marriages of the atmosphere
> are worth celebrating
>   where Tudor City
> catches the sky or the glass side
> of a building lit up at night in fog
> "What is that gold-green tetrahedron down the river?"
> "You are experiencing a new sensation."
>
> > *if the touch-me-nots*
> > *are not in bloom*
> > *neither are the chrysanthemums*
>
> The bales of pink cotton candy
> in the slanting light
>   are ornamental cherry trees.
> The greens around them, and
> the browns, the grays, are the park.
>
> It's. Hmm. No.
>   Their scallop shell of quiet
> is the S.S. *United States*.
> It is not so quiet and they
> are a medium-size couple who
> when they fold each other up
> well, thrill. That's their story.[37]

Schuyler's poem slides along the Manhattan vistas from an elevated vantage point (his apartment window, no doubt). It gazes at skyscrapers, into the park, out into the harbor. His lines hang delicately around the verb "to be," enacting through metaphor, painterly description, or qualification the poetic effect Schuyler is famous for, that of imaginatively transforming his environment in the act of perceiving and then describing it poetically. Here is New York landscape as a series of transformations: a building in the light and fog becomes "a gold-green tetrahedron"; "ornamental cherry trees" become "bales of pink cotton candy" and then "a medium-size couple"; the park ("[h]mm," or is it?) gets represented by greens, grays, and browns; "the scallop shell of quiet" surrounding the trees "*is* the S.S. *United States*" (my emphasis on "is"), a luxury liner that often docked in the New York harbor. One recognizes immediately while reading "Freely Espousing," a favorite of Schuyler critics, why they emphasize the painterly qualities of his poems, his play with sound and citation, and his skill as a poet of the everyday.[38]

Yet, Schuyler's poem, no less than di Prima's, situates itself in relation to politics and history. The "marriages of atmosphere" he celebrates are not just features of the poem's representational surface; they are ways of thinking through the "new sensation[s]" created by the built environments of the postwar urban metropolis while thinking simultaneously about the freedoms granted or refused to Americans in the 1950s. The freedom to "espouse" in this poem, framed explicitly as a question of aesthetics, is equally—if somewhat more subtly—a question of sexual politics, of being able to couple however one chooses. This connotation of "espousing," echoed in the poem's puns on "commingling" and "marriage," and in its mention of "forbidden . . . act[s]" and "inescapable kiss[es]," snaps into place in the poem's final stanza, with its sudden focus on the "medium-size couple" surrounded by the ponderous weight of an American ideology—the S.S. *United States*—eager to christen its ships as patriotically as possible. Slipping quietly away from this weight, "Freely Espousing" closes with a vision of queer coupling at once open and closeted, unapologetic and oblique.[39] It closes as well with an alternative image of the nation, in which visible symbols of American prosperity and military might—a stupendous luxury liner built to be repurposed, if the need arose, as a troop carrier—are recast as the enfolded thrill of male-male affection.

We can distinguish the approach to history implied by poems like di Prima's "More or Less Love Poems" and Schuyler's "Freely Espousing" from that of poets writing earlier in the twentieth century and from that of important figures among their contemporaries. With their variable pivots, shifting atmospheres, and fondness for self-deprecating tones, these poems convey none of the modernist confidence, evinced in the work of Pound or T. S. Eliot, that poets with a sufficiently comprehensive understanding of the literary past might reorder for us "the . . . futility and anarchy which is contemporary history."[40] Similarly, they resist Robert Lowell's authoritative pessimism about the 1950s and 1960s, as well as the New Critical contention—still dominant at the time—that poems should be valued precisely for their ability to transcend current ideological debates. As I argue in chapter 4, for example, Ginsberg's unapologetic embrace of communism was central to his most popular and influential early poems. And yet it was utopic and nostalgic rather than directly engaged in any party or political organization, a queer communism setting him at odds not just with U.S. foreign policy but also with communist governments in Cuba and Czechoslovakia.[41]

Not surprisingly, then, the poems I read in *Poetics of Emergence* tend to be open-ended or interrogative; depressed, self-critical, or speculative; silly, vatic, or hip. Though they respond willingly to current events and ideological conflicts, their attempts to imagine a speaker's relation to a set of larger forces and economies of power are often inconclusive, subject to revision. Powerfully felt, these forces remain difficult to name definitively from the speaker's perspective, anchored as it is in its own emotional orbit and immediate surroundings. As affect theory has argued, beginning with Williams's meditations on "structures of feeling" and passing more recently through theorists like Berlant, Flatley, and Ngai, a fuller analysis of the complexities and ambivalence of this impasse means moving beyond the purely cognitive and conceptual to consider the expanded repertoires of affect, gesture, and tone that we claim as representations of our own historicity. The poems I read in this book seem to anticipate these insights, and to imagine their own historical situation as a set of problems and potentialities that have yet to be resolved, and that are felt as vividly as they are thought. As they pivot and shift, these poems register history as it emerges and makes itself present to us in the first place, not as a discrete and verifiable set of systems or events, but rather as a quality of experience, mediated by affect, perpetually updated and emended.[42]

Like Baudelaire in Benjamin's essay, postwar poems by O'Hara, Ginsberg, Baraka, and di Prima meditate implicitly on how the lyric needs to change in order to sustain its capacity to register experience in the face of rapid historical change. They help develop a new, rapidly composed, spontaneous lyric approach as a means of responding to what they perceive as substantial threats to their ability "to assimilate the data of the world" around them into something like their own characteristic set of memories, desires, perceptual and cultural responses, and collective affiliations.[43] These threats include social insult, isolation from any enabling experience of collectivity, the pressures of a more and more heavily administered world, and the overwhelming flow of stimuli their poems catalog so persistently (advertisements, newspaper headlines, radio broadcasts, anonymous encounters, consumer choices, traffic, construction projects, and so forth). While the historical experience registered in their poems differs markedly from the more catastrophic "shock experience" Baudelaire confronts in a nineteenth-century Paris suddenly transformed by industrialization, essential features remain: the crowds, the anonymous encounters, the commodities, the flânerie, the erotic charge of urban life, the psychological pressures of thinking one's way through "giant cities and the web of their numberless interconnecting relationships."[44] Illuminated against a backdrop of artistic exuberance and acute historical disorientation, these poems begin to suggest something like the distinctive and contradictory atmosphere of the United States in the 1950s and 1960s.

✼ ✼ ✼

Scholars have long emphasized the large-scale economic, structural, and ideological transformations that defined U.S. social and intellectual life in the two decades following World War II, changes felt with particular intensity in Manhattan, where O'Hara, Baraka, di Prima, and Ginsberg all established themselves in the 1950s (Ginsberg drifting off to Cuba, Mexico, Berkeley, Paris, and India, but always drifting back). In an era of unprecedented economic growth in the United States—of suburban and infrastructural expansion, expanding consumer demand, and a historic boom in higher education—change seemed to accelerate at an even faster pace in New York. As European economies struggled to recover from World War II, Wall Street consolidated its position as the world's financial capital; on Madison Avenue, the advertising industry reinvented itself for television, its profits soaring as companies raced to push products in American living rooms. Though still an industrial city, New York began to feel more and more like a global capital of finance and culture: a city of banks, corporations, advertising firms, television studios, art museums, music venues, recording studios. It was also a city being rebuilt faster and more ambitiously than any other. "By 1957," Robert Caro writes, "$133,000,000 of public monies had been expended on urban renewal in all the cities of the United States with the exception of New York; $267,000,000 had been spent in New York."[45] There was no more striking emblem of U.S. influence in world affairs than the United Nations Building, completed in 1950 and immediately a favorite image for New York poets like Schuyler and O'Hara, who shared an apartment nearby in the early 1950s. "Is there at all anywhere / in this lavender sky / beside the UN Building / where I am so little," O'Hara asks in "October," "a fragment of the paradise / we see when signing treaties / or planning free radio stations?" (CP, 110). Here and elsewhere in the poems of the era, the excitement of being near the center of the action—so close to all the talk of freedom and transformation—is accompanied by feelings of historical insignificance. One feels little, and perhaps a little cynical, living in the shadows of postwar financiers and decision-makers.

In the meantime, however, New York's postwar expansion had its advantages. Apartments were cheap—painters and musicians could afford studio space in downtown Manhattan—and jobs readily available. Ginsberg worked in marketing research in the early 1950s, spending several months on a campaign for Ipana toothpaste; O'Hara arrived in New York in 1951 and found a job that winter selling tickets and postcards at the front desk of the Museum of Modern Art, a move calculated to keep him as close as possible to the new Matisse retrospective. Di Prima worked in a bookstore, as a model for artists, as a hostess of sorts for a publicity man with mob connections. Baraka arrived in the Village in 1957 and before long was hired as shipping manager for the

Record Changer, a small magazine for collectors of early jazz recordings. There he met Hettie Cohen (later his wife Hettie Jones), who worked at the *Record Changer* until she moved on to take a job as subscription manager for *Partisan Review*.

Having a job and an apartment in Manhattan in the 1950s or early 1960s, even a cold-water flat in an old tenement building, gave one access to a propulsive set of artistic movements and events. The excitement projected in memoirs and biographies of the era about the jazz then being played in New York—Monk and Coltrane at the Five Spot, Billie Holiday at Carnegie Hall, Miles Davis and Charles Mingus trading sets at the Cafe Bohemia—remains striking. Descriptions of the art scene flourishing in the 1950s in museums, small galleries, downtown bars, and studios now read like hymns to a golden age, during which abstract expressionism helped establish New York as the new capital of modern art and the city's creative spirit seemed endless. O'Hara raced from gallery openings to watch Tallchief dance for Balanchine in the New York City Ballet; Baraka became a leading critic and proponent of the new jazz movement he heard developing in neighborhood jazz clubs and downtown lofts; di Prima joined with four other friends, including Baraka, to found the New York Poets Theatre, which ran for four seasons performing one-act plays by poets.[46]

Alongside all this propulsive energy and assurance, accounts of the era contain sharp notes of dissatisfaction. America's newfound wealth and growing sense of opportunity was hardly universal, a basic fact motivating the civil rights movement and, by the 1960s, antipoverty and women's rights movements. Even middle-class white men, the most immediate beneficiaries of postwar economic growth, felt increasingly apprehensive about their own perceived loss of independence, an apprehension expressed in fiction as well as sociology, where representations of loneliness and conformity proliferated.[47] Hovering over everything was a Cold War foreign policy that manifested itself domestically in what Alan Nadel has called "containment culture," wherein a healthy U.S. democracy was seen as inseparable from the patriotic enthusiasm of middle-class families, whose economic successes were assumed to be the just reward for their unswerving commitment to both religious values and traditional gender roles and courtship rituals.[48]

In spite of its apparent cheerfulness, such a culture generated pervasive anxiety, even paranoia. Nuclear catastrophe seemed imminent, and anyone engaging in or even defending behavior construed as subversive or perverse might be investigated or accused publicly of "un-American activity." Nor were the threats of surveillance or criminal charges merely an abstraction for the poets in my study. Ginsberg's stay in the Columbia Presbyterian Psychiatric

Institute, the result of a 1949 arrest, features centrally in "Howl," whose un-apologetic references to gay sex made it, in 1957, the subject of a well-known obscenity trial. Baraka also stood trial for obscenity charges. "Treasury agents, FBI, and police" showed up to arrest him in 1961 for material he had published in *The Floating Bear*, the little magazine he was editing with di Prima.[49] Carl Solomon, whom Ginsberg had met while institutionalized in 1949 and to whom "Howl" is dedicated, meditated on U.S. hypocrisy, inequality, and repression in his own 1961 contribution to *The Floating Bear*. "Only in America and from America came the slogan: Freedom," Solomon writes. "The slogan," he concludes, "meant white supremacy and the suppression of every movement for human hope on the face of the planet."[50]

I will return in a moment to this seemingly constitutive tension, in accounts of the 1950s and 1960s, between optimism and dissatisfaction, artistic exuberance and paranoia. First, though, I want to underscore how frequently accounts of postwar dissatisfaction were fused with descriptions of a more widespread and debilitating loss of historical grounding and agency. This discourse takes shape partly as a critique of conformity, the diagnosis from various perspectives—from Frankfurt School sociology to business writing to emergent feminism—of the decline of robust individualism or critical thought, and of the narrowing and falsification of human freedom. Expanding bureaucracies, mass entertainments, and suburban family life, critics worried, presented themselves as the benevolent results of a culture of affluence and thus managed to disguise the limits they imposed on social lives and political horizons. Midcentury corporate culture, William Whyte remarked in 1956, strove to make conformity feel like "a . . . moral imperative," while outside the living rooms of the burgeoning middle class change now occurred too quickly and on too global a scale to be grasped with any certainty; the forces that directed it seemed distant, mystified, systemic.[51] Echoing this critique at the close of the 1950s, the influential sociologist C. Wright Mills warned that "the very shaping of history now outpaces the ability of men to orient themselves."[52]

From Mills's perspective, average men and women in the 1950s had little control over their own lives. Shaped by social, political, and economic forces they could "neither understand nor govern," they had lost their sense of purpose and agency in a country directed by a small handful of corporate, governmental, and military decision-makers.[53] In the developing world, the pace of change was startling; feudal cultures were transformed, "in the course of a single generation . . . into all that is modern, advanced, and fearful."[54] In "the overdeveloped world," whether communist or capitalist, "the means of authority and of violence [had] become total in scope and bureaucratic in form."[55] Even Mills's academic discipline, sociology, was threatened by the "bureaucratic ethos" that hovers everywhere in his work, like a great shadow over human freedom. Social scientists, he worried, were now encouraged to gather empirical data that served the political and administrative interests of the organization supporting the study; the studies they generated were divorced from broader contexts or serious analysis of historical causes.[56]

This was a particular problem, Mills argued, for intellectuals on the left, or for anyone committed to criticizing abuses of power in a world of seemingly unlimited yet decidedly unequal prosperity. For corporations, governmental bureaucracies, and established political parties, it hardly seemed a problem that most Americans were complacent about the erosion of their own influence or the narrowing of their political options. On the contrary, the fact that consumer-citizens tended to confuse their own career advancement with "the quality and condition of social justice" as a whole was enormously advantageous, as was the conversion of once relatively independent classes of artists and intellectuals into corporate-sponsored producers of culture or members of "research cartels."[57] For anyone still invested in the idea of a self-reliant, truly international left, however, the situation seemed disastrous. Communism, once a definitive compass point for intellectuals in both the United States and Europe, now seemed nationalized and dogmatic; one had to separate the force of communism as an idea, or as an expression of ongoing revolutionary potential, from the policies of the Soviet elite. And though "cultural activities" in the United States were "formally quite free," artists, scientists, and intellectuals—whether employed by corporations, government-funded organizations, or major universities—were strongly encouraged "to divorce intellectual activities from politics or any sort."[58] The "means of distribution, and, increasingly, of cultural production," were being taken out of their hands in the interests of bureaucratic efficiency and market profitability.[59] "In our time," Mills wrote in 1959, "there is no Left establishment anywhere that is truly international and insurgent."[60]

Though Mills's popularity in the 1950s and influence on the New Left in the 1960s make him an appropriate figure through which to characterize the historiographic imagination of the era, he was by no means the only thinker to diagnose an overwhelming sense of conformity and lack of historical and intellectual agency in the decades after World War II. One might begin instead with Herbert Marcuse, Hannah Arendt, or Clement Greenberg, for example, all of whom published enormously influential work in the 1950s and 1960s, proposed epochal shifts (the rise of postindustrial society, the shock of global totalitarianism, the triumph of painting over all other arts and of aesthetic form over content), and diagnosed what they characterized as dramatically altered conditions for human freedom and creativity.[61] It is the combination of all these speculative energies, one might say—new efforts to describe the immersive sprawl of consumer culture, the global ambitions of power, the purification and sublation of modernism as an ideology—that Fredric Jameson would describe some two decades later as a new, postmodern cultural dominant, one dedicated to new styles and a commodified nostalgia for old ones but fundamentally incapable of real (which is to say critical and potentially utopic) historical thinking.[62] Recent critiques of postmodernism, such as Andrew Hoberek's perceptive suggestion that it falsely universalizes the plight of the American middle class, help us better understand the devil's bargain at the heart of postwar prosperity, in which the short-term economic benefits of white-collar employment lead to the significant erosion of economic and political agency in the long term. As Hoberek himself acknowledges, however, such critiques hardly mitigate the contemporaneous experience of attempting but failing to fully comprehend that transaction as it occurred.[63] What I hope to emphasize in invoking Marcuse, Mills, Greenberg, and Arendt is the shared sense among intellectuals working during the 1950s and early 1960s that the increased pace and global scope of change in the decades following World War II created deep historiographic uncertainty and a mood of both crisis and opportunity, "reckless optimism and reckless despair."[64]

* * *

Particularly where New York poets are concerned, as I have already argued, overarching characterizations of the 1950s and 1960s swing dramatically between depression and optimism, or between descriptions of the social insults and paranoia of Cold War culture and celebrations of the remarkable creative ferment of the era. In one account, we step into "the paint-happy 1950s," where poets and abstract expressionists walk, talk, and drink together at the Cedar Tavern, "immersed in their own glorious reimaginings of art and life in New York City, secure in the knowledge that they would make everything new."[65] In another, New York School poetry originates "during . . . a particularly repressive and paranoid period of American history" or "arguably the single most actively homophobic decade in American history," one forever associated with McCarthyism and during which homosexuality, like communism, was construed as a national security risk.[66]

Though when juxtaposed these accounts may seem difficult to reconcile, I want to argue that both are borne out by the poems I discuss in the following chapters. Indeed, this juxtaposition captures something vital about New York in the 1950s and 1960s, when artists felt confident, even recklessly so, about the transformative potential of experimental art while also feeling remarkably depressed about the wider culture. Ashbery, for one, has characterized the mood of the early 1950s as debilitating for artists whose work or personal life was in any way unconventional. Somewhat paradoxically, he has also argued that the historical atmosphere of depression, doubt, and risk became an incitement to produce experimental art:

> [I]n the early 50's I went through a period of intense depression and doubt. I couldn't write for a couple of years. I don't know why. It did coincide with the beginnings of the Korean War, the Rosenberg case and McCarthyism. Though I was not an intensely political person, it was impossible to be happy in that kind of climate. It was a nadir.[67]

> At that time I found the avant-garde very exciting, just as the young do today, but the difference was that in 1950 there was no sure proof of the existence of the avant-garde. To experiment was to have the feeling that one was poised on some outermost brink. In other words if one wanted to depart, even moderately, from the norm, one was taking one's life—one's life as an artist—into one's hands.[68]

The logic and implied resolution of this contradiction will of course seem familiar to students of the avant-garde. Work remains incomplete because a potential artist's personal mood is so depressed, creating a kind of incapacity and self-doubt that is difficult to attribute to any single cause but that one associates intuitively with a larger political atmosphere. The other side of the coin, however, is that this same debilitating atmosphere becomes a source of excitement, for it seems to guarantee, in a way that may not be true in moments of greater freedom and tolerance—or of corporate investment in new styles and marketable nonconformities—that experimental art-making feels like a substantial risk or provocation, an attempt, even if modest or not fully comprehended at the time, to use art to imagine that politics or social relationships might be differently configured. There is an affective circuit in postwar art, as these two Ashbery quotes indicate, that runs continually between a firm belief in the cultural and existential vitality of new poetic forms and an equally insistent pessimism about larger systems. "Howl" remains perhaps the most iconic, widely circulated articulation of this circuit in postwar poetry, its investment in the subversive practices of a small, bohemian cohort set in opposition to "Moloch," that sprawling, nightmarish figure of loneliness, repression, and military-industrial expansion. Yet it is far from the only poem I focus on whose emotional textures seem to hinge upon this movement between ecstatic self-confidence about art making and anxiety about what O'Hara in "Rhapsody" calls the "rancid nourishment" of American life (*CP*, 326).

For the most part, I will argue that such contradictions exist synchronically, in the poems by New York poets from any given year from about 1950 to 1965. Other commentators have explained them diachronically, however, as the difference between the 1950s and 1960s, for instance, or between the repressiveness and conformity of the early 1950s and the social unrest that became increasingly palpable during the final years of the decade. Remembering 1957 in his autobiography, for instance, Baraka describes it as "a time . . . of transition. From the cooled-out reactionary 50's, the 50's of the Cold War and McCarthyism and HUAC [the House Un-American Activities Committee], to the late 50's of the surging civil rights movement."[69] This sense of movement and change across the period I describe remains important, for it carries with it the electric charge of internal differentiation, of change over time, of internal shifts within a relatively brief historical period. It carries as well the charge of the new social movements: of the emergence of feminism in the mid-1960s, the rise of black separatism, the appearance of an explicit and openly politicized gay rights movement at the end of the 1960s. Even when I fall back, as in chapters 2 and 3, on narratives of progress and development (from art to activism, for example, or from the cultural politics of bohemianism to the more explicitly political insurgencies of the 1960s), I hope to place the accent just as strongly on a set of ongoing cultural dynamics, processual and affectively mediated, that I discover in poems from across the periods in question. This includes the double movement between the hypocrisy and coercion of American culture, on the one hand, and the continued investment in experimental forms, on the other. Whether I am reading a poem from the middle of the 1950s, like Ginsberg's "In back of the real," or from the mid-1960s, like Baraka's "Kenyatta Listening to Mozart," I concentrate most intently on their shared insights into the problem of orienting ourselves historically through the aesthetic projection of moods and collectivities.

The chapters that follow examine a series of discrepant but identifiable structures of feeling: O'Hara's cognitive and affective maps; Baraka's self-critical musicality; di Prima's hip detachment from threats and insults; Ginsberg's sentimental attachments to lost political formations. These structures, like the poems they inhabit, may now strike us as misguided, exaggerated, or less subversive than we might once have thought. And yet they can hardly fail to address us, if we will only listen for the experience of the present, ongoing and emergent, they once tried to imagine for us and to set down as a poem.

Frank O'Hara's Twentieth Century

I am ashamed of my century
for being so entertaining
but I have to smile.
—Frank O'Hara, "Naphtha"

No poet captures the emergent historicism I outline in my introduction more deftly than Frank O'Hara. His poems ground themselves in representations of the rhythm and fabric of everyday life and then skip suddenly toward larger historical frames, all the while proposing a series of emotional atmospheres that also shift constantly as the poem unfurls, as in the move from shame to amusement in my epigraph.[1] Comparative global or historical perspectives pop up continually in O'Hara's poems, emerging from their own paratactic and imaginative movements to recontextualize our perspective within a wider historical field. In "Memoir of Sergei O. . . .," a twentieth-century Russian exile compares himself to a princess at the start of the French Revolution; in "Rhapsody," a New York poet has questions for the Dalai Lama; in "Poem (Khrushchev is coming on the right day!)" the poet imagines himself traveling through New York City at the same moment as the Soviet premier. Such juxtapositions seem all the more unexpected considering how mesmerizing and unforgettable are those aspects of O'Hara's poems that encourage us to think of him as a poet of everyday experience and minute, micropolitical negotiations rather than a poet of global reach or historically expansive vision.[2]

And yet one of the fundamental tricks of O'Hara's poems is to capture simultaneously the lower-level strata of historical experience—mundane, forgettable, surreptitiously hidden away from the realm of significant events—and the utopian hopes, explanatory impulses, and glimpses of collectivity or historical significance that emerge suddenly from the field of the everyday and hold out the promise of transforming it. The historical present, as Lauren Berlant argues, "is perceived . . . affectively . . . before it becomes anything else, such as an orchestrated collective event or an epoch on which we can look back."[3] This is an insight that O'Hara seems to anticipate, expanding the field of historical thinking to accommodate all the various gestures and tones (boredom, attentiveness, depression, intimacy, expertise, bemusement, delight, spite, anxiety, exhaustion, and so on) that accumulate in his poems. O'Hara's pivots between perspectives or levels of historical presentation are in fact mediated by affective surrounds. Diverse, often strangely precise accounts of emotional states—"quandariness," "impossible eagerness," "inexorable" joy, "concrete . . . obscurity of emotion"—accumulate in his poems and hold out the promise of understanding them (*CP*, 325, 326, 331, 340).

We might describe O'Hara's aesthetically and ideologically dexterous leaps as poetic versions of what Fredric Jameson calls "cognitive mapping," his term for the process through which individuals overcome paralysis by generating productive images of their own relationship to "that vaster and properly unrepresentable totality" of national and international social relations.[4] Jameson's description of this process builds on an important postwar work of urban planning, Kevin Lynch's *The Image of the City* (1960), expanding Lynch's examination of the challenges of forming usable mental images of midcentury American cities to encompass the challenges of ideology writ large. In Lynch's account, the more "legible" and conducive to "way-finding" the city, the more successfully its residents can form functionally reliable maps of their surroundings, thus allowing them to get where they need to go and to feel relatively confident in doing so.[5] Something similar is true, Jameson argues, about our attempts to create for ourselves "some new heightened sense of [our] place in the global system."[6] Cognitive maps of an increasingly layered, expansive, and rapidly shifting set of economic and social relations entail frequent leaps between local itineraries and overarching structures and ideologies. These are leaps we continue to make, even as we suspect that our maps, though functional, will never capture the global system accurately or completely.[7]

O'Hara's poetic representations of these processes, as I have suggested, demand an expanded description of affect, or of those structures of feeling that mediate our cognitive and ideological movements and allow us to invest in them in the first place. Our chosen itineraries through a city, as Jonathan Flatley argues, are shaped as much by how we feel about places as they are by our ability to remember how one street connects to another.[8] The same can be said of our own relationships to political processes or change over time, which are mediated just as powerfully by affect as they are by understanding. The likelihood that we will commit to one or another form of politics or description of the present depends on interest and attachment. "Insights about one's political oppression," Flatley observes, "are unlikely to motivate resistance unless they can be made interesting and affectively rewarding."[9] Day by day and year by year, we adjust our levels of optimism and pessimism, our attunement to various objects, ideas, and aesthetics. Particularly in moments of "rapid social change and upheaval," or of significant changes in our own personal lives, we struggle to redraw our existing "affective maps."[10] Attempting to do so, and succeeding where we can, allows us to sustain our engagements in the world and to imagine there might be others who share them.

One can read O'Hara's poems as records of such adjustments and attempts to sustain interest and engagement. In keeping such a record, and in combining it with the effort to occupy or imagine perspectives from which he might locate himself in relation to broader structures or overarching historical narratives, O'Hara tries, to steal a phrase from Christopher Nealon, to "feel historical." He works to convert identifiable forms of isolation or disabling exclusion—often related to sexuality, though not always or exclusively—into expressions of collectivity and connection with a range of figures whose mood or perspective he imagines mirrors his own.[11] When these attempts fail, as they often do, the failure tends to result in further attempts, which is to say in more poems and more dynamic accounts of historiographic uncertainty. And though failure sometimes leaves O'Hara feeling stuck—or commenting on his own depressing inability to transform his mood—just as often it sends him plunging back into the pulsating, disorienting middle of the twentieth century, a century, as my epigraph suggests, as entertaining as it is shame-inducing.

As an illustration of this plunge, consider the following excerpt from "Memoir of Sergei O. . . .," written in the voice of the Russian revolutionary poet Sergei Esenin:

and there are no chandeliers and there
are no gates on the parks so you don't
know whether you're going in them or
coming out of them that's not relaxing
and so you can't really walk all you can
do is sit and drink coffee and brood
over the lost leaves and refreshing scum
of Georgia Georgia of my heritage
and dismay meanwhile back in my old
country they are renaming everything so
I can't even tell any more which ballet
company I am remembering with so much
pain and the same thing has started
here American Avenue Park Avenue South

Avenue of Chester Conklin Binnie Barnes
Boulevard Avenue of Toby Wing Barbara
Nichols Street where am I what is it
(CP, 434)

Here O'Hara conveys melancholy with tragic hilarity, the humor hinging on his representation of the failure of his speaker's cognitive and affective maps. The failure is so extreme, in fact, as to constitute a new map, or at least a kind of clarity about the speaker's own vivid sense of despair. Written as if during Esenin's visit to the United States in the early 1920s with the dancer Isadora Duncan (whom Esenin married in 1922 and left to return to Moscow in 1923), the poem associates the twentieth century with displacement and historical dislocation.[12] Not only has the speaker "never been comfortable" since he left Russia for the United States, a "foul country" where the parks have no gates and "even the chairs are upholstered to a / smothering perfection of inanity" (CP, 434), but back in Russia everything has changed since the revolution. He no longer knows, when he hears the name of a ballet company, which one he should be remembering "with so much / pain." To make matters worse, this disruption of the affective maps he once depended on finds itself reproduced in the United States, where they are renaming already barely distinguishable streets ("American Avenue Park Avenue South / Avenue") after film actors. The poem's unpunctuated, composite list of actors further betrays the effects of historical disorientation and drift; the list runs without pause or distinction from Chester Conklin, a comedian already famous in the silent era of the 1910s, to Barbara Nichols, a buxom pin-up girl and supporting actress in films from the 1950s and 1960s, whom O'Hara would have known well but Esenin, who hanged himself in 1925, would never have seen. It functions ironically as well, proposing actors, like Nichols or the B-movie star Toby Wing, hardly famous enough to have streets named after them in the first place.

"[M]eanwhile back in my old / country": the pivot in the middle of the excerpt shifts our attention away from the speaker's static brooding and "dismay" in the United States toward the active work of renaming taking place in Russia, soon to become the Soviet Union. Unlike the sonnet's volta, or the single dramatic pivot that retrospectively reshapes all the previous movements in O'Hara elegies such as "A Step Away from Them" or "The Day Lady Died," in "Memoir" this pivot is just one in a larger field. It echoes the syntax of an earlier shift in the poem, which makes an even greater historical leap, this time from twentieth-century Russia and the United States back to Paris at the start of the French Revolution, where "they were stumbling toward the Bastille." The unpunctuated, paratactic rhythms of the poem carry us quickly from one syntactic and geographical pivot to the next ("meanwhile back in France," "I still hated to move," "little did I know," "meanwhile back in my old / country," "and the same thing has started here") skipping colloquially between continents and historical periods before finally settling in the United States, with the joke about boulevards being renamed for second-tier film stars. "[Y]ou are ruining your awful country and me," the poem concludes: "it is not new to do this it is terribly / democratic and ordinary and tired" (*CP*, 434).

The tone that floats across these pivots is campy and melodramatic; it allows the poem to perform homesickness with a stubbornness and wit designed to amuse readers even as it takes seriously the problem of cultural dislocation. While sympathizing with Esenin's critique of America and his longing for home, the poem nevertheless exaggerates the peasant-bohemian Romanticism of its speaker, entertaining us with his criticisms without necessarily having to endorse them all. O'Hara plays with features critics have long identified with camp: its artifice, its theatrical approach to insecurity and social insult, its pseudo-aristocratic (here bohemian-revolutionary) posing, its versatility as a strategy for intervening in questions of taste in the era of avant-garde and kitsch, middle-brow and masscult.[13] His quintessential camp move is to appropriate the voice of the Russian poet, melodramatic and condescending, in an effort to respond to recognizably American, urban, consumerist forms of historical drift. Issuing judgments of taste whose melancholic arrogance he takes pleasure in imitating, O'Hara dwells on exile as a way of theorizing the historical disorientation produced by Manhattan's endless proliferation of streets and street names, or by Hollywood's endless parade of starlets, named and rendered obsolete in the same breath. (In another quintessentially campy maneuver, O'Hara tries to rescue starlets like Nichols and Wing, holding them within his poem's own enduring memory even as he alludes to their inevitable disappearance from marquees and celebrity columns.) "[W]here am I what is it," Esenin queries near the end of the poem. He is immersed, as O'Hara is, in the experience of cultural transition, and in the struggle to redraw his affective maps of a world that refuses to stop changing.

Though New York in the late 1950s is not Russia in 1917 or Paris in 1789, O'Hara longs to see it saturated with its own equivalent historical significance. Having the Russian revolutionary poet comment on the incomprehensibility of American streets and pop cultural stimuli, the inane and "smothering perfection" of its chairs, and the ordinariness of democratic life is a way of indexing an experience of historical dislocation different from that of a sudden crisis or upheaval but equally in need of aesthetic description. Revolution thus seems at once crucially important and belated in "Memoir of Sergei

O. . . .," like a previous version of social transformation meant to set off, by way of comparison, the extended pleasures and insecurities of the present. This is a present O'Hara touches on even in the voice of Esenin, and that he contemplates less obliquely in famous lyrics such as "Personal Poem," "Poem (Lana Turner has collapsed!)," or "The Day Lady Died." In these poems, melancholy and insecurity are combined with enthusiasm for those very aspects of American daily life and culture that Esenin would have criticized. The persona O'Hara adopts with such verve in a dramatic monologue like "Memoir" is replaced by a seemingly transparent yet still cleverly constructed version of his own personality, what Charles Bernstein has called a "propose[d] . . . domain of the personal."[14] And yet the movement between O'Hara's persona poems and his better-known autobiographical and occasional poems, or what he famously called his "I do this I do that" poems, is itself significant.[15] As O'Hara moves between one voice and the other—autobiographical and assumed, contemporary and anterior, foreign and American, revolutionary and belated—he manipulates a shift between historical frames not dissimilar to the shifts he offers in any individual poem. In "Memoir," as in so many of O'Hara's poems, the "push and pull" Marjorie Perloff has identified in his work, or the "ongoing process of decisions" Charles Altieri discovers there, reveals itself as not just as a formal effect but as a trick of the historical imagination.[16] The storming of the Bastille, Russia before and after the revolution, the United States in the era of movie stars and urban renewal: O'Hara's poems push us from one historical location to the next, shifting moods according to the circumstances they invoke or the historical frames they bring to bear on the present.

* * *

As the best recent criticism on O'Hara has argued, two of the historical frames O'Hara's poems invoke most insistently are those related to his work life at the Museum of Modern Art (MoMA) and to his unapologetic yet complexly articulated queerness, a kind of running commentary on the sexual politics of the 1950s and 1960s. O'Hara's poems move deftly and intuitively to combine these two historical frames, considering them simultaneously or exiting one to wander into the other. The cognitive and affective maps that result, as I have already suggested, remain speculative and preliminary, works of art rather than fully elaborated critiques. They gather objects and observations, literary references and scenes from films, buildings and buses and neon signs, snippets of voice and conversation. They offer their own ongoing meditations on the work of remaining engaged by and optimistic about social life as it unfolds, one encounter after another, a set of historically specific textures that have yet to be woven into any one narrative or consolidated as fact.

It was hardly self-evident, for example, while O'Hara was alive and composing poems, or even a decade after his passing, that he would one day be thought of as the preeminent white-collar poet of the era. And yet no poet speaks more eloquently about the changing shape of labor after World War II, when blue-collar employment was booming but white-collar jobs increased even more dramatically.[17] Hired in 1955 by the International Program at MoMA, by the time of his death in 1966 O'Hara had been promoted to associate curator. His professional life tied him to a repetitive, institutional schedule and embedded him as deeply as any other postwar poet in the bureaucratic culture of the era. He was up early for work, out for drinks after, traveling to Long Island for the weekend. As recounted by colleagues and friends, and as reflected in his poems, O'Hara spent his days making phone calls, circulating memos, organizing exhibits, managing official correspondence, considering budgets, writing grant proposals. If O'Hara refashioned the nine-to-five workday to better fit his own tendencies, "steam[ing] in late and smelling strongly of the night before," as James Schuyler remarked, he nevertheless devoted himself with diligence and efficiency to the tasks at hand. "[H]e was highly organized," Schuyler writes, "with a phenomenal memory. When I say 'he got down to work,' I mean it; he worked, and he worked really hard."[18] He was also remarkably adept at fitting poems into the pauses of the workday; famous, as John Ashbery put it, for "[d]ashing the poems off at odd moments—in his office at the Museum of Modern Art, in the street at lunchtime or even in a room full of people."[19]

In Jasper Bernes's reading, O'Hara writes white-collar poems for white-collar workers; more specifically, he reimagines the lyric for "the service sector."[20] His "charisma is the charisma of the salesperson," "providing a human face to abstract, alienating, and often overwhelming systems, personalizing them and making them sensible and coherent."[21] We can understand his lyric tones and strategies in relation to both his curatorial work at MoMA—where he made choices for museumgoers in order to "craft and refine [their] experience"—and to the strategies of postwar advertisers, who hoped to produce for consumers the same vivid textures of experience and desire O'Hara conjures for us in his poems.[22] Indeed, Bernes is explicit in his judgment that the techniques O'Hara's lyric models for admen and corporate executives outweighs the experience of the poems themselves, which to my ear strain to express something different from the language of advertising, or at least to imagine modes of connection and collectivity that depart from the logic of profitability and manipulation it entails.[23] This is the emergent murmuring I listen for in the readings that follow: comfortable then confused, dispirited but then re-engaged, its street-level moods giving way to sudden utopic flights. If this murmuring hardly constitutes a revolutionary program of the sort Esenin once supported, it is also true that there was no equivalent position, at the height of the Cold War, for O'Hara to endorse.[24] His position was rather that of measuring the era's distance from revolution while charting the surfaces and depths of the present as it unwound, moment by moment and line by line.

This is the process that leads to sudden bursts of collectivity in O'Hara, or to poetic images of what Michael Clune describes as "common life" or "the nervous system of a collective body."[25] And if this nervous system expands with the free market in Clune, in other perceptive readings of O'Hara our social and economic circulation—how we move through the city; what we buy; who we live with and where; who we meet for dinner, visit on weekends, or call on the telephone—gets reshaped according the logics of male-male sexual attraction, camp, alternative models of kinship, intimacy and publicity, queer futurity.[26] It is in queer theoretical readings of O'Hara that one feels most keenly both the sting and shame of social life as he represents it and the alternative possibilities it presents, from the "unauthorized selves" made repeatable (and thus illicitly social) as gossip in Chad Bennett's account to the "vast lifeworld of queer relationality . . . and utopian potentiality" that José Esteban Muñoz overhears in "Having a Coke with You."[27] As determined as O'Hara's lyrics may be by an institutional schedule, they are also cruising poems, aesthetic and affective portraits of (mis)recognition and desire, and of O'Hara's movements, lived and imagery, through the alternately generous and punishing spaces of midcentury New York.

As these remarks indicate, it is important to take note of all those moments in O'Hara's poems when engagement is interrupted, and when the clash of particles that allows for jolts of sexual and imaginative energy suddenly comes to a halt. We experience just such a disruption in "Music," from 1954, the opening poem from O'Hara's best-known collection, *Lunch Poems* (1964). As Perloff observes, "'Music' fuses realism with surrealism, the literal with the fanciful," employing "a series of cuts and dissolves, whether spatial, temporal, or referential" in order to represent "the poet's perceptions" and to capture "the sense of magic, urgency, and confusion of the modern cityscape."[28] The poem begins with the literal, realistic details of a particular "early afternoon"—telling us where the speaker is, what he sees, what he has eaten for lunch—before flooding these details with a series of metaphorical improvisations. The metaphors seem to proceed by chance, or according to the needs of the specific poetic or compositional moment, rather than according to some more synthetic logic. That the speaker is "naked as a table cloth" in line 6, for instance, does not have to jibe with his remark in lines 10 and 11 that "gusts of water spray over the basins of leaves / like the hammers of a glass pianoforte" (*CP*, 210). Instead, these two similes help represent the changes in the speaker's perceptual focus and/or state of consciousness from one moment to the next.

And yet there is an emotional arc to "Music" that pulls its jump cuts and its dissolves into sharper focus, making clear how its shifting perspectives and contradictory images and responses to the cityscape are connected. O'Hara is exploring something specific in this poem: the difficulty of sustaining any sort of focused emotional and intellectual engagement with a cultural environment hostile to one's desires. Like so many of O'Hara's poems, "Music" records his rapidly shifting affective engagement with the city, his struggle to remain, as he says in "Personal Poem," "happy for a time and interested" (*CP*, 335). And while "Music" represents an even faster-paced set of affective movements than does "Personal Poem," it culminates not in happiness and interest but rather in a kind of aimless unhappiness.

"Music" immediately registers the speaker's openness to his environment, and it expresses as well the city's tendency to energize him, to inspire the kind of imaginative engagement that begins with his verbal reproduction of the optical illusion directly before him, in which an angel seems to lead the bronze horse of a statue "into Bergdorf's."[29] The speaker is "naked as a table cloth, [his] nerves humming": throughout the poem he will retain both his "naked" openness to the city's flood of perceptual and cultural stimuli and his nervy, buzzing poetic commitment to the immediate imaginative transformation of as many stimuli as possible. Near the middle of the poem—where the "gusts of water . . . over leaves" become "the hammers of a glass pianoforte," where the speaker sees his own "lavender lips" under "the leaves of the world," and where he figures late autumn as "a locomotive on the march"—he seems to give himself up fully to this process by which he attempts to transform, instantly and most often metaphorically, his every thought and perception.

All the speaker's humming energy and imaginative engagement, however, finally add up to only a vague sense of loneliness, resignation, dissipation. "The fear of war" in line 5 fades into the "meaningless" eating of line 6, the "distress and clarity" of line 12, the "tear" of line 15, and finally the terrible lateness of the poem's last line. Unlike so many of O'Hara's *Lunch Poems*, there is no one moment of imagined solidarity in "Music," no single moment in which the ubiquitous energy of the city is concentrated in one cultural message or perceptual stimulus (as is the case with the headline "LANA TURNER HAS COLLAPSED," for instance, or the *New York Post*'s announcement that Billie

Holiday has died in "The Day Lady Died").[30] Instead, the speaker's seemingly desultory engagement ends with him watching his "daydreams walking by with dogs in blankets" before making a final gesture toward the frozen exteriors and endless shopping of the fast-approaching holiday season. And though the speaker calls out to his often sexualized city for some form of affection or sympathy—"Clasp me in your handkerchief like a tear," he pleads—it offers no response, and O'Hara is left to face an oppressive chorus of institutional discourses, a chorus that bears down upon him, methodically, "like a locomotive on the march."[31]

One way to explain O'Hara's failures of mood and attunement in "Music" is to read it in relation to Eve Sedgwick's meditation on "the Christmas season . . . when all institutions are speaking with one voice." The voice Sedgwick describes is the state- and church-sanctioned, commercially supported voice of "the family, an impacted social space" that comes to stand for a nearly endless series of normative assumptions about the wholeness and stability (at once economic, sexual, reproductive, patriotic, religious, and so forth) that the family is said to offer us.[32] It is a voice that marks O'Hara (gay, nonmonogamous, an atheist, without children, always renting, never buying) as perverse, abnormal, excluded. It marks him as failing to participate. And while "Music" does not describe this sense of exclusion in the explicitly political and ideological terms that Sedgwick employs, I would argue that its speaker's "distress" grows out of his confrontation with a pre-Christmasy Manhattan that suddenly dulls his capacity to intuit attachments or connection and renders impossible the sudden pivot toward collectivity or historical belonging that pops up with such frequency in his poems. Instead of opting for some more literal description of the effects of the exclusionary messages that confront him here, O'Hara constructs a sort of poetic allegory for the way overwhelmingly compacted, self-reinforcing ideological discourses and material structures of inclusion and exclusion interfere with his own personal and artistic commitment to openness and imaginative transformation. Visions of angels, Christmas trees, and late evening shopping finally overwhelm his capacity for imaginative engagement with the city; once "all those coloured lights come on," the speaker suggests with understated portent, his daydreams will end.[33]

* * *

If "Music" reads like an allegory for the depressing, energy-sapping, poetry-killing effects of the Christmas trees, nuclear families, and mandatory consumerism, many more of O'Hara's poems beg for something closer to what Sedgwick calls a "reparative reading."[34] They celebrate art, culture, wit, friendship, and everyday vernacular practices as means of sustaining lives marked, as in "Music," by insult and discouragement. They view poetry as "additive and accretive," an orientation toward an ongoing present with potentially utopic horizons. And they help us understand camp as Sedgwick argues we should, not as self-hating parody but rather as "the communal, historically dense exploration of a variety of reparative practices."[35] As I argued in my reading of "Memoir of Sergei O. . . .," O'Hara engages camp as a way of performing his attachments to miserable poets and divas who have failed to get their due; approaching painful experiences in writing packed with humor and wit; and proposing speculative historical comparisons, or what Sedgwick might call "alternative historiographies."[36] What do postwar Manhattan streets—with all their synesthetic fullness of street names, open parks, shoppers, construction workers, "hum-colored / cabs" (*CP*, 257), and white collar employees— have to do with moments of grand historical upheaval like the French or Russian Revolution? O'Hara's speculative, even counterfactual, historical pivots and comparisons demonstrate the dash and vitality of an emergent, historicist poetics that begins with description and then drifts insistently toward points of convergence and implied collectivity.

No single poem demonstrates O'Hara's distinctive approach to history more keenly than "Rhapsody," and none captures more beautifully the constant intermingling we discover in his poetry between sexual desire and institutional structure. O'Hara's speaker in "Rhapsody" contemplates his embeddedness in the ebb and flow of everyday work life and social relation while still longing for a higher, clearer perspective from which to understand it, or for a comparative historical vision that might somehow redeem his experience of New York streets and sociality. There is an exquisite longing in this poem for just such a perspective, and for an expansion of sexual desire beyond any one potential encounter. Imaginative and sexual energies merge in "Rhapsody" with Manhattan buildings and the flow of traffic through the island; they float up out of "the . . . labyrinth," into the sky, and around the world to Tibet.

Written during O'Hara's most productive period as a poet, "Rhapsody" sings of O'Hara's movements to and from work. Its opening lines give us the address of a building near MoMA that O'Hara would have passed on his way to work, and the rest of the poem floats across a Manhattan geography stretching from MoMA to his apartment near Tompkins Square Park. As clarified in the notes to O'Hara's *Collected Poems*, the façade of the building O'Hara has in mind as the poem opens faces 53rd Street, around the corner from Madison Avenue and a few blocks east of the museum.[37]

515 Madison Avenue
  door to heaven? portal

stopped realities and eternal licentiousness
or at least the jungle of impossible eagerness
your marble is bronze and your lianas elevator cables
swinging from the myth of ascending
I would join
or declining the challenge of racial attractions
they zing on (into the lynch, dear friends)
while everywhere love is breathing draftily
like a doorway linking 53rd with 54th
the east-bound traffic with the west-bound traffic by 8,000,000s
o midtown tunnels and the tunnels, too, of Holland
(*CP*, 325–26)

"Rhapsody" opens with a workaday, professional setting it then reshapes through metaphorical substitution and virtuosic associative rhetoric. It offers us a specific business address, the façade of a building, and, beyond that, the elevator that would carry executives and administrators, lawyers and secretaries, managers and salesmen up to their offices at the start of the day. As C. Wright Mills and others argued in the 1950s, it was a culture of cooperation and efficiency, which discouraged serious thinking about historical causes and effects.[38] Pulling this setting into its associative flow, however, the poem transforms it into a broader geography of social connection and sexual desire. Let us suppose that there is a black elevator operator here as well, barely disguised behind O'Hara's references to "racial attraction" and his "impossible eagerness" to step into the elevator and ascend in cruisy, lascivious bliss. The elevator operator is imagined as a potential lover, someone O'Hara might once have approached with offers of sex, as he once approached the security guard at the United Nations or the coin clerk at a Queens subway station.[39]

The opening stanza's tone of nonspecific longing, however, complicates an explicitly cruisy reading of this poem, or at least one focused on a single lover, as does its rhythm of questioning, qualification, and digressive response. Is the door to this building the "door to heaven," the poem asks, a "portal" within which "realities" stop and are replaced with "eternal licentiousness"? Might it also be the case that licentiousness disperses so widely once one passes through the door that it becomes indistinguishable from other forms of affection and affiliation? O'Hara's lineation, lack of punctuation, and ambiguous syntax make multiple responses available to us. We can connect the different parts of the poem differently, according to the logic of multiple attractions and overlapping possibilities that seems to characterize O'Hara's social and sexual instincts as well. By the end of the stanza, questions and qualifications are replaced by the confident assertion that "love is breathing draftily" through that midtown block, linking it with other blocks, expanding with the flow of traffic and moving underground on its way—love's way—off the island. The tunneling here is as erotic as it is connective, expanding through chiasmus and repetition to the sounds of "t" and "n," "oo" and "o." In the middle of the stanza, however, the speaker's assertions don't seem as confident, and the upward movements of the poem are troubled by racial difference. "Into the lynch, dear friends," O'Hara remarks self-critically, suggesting that the same jungle imagery and mythologies of licentiousness that subject African Americans to threats of racial violence might well have tainted his longings for interracial connection.[40]

"[W]here is the summit where all aims are clear," O'Hara asks at the start of the poem's second stanza, "the pin-point light upon a fear of lust." Here the interrogative tone of the poem's opening lines returns, as well as O'Hara's upward drift and apparent longing for a standpoint from which to understand more clearly his own motivations as they intersect with the politics of social division and desire. Why should lust inspire fear? Can we pinpoint the reasons and the results? Or, to raise an overlapping question, one that shapes the final stanzas of "Rhapsody," why should alternative practices and modes of desire—spiritual as well as sexual—call down violent reprisals from ruling regimes, as was the case with gay men in New York as well as with Tibetan Buddhists, whose recent uprising against the Chinese communist government had been repressed by military force?

True to its emergent procedures, the poem responds to such questions not with explicit answers but rather with improvised descriptions of the feelings and events that inspired the questions in the first place. This is, after all, a rhapsody, which for Rachmaninoff or Prokofiev (two more Russian Sergeis and two of O'Hara's favorite composers) would indicate both emotional intensity and the episodic, nearly improvisatory shifts a poem or musical composition would pass through over the course of a single, extended movement.[41] Whereas the jump cuts and dissolves of "Music" seem to respond to a single moment ("If I rest for a moment near the Equestrian") during which O'Hara observes an urban setting he then proceeds to transform imaginatively and metaphorically, "Rhapsody" skips paratactically between episodes, settings, and affective atmospheres. It moves exuberantly and then in more melancholy tones from one geographical reference to the next (Holland, Canada, Niagara Falls, Victoria Falls, "the Gulf of Guinea near the Menemsha Bar," the "beautiful urban fountains of Madrid"), all the while grounding itself in the specific geography of Manhattan in the late 1950s: "getting into a cab at 9th Street and 1st Avenue," "passing Madison Avenue," or "lying in a hammock on St. Mark's Place sorting . . . poems" (*CP*, 326).

In the third and fourth stanzas of "Rhapsody," O'Hara catches a cab in the East Village, rides uptown on his way to work, and then hovers in the midtown of MoMA and Madison Avenue. But in the poem's final stanza he plunges back downtown:

> I have always wanted to be near it
> though the day is long (and I don't mean Madison Avenue)
> lying in a hammock on St. Mark's Place sorting my poems
> in the rancid nourishment of this mountainous island
> they are coming and we holy ones must go
> is Tibet historically a part of China? as I historically
> belong to the enormous bliss of American death
> (*CP*, 326)

"I have always wanted to be near it," the speaker assures us, invoking all at once Manhattan, the quality of light there, and the tensions and potential connections that the city invites. The day is long for New Yorkers hoping to combine a full workday with the promise of social life, sexual bliss, creative endeavor. Further, the hierarchies of race and class invoked in this poem, like the homophobic insults and exclusions of "Music," can turn the nourishment the city offers rancid. In response to such insults, O'Hara turns both to poetry and to the sustaining holiness of historical belonging, in particular those forms of belonging forged in response to oppression and exploitation, which thrive with the economy in this poem, and with sanction from the state.

The poem's closing reference to Tibet's recent uprising and the Chinese government's subsequent crackdown clarifies a great deal about the poem and in fact retroactively alters the imagery of the preceding stanzas. O'Hara draws here upon an important Cold War event and constructs the quotidian around it, to borrow Michael Davidson's formulation, using it to shape his meditations on his own workday itineraries and on U.S. culture as an internally contradictory proposition, a spectacular combination of repression and permissiveness, catastrophe and bliss. Though O'Hara's sympathy for the Dalai Lama, who had fled Lhasa under threat to seek asylum in India, aligns in this case with American interests, he nevertheless proposes in "Rhapsody" something like the "alternate register" Davidson identifies in "Poem (Khrushchev is coming on the right day!)." He fashions a "queer, celebratory" voice that displaces official Cold War accounts of the Chinese crackdown on Tibet, which American journalists and government officials criticized as a sign of the heavy-handedness and intolerance of China's communist government.[42] Indeed, the repressive decisions of the Mao government are not addressed directly in the poem but referred to obliquely, in the poem's mention of "run[ning] the gauntlet" and in its indefinite mention of a "they" who "are coming," thus forcing the "holy ones [to] go." These lines, I would argue—when placed in the larger context of the poem—seem to refer more pointedly to oppression and inequality in the United States than they do to the political situation in Tibet.

The Dalai Lama smiles out from the pages of the *New York Times* in a feature on "The God-King of Tibet" published in April, some four months before O'Hara wrote "Rhapsody" (dated July 30, 1959). He is described in the feature as projecting "an almost overwhelming gentleness," the kind of calm one might associate with someone believed to be "a living god, the incarnation of the Lord Buddha himself."[43] O'Hara echoes such descriptions when he writes, at the start of the poem's penultimate stanza, "you were there always and you know about all these things / as indifferent as an encyclopedia with your calm brown eyes" (*CP*, 326). Queering the god-king, O'Hara depicts him in this stanza as a queen, smiling and preternaturally calm but also spitting fiercely—gorgeous as a fountain or waterfall—while running the gauntlet out of Lhasa and south into India. From the start ("into the lynch, dear friends") the poem invokes threats of physical violence and harassment endured not just by the Dalai Lama but by the gay and black, working-class New Yorkers who populate the poem, and indeed by African Americans in the South, running the gauntlet of white racists in their attempts to integrate schools or sit down on a bus. The threats are not debilitating to any of these groups, however, at least not in "Rhapsody." The poem's own reparative accents fall instead on the historical belonging it associates with poetry itself, and with all those communities made holy by their ability to carry on in the face of insult and coercion.

* * *

O'Hara's poetry thus opens a discursive space in which comparative global and historical perspectives—Russian poets lost in American parks, Khrushchev on the train to Penn Station, birds flying high over Paris, the Dalai Lama fleeing Tibet—push off suddenly from an embedded social world and then linger speculatively in the atmosphere. A quick survey of O'Hara's poems adds numerous other instances to this list: Jean Dubuffet in the Eiffel Tower in 1922, Iroquois workers on New York skyscrapers at the start of the century, Buddhist artworks addressing the people of West Germany, and so forth. This array of perspectives bespeaks O'Hara's longing, if not to map his position cognitively, in relation to some larger, impossibly complex circuit of social relations, at least to keep generating those alternative historiographies to which he has become so attached, and whose reparative powers seem so evident. (How would one go about describing, for that matter, the relationship between O'Hara and the Dalai Lama, sexual freedom in postwar New York and religious and cultural freedom in Tibet?) Even in the absence of the capacity for cognitive mapping, furthermore, O'Hara continues to map his world affectively, offering a remarkably detailed and prolific catalog of how he feels about people, places, books, buildings, poems, paintings, films, countries, historical events, specific commodities, celebrities, seasons, and the mood on the sidewalk as he hurries past.

What would such a reading look like when applied to O'Hara's most famous "I do this I do that" poem, a lyric more often read as an elegy or as an energetic portrait of late-1950s Manhattan than as a serious meditation on the historical imagination? "The Day Lady Died," as critics have quite rightly insisted, reoriented the elegiac tradition, issuing it abruptly into the era of mass culture, in which we learn about the death of famous people by way of newspaper (now internet) headlines and struggle in real time to articulate our response to their passing.[44] It is also a subtly perceptive poem about an everyday life transformed by consumer culture, which renders politically alternative communities infinitely rarer and more vulnerable without, however, rendering them impossible. Within the postwar market economy, the various modernisms in which O'Hara remains invested need to be sewn into the fabric of some deeper sense of personal or collective memory if they are going to retain any of their explanatory force or political significance.

The day that Frank O'Hara wrote "The Day Lady Died," one might say, revolution was in the back of his mind. Writing his famous elegy for Billie Holiday while sitting in his office at the Museum of Modern Art on July 17, 1959, he returned subtly but repeatedly to images of political upheaval and transformation.[45] Here is Bastille Day in the poem's second line, a reference to Ghana's recent struggle for independence in lines 9–10, an invocation in lines 16 and 17 of two different Jean Genet plays meditating on historical violence and rebellion, *Le Balcon* (1957) and *Les Nègres* (1959), alongside a reference to "Brendan Behan's new play"—*The Hostage* (1958)—set in a brothel and against a background of political violence and unrest between Britain and the Irish Republican Army. Buying a hostess gift "for Patsy," whom he'll see on Long Island that weekend, O'Hara's speaker decides against the two Genet plays and instead picks out a book of Verlaine poems illustrated by Bonnard, "after practically going to sleep with quandariness" (*CP*, 325). Though the imagination in this poem seems drawn to scenes of revolution, finally it chooses something else, something less like political art and more like an art book for a friend. Indeed, one might argue that it's appropriate that the poem is set "three days after Bastille day," in a distant or belated relationship to the histories of political rupture that still shaped modern intellectual culture in late-1950s New York. If Amiri Baraka (then LeRoi Jones) was electrified, as I'll discuss in chapter 2, by the Cuban Revolution and by postcolonial independence movements in Africa and Asia, for O'Hara such movements seemed farther away, less like immediate possibilities and more like "spirits" one might call to and then contemplate in relation to everyday life in Manhattan (*CP*, 305).

And yet O'Hara's poem seems equally inconceivable without the continued presence and possibility of the revolutionary event, and of the new identities and collectivities it might inspire. References to Ghanaian independence and to the poems it inspired, or to Genet's revolutionary settings, frame the dramatic transformation of O'Hara's speaker's consciousness and sense of temporality in "The Day Lady Died." As many readers know already, all of O'Hara's lunchtime preparations for leaving town for the weekend (eating lunch, shopping for friends, buying cigarettes, withdrawing cash, having a shoeshine) are interrupted by the sort of media event that now seems familiar to us (after JFK, after Malcolm, after MLK, after Lady Diana, after Kurt Cobain, after Michael Jackson, after Whitney Houston, after Prince) but that O'Hara captured for the first time in literature.[46] Seeing the headline and front-page photo in the *New York Post* announcing Billie Holiday's death provokes a sudden epiphany in the speaker, who is swept out of the ongoing present of midday errands and returned to the memory of having seen Holiday perform some months before at the Five Spot:

> and I am sweating a lot by now and thinking of
> leaning on the john door in the 5 SPOT
> while she whispered a song along the keyboard
> to Mal Waldron and everyone and I stopped breathing.
> (*CP*, 325)

With improvised brilliance, O'Hara's line breaks pull us down the page and back into the whispered past of memory, where the felt sensations of the speaker's own stopped breath and leaning body respond to the ethereal physicality of Holiday's song as it travels quietly across piano keys to both audience and accompanist. O'Hara's final quatrain in "The Day Lady Died" is remarkable for the sense of immediacy and radical intimacy it creates. The sudden pause or syncopation punctuating Holiday's performance ("and everyone and I stopped breathing") mirrors the interruption in the poem's narration of everyday consumer decisions and its abrupt movement into the space of elegiac memory. This pause—an inhaling of breath by the audience in response to the distinctive whispers and hesitations that characterized Holiday's own performance late in life—hints at the transformation of the isolated, individual decisions of the poem's first twenty-five lines into a space of shared emotion and communal desire. The possibility emerges in the poem's final lines that the speaker's "quandariness" about his own social life might be redeemed by a moment of solidarity and brief but nonetheless utopic community.

Such moments—of abrupt solidarity, of intimate connection and collectivity—occur frequently in O'Hara's poems. They are not "economic fiction[s]" in Clune's sense of the term, according to which O'Hara would give himself over to a market that then structures agency and collectivity for him, regardless of his own personal preferences or attachments (and regardless of "the constraints of . . . the social sphere").[47] They are rather moments during which the contingencies of the market and the larger universe of social relations—the sudden appearance of a newspaper headline announcing the death of someone he feels attached to, for instance, at the moment he stops to buy cigarettes—are given new meaning the instant they come into contact with his own memories and affective commitments. They are transformed in part because these memories and attachments let O'Hara imagine that he might be connected to others who feel similarly. There are people out there, O'Hara's poems seem to be telling us, who share our feelings about poems, songs, public bathrooms, political discourses, historical events, or—in this instance—about the death of someone we admire.

Such moments of potential solidarity are not without their ambiguities and hesitations, as is indicated by the famously uncertain syntax of the final line of "The Day Lady Died." Does Holiday whisper a song to Mal Waldron while the speaker holds his breath along with everyone else in the basement club, at the same instant and in a moment of intensity and transformative collectivity? Or does she whisper her song to her accompanist and to everyone else, while the speaker, alone against the john door, contemplates his own isolation and, ultimately, his own death? These are tensions the poem creates and then holds open, the speed and flexibility of its syntax encompassing multiple possibilities rather than resolving them into a singular vision. In so many of O'Hara's poems, as in the poems by Baraka, Diane di Prima, and Allen Ginsberg that I will go on to discuss, the point is not just to conjure for us the existence of new collectivities but to remake art in relation to their complexities, vulnerabilities, and sudden appearances on the horizon.

LeRoi Jones, Editor

Kulchur Magazine and the Poetry of Cultural Politics

> some possible image
> of what we shall call history.
>
> –Amiri Baraka, "A Poem for Neutrals"

History, as Hayden White reminds us, is made up of the stories we tell ourselves about the past, and about how it shapes our present and potential futures.[1] History looks and feels different, however, when offered to us not as narrative but rather as an extended poetic and editorial performance located, as Fred Moten puts it, "in the break, in the scene, in the music."[2] Such is the case with Amiri Baraka's (then, LeRoi Jones) poems, essays, and editorial activity at the start of the 1960s, in which the historical imagination expresses itself both aesthetically and as active social practice, in dialogue with a downtown scene dedicated—from drama to dance, from visual art to art criticism—to renovating American culture. True to the collaborative and multimedia experiments of the era, and to the Beat, Black Mountain, and New York School poets who influenced him, Baraka invents a fragmented, syncopated, avant-garde aesthetic for his poetry, one that echoes and overlaps with his historical speculations in other genres.

As I argue in this chapter, echoing Baraka's own accounts of his development, these historical speculations tend increasingly toward ideas of revolution.[3] They tend toward an increasingly political art, inspired by the most vociferous and uncompromising resistance to U.S. racism at home and by postcolonial revolutions abroad. That this development remains tense and inconsistent constitutes an essential feature of Baraka's work, one that both he and his most perceptive critics have often remarked upon.[4] The revolutionary cast of his thinking takes shape in poems that vacillate between what he once called "pure lyrics," on the one hand, and poems that "take . . . some kind of specific social attitude."[5]

Nor is it just in his poems that Baraka strives to respond actively to feelings of frustration about his own life or about the larger forces impinging on him. Indeed, few critical statements on the art forms and affects of the postwar moment are as illuminating as those Baraka offers on black music. In *Blues*

People: Negro Music in White America (1963) and in the essays and reviews collected in *Black Music* (1968), Baraka gathers the dissatisfactions and historiographic confusions of the 1950s and pushes them toward the increasingly audacious claims of the late 1960s. In the case of *Black Music*, the endpoint is the revolutionary-utopic structure of feeling of black nationalism as captured in the live and recorded performances of free jazz. From Baraka's perspective, the extended improvisations and rhythmically and harmonically expansive compositions of Ornette Coleman, Cecil Taylor, Archie Shepp, Sun Ra, Sonny Rollins, John Coltrane, Eric Dolphy, Max Roach, and Abbey Lincoln, among others, managed to reinterpret the history of African American music, expressing its "consciousness of social reevaluation and rise, a social spiritualism" that unified the avant-garde and the popular, "jazz and blues, religious and secular."[6] The jazz avant-garde in this formulation remains connected to "the straightest R&B," the two forms intersecting and mutually reinforcing one another: "James-Ra and Sun-Brown" (*BM*, 180, 211). Joined by their shared embodiment of "the blues impulse," both free jazz and R&B refuse the whitening of black American music and free themselves and their listeners from "American white cocktail droop, tinkle" and "[t]he strait jacket of American expression *sans* blackness" (*BM*, 180, 209).[7]

On the way to his Black Nationalist stance of the late 1960s, Baraka articulates a theory of affective and stylistic change over time that echoes Raymond Williams's contemporaneous articulation of the concept of the "structure of feeling."[8] Baraka's critique of existing jazz criticism and defense of blues, bebop, and free jazz depends fundamentally on the idea that the formal innovations of black musicians express a set of lived "attitudes" or "redefined emotional statements," affective stances that reflect changes in racial experience over time (*BM*, 14, 19). The first essay in *Black Music*, for example, "Jazz and the White Critic," originally published in *DownBeat* in 1963, makes a case for the emergence of critics like Baraka and friend and fellow poet and small magazine contributor A. B. Spellman, black critics in their twenties who understood what was at stake in free jazz. While white critics like John Tynan and Leonard Feather disparaged the "anti-jazz" turn taken by John Coltrane in the early 1960s, Baraka and Spellman strongly identified with this change, which was bolstered by a growing circle of musicians playing what was first called "the new thing" or "the jazz avant-garde," and which seemed to Baraka and Spellman to gather up and give shape to the present. Central to Baraka's response to "anti-jazz" critics and defense of the new genre was a sense of history, one marked by the absence of a jazz criticism capable of understanding the music's development over time and in relation to the changing conditions of black lives. The white critics who had produced the bulk of jazz criticism to that point had failed to frame the rise of newly experimental jazz within an accurate understanding of history. Then as in the past they misunderstood the social implications of the music they listened to. They offered "strict musicological" or "narrow sociological analysis" without managing to understand the emotional impact of the music, "the attitudes which produced it" (*BM*, 14). "Coltrane's cries are not 'musical,' but they *are* music and quite moving music," Baraka asserts. "Ornette Coleman's screams and rants are only musical once one understands the music his emotional attitude seeks to create" (*BM*, 15). White critics like Tynan and Feathers misunderstood the honks, cries, and collective improvisations of free jazz just as their precursors had misunderstood bebop, which to Baraka's ear "carried with it a distinct element of social protest" and whose "anarchy," "excitement," and rhythmic invention free jazz reapplied in the present (*BM*, 16, 23).

In an earlier essay, "The Jazz Avant-Garde," first published in 1961 in *Metronome*, Baraka sets forth the initial terms of an argument he will continue to make—in poems as well as criticism—well into the 1970s. Bebop and the blues are "the *roots*" of the new jazz, and these roots "are emotion." "The *technique*, the ideas": these constitute "the way of handling that emotion" (*BM*, 72). The avant-garde in Baraka's formulation thus consists of the ability to make vital aesthetic and conceptual use of historical resources, to reinterpret mediating emotional structures and forms in relation to the present. The answer to the question of how to play "exactly what I feel," Baraka argues, "is a *technical* consideration," where technique is understood as expansively as possible, as the ability "to use what important ideas are contained in the residue of history or in the now-swell of living" (*BM*, 71). "To my mind," Baraka writes, "*technique* is inseparable from what is finally played as content." "A *bad* solo," he continues, "no matter how 'well' it is played is still *bad*" (*BM*, 71).

* * *

These arguments about the active, technical expression of contemporaneous affects are applied forcefully by Baraka in both his poetry and his little magazines.[9] The three little magazines Baraka, then LeRoi Jones, either cofounded or helped edit from 1958 to 1965—*Yügen*, *The Floating Bear*, and *Kulchur*— offer snapshots of the cultural terrain to which Baraka responds, including new jazz records, pressing intellectual debates, recently published essays, and reports of civil rights activism at home and political conflict abroad. Significant events stand out, as the Cuban Revolution does when one reads early issues of *Kulchur*. Reading these little magazines in sequence, moreover, from the first issues of *Yügen* to the final issues of *The Floating Bear* and *Kulchur* with which Baraka remained directly involved, allows us to reconsider the familiar narrative of Baraka's transition away from primarily aesthetic notions of poetry and toward a tense and increasingly contentious version of poetry as cultural politics, tense in part because it refuses to abandon notions of style and aesthetics—of technique—and must then expand to accommodate increasingly political demands. It is as if we are hearing a new arrangement of an old tune, or hearing it reinterpreted by a new ensemble.

Just as Frank O'Hara's poems do, Baraka's poems from the late 1950s through the mid-1960s shift rapidly between scenes of personal life and its various cultural and historical frames. They skip from one frame to the next, their non sequiturs held together by the poem's overall mood or emotional atmosphere. Consider, for instance, these excerpts from "Look for You Yesterday, Here You Come Today," an important poem from Baraka's first published volume, *Preface to a Twenty Volume Suicide Note* (1961):

> Part of my charm:
>   envious blues feeling
>   separation of church & state
>   grim calls from drunk debutantes
>
> Morning never aids me in my quest.
> I have to trim my beard in solitude.
> I try to hum lines from "The Poet in New York"
>
> [. . .]
>
> It's so diffuse
> being alive. Suddenly one is aware
>   that no one really gives a damn.
>   My wife is pregnant with *her* child
>   "It means nothing to me," sez Strindberg
> [. . .]
> I would take up painting
> if I cd think of a way to do it
> better than Leonardo. Than Bosch.
> Than Hogarth. Than Kline.
> [. . .]
> All the lovely things I've known have disappeared.
> I have all my pubic hair & am lonely.
> There is probably no such place as Battle Creek, Michigan
>
> Tom Mix dead in a Boston Nightclub
> before I realized what happened.

[. . .]

THERE MUST BE A LONE RANGER!!!¹⁰

As these excerpts suggest, "Look for You Yesterday, Here You Come Today" rides its speaker's free-floating "blues feelings" and "maudlin nostalgia" from one reference to another, skipping from poetry to visual art, modern drama, World War II, narratives of modernization, film genres, popular radio shows, advertising, and back to the blues. It offers us an "avalanche of words" and poetic stanzas, improvised and loosely connected, all indulging in the speaker's sense of himself as never quite present—dispersing instead into memory and failing to ground himself permanently in any of the cultural frames he invokes. Tom Mix, star of early Westerns, has passed on. Battle Creek, Michigan, a town associated with the cereal box top rewards of Baraka's youth, likely never existed, at least in the drifting, obsessively self-conscious logic of the poem. Similarly, Baraka's speaker finds that his own past selves are now lost to him, and he waits in vain for some new identity to coalesce. He quotes a classic blues lyric ("Look for you yesterday / Here you come today") that, in the context of this poem, substitutes a story of self-discovery perpetually delayed for a scene of frustrated romantic longing. The speaker searches for but never manages to discover himself in this ongoing series of activities, historical locations, and texts.

If Baraka's poems begin with something very much like O'Hara's continual pivots and emergent historicism, as the 1960s go on his poems demonstrates a much greater enthusiasm than O'Hara's for reimagining poetry as mode of explicit confrontation. O'Hara's poems, as I have argued in chapter 1, mostly go about their business. They swing between scenes of intimate friendship and sudden vistas of collectivity, happy to be overheard but unlikely to challenge readers directly. They situate friendship, coterie, and collectivity in historical context, as critics like Andrew Epstein and Lytle Shaw have argued, but their cultural politics and moments of critique most often reach us through subtlety or misdirection. O'Hara, as Shaw puts it, enters into "public social discourse from a position often misunderstood as private."¹¹ Baraka's treatments of everyday experience, on the other hand, are more immediately confrontational; by the time he publishes his second volume of poetry, *The Dead Lecturer* (1964), he favors poems that set out to identify and critique a group of hypocrites. This procedure is evident from the poems' titles: "A Poem for Neutrals," "Short Speech to My Friends," "The Politics of Rich Painters," "A Poem for Democrats," "A Poem for Speculative Hipsters." Again and again, Baraka pushes past the moment during which a poem gathers up the details and emotional contours of a felt historical location and begins to stake out positions in a set of public debates.[12] "Luxury," he writes in "Political Poem," opening with a tone of direct confrontation that rarely appears in O'Hara's work, "is a way of / being ignorant, comfortably / An approach to the open market / of least information" (*T*, 107).

Echoing the arguments of other New Left intellectuals, Baraka used the poetry, fiction, essays, editorials, and music reviews he published in his little magazines to expand politics into the field of culture, itself expanding rapidly after World War II. It is at precisely this moment, as Fredric Jameson, Michael Denning, Marianne DeKoven, and others have argued, that popular culture is transformed irrevocably into mass culture, leisure activities become as fully commodified as manufactured goods, and art feels itself being swallowed up by advertising.[13] As Denning writes,

> It was not that there had been no culture before 1950, but it was always in a period's background. Historians dutifully included it in a supplementary chapter on arts and culture as they surveyed the age of Jackson or Victoria. But suddenly, in the age of three worlds, everyone discovered that culture had been mass produced like Ford's cars; the masses had culture and culture had a mass. Culture was everywhere[.][14]

Late capitalism in what Denning calls "the age of three worlds"—another way of describing the Cold War's portioning of the world into communist, capitalist, and so-called "third world" countries—ushers in an unevenly developed yet perceptibly postindustrial economy, one now difficult to distinguish from consumer society. International conglomerates and state ideological apparatuses begin not just to regulate economic and foreign policy but to profit from the very lifestyles they market and promote. "America," Allen Ginsberg asks of his country in 1956, "Are you going to let your emotional life be run by Time Magazine?"[15]

Like other intellectuals of the era, Baraka responds to the coercions of mass society by fusing his analysis of everyday hypocrisies—by racists, bohemian intellectuals, or the black bourgeoisie, for example—with critiques of the systems and ideologies that sustain them. He attacks what Herbert Marcuse would have called "one-dimensional" thinking, what C. Wright Mills characterized as "the power to manage and manipulate the consent of men," or what Betty Friedan described as the consolidation of discourses (expert, traditional, commercial, institutional) all aimed at delivering the same debilitating message.[16] In the United States, Baraka argues in 1960 in his "Cuba Libre" essay, intellectuals and average citizens alike are cowed by "the thin crust of lie [they] cannot even detect in [their] own thinking," thus leaving them ignorant about global events and complacent about their own lack of political agency and influence.[17] In response, the first goal of intellectuals has to be to reassess, critique, and raise consciousness, drawing for one another what Jameson would later describe as "cognitive maps" of a simultaneously disorienting and seductive cultural terrain.[18]

Baraka's little magazines, as they connected postwar experimental poets to a larger community of New York critics and intellectuals, became an important site for this kind of cognitive mapping. Indeed, alongside their impact as venues for some of the most important poems of their era, the little magazines Baraka edited should be thought of as active, collaborative attempts to gain some leverage on a set of historical conditions and ideological pressures he and others saw as profoundly disempowering. "What do we do now?" Baraka asks in "Milneburg Joys," a critique of bohemian conformity that adds crackle and intensity to *Kulchur* 3: "New York City, March 1961. The world here, almost as we have made it."[19] Baraka's little magazines, and *Kulchur* in particular, scramble to relate developments in one artistic medium to contemporaneous developments in other media, and to set them beside cultural and political events adduced as historical context. Implicitly and explicitly, they work to establish the little magazine among a more and more widely proliferating set of choices and styles—in literature or on television, in dance performances or as expressions of subcultural dispositions such as hipness and camp. They attempt to explain how experimental art might still help to outline a critical and enabling sense of the historical situation, reinforcing the notion of emergent historicism—with its love for pivots and its expanded range of affect—that I outlined in my introduction and the first chapter on O'Hara.

Even as Baraka insists on collaboration, however, his deployments of affect retain something distinctive. In his poetry as well as in his critical and editorial writings, Baraka invokes skepticism and intellectual rigor as forms of resistance to the seductions of lazy consensus, whether among downtown bohemians or Cold War Americans as a whole. As he reiterates in poem after poem, however, skepticism and critical intelligence often begin as emotional responses: as feelings of dissatisfaction, for instance, with a poem, a piece of music, an existing description of a cultural field, a platitude about racial progress, or a popular explanation for U.S. foreign policy. Nathaniel Mackey has underscored this dialectical movement in Baraka's poems between rational (abstract and philosophical) perspectives, on the one hand, and, on the other, the invocation of emotional truths meant to undermine supposedly thoughtful, confidently logical positions Baraka nonetheless considers false. Invoking strong feelings in order to protest and deconstruct familiar ideologies constitutes what Mackey describes as an "anti-reflective position, . . . having been arrived at by way of reflection," "not so much a repudiation of thought as an effort to rethink, to as it were *un*think the perversions of thought endemic to an unjust social order."[20] "Forget me, or what I say," Baraka writes in "Tone Poem," "but not the tone, and exit image," and indeed the tone and imagery of Baraka's poems are often the features we remember best (*T*, 131). Similarly, in the editorials he writes for *Kulchur* and *The Floating Bear*, his critiques tend to hinge on the tone they produce, or the frustration they convey with political positions or aesthetic judgments he then proceeds to deconstruct on intellectual grounds.

* * *

Yügen, *The Floating Bear*, and *Kulchur* offer a wide lens through which to consider Baraka's diverse, overlapping approaches to history, including his production of music criticism; his commitment to building a shared, alternative poetry movement; and his more and more explicit embrace of poetry as a form of cultural politics. These magazines also stand as important cultural documents in their own right: tangible evidence of the poetic energies, political concerns, and literary-bohemian social formations of the late 1950s and early 1960s. *Yügen* and *The Floating Bear* began as underground poetry initiatives, collectively produced and circulating locally or among small groups of friends and fellow poets; they remained so throughout their publication. *Yügen*, on the cover of its first issue, promised readers "a new consciousness in arts and letters." *Kulchur* moved beyond aesthetic promises and into the realm of cultural critique. By its fifth issue, *Kulchur* was billing itself as "the only vanguard magazine devoted principally to / Criticism and Commentary," and as a source for "essays on literature, art, jazz, politics & pop culture / by leading poets."[21]

As in previous and subsequent avant-garde movements, experimental poets establishing themselves in the 1950s and early 1960s did so by founding magazines and cultivating the social ties and opportunities for collaboration they provided. Diane di Prima, with whom Baraka cofounded and coedited *The Floating Bear* during its first years, has commented perceptively, for example, on their early, symbiotic relationship with the poet Charles Olson:

> I remember that the last time I saw Charles Olson in Gloucester, one of the things he talked about was how valuable the Bear had been to him in its early years because of the fact the he could get new work out that fast. He was very involved in speed, in communication. We got manuscripts from him pretty regularly in the early days of the Bear, and we'd usually get them into the very next issue. That meant that his work, his thoughts, would be in the hands of a few

hundred writers within two or three weeks. It was like writing a letter to a bunch of friends.[22]

Alongside the voluminous correspondence these same poets maintained with one another, their little magazines offer a vivid impression of their shared, often urgent sense of purpose. They reinforce our sense of a poetic movement founded on mutual enthusiasm and self-interest, built from the ground up, if often orchestrated by central figures within a set of overlapping poetic groups. Thus Olson and Robert Creeley supported other Black Mountain poets in print and in their letters, for instance, while Ginsberg worked tirelessly to promote the writings of Jack Kerouac, William Burroughs, Gary Snyder, and Gregory Corso (all of whom became prominent Beat figures thanks in part to Ginsberg's efforts) as well as the work of poets like Anselm Hollo and Ron Loewinsohn.

Ginsberg's correspondence in the early 1960s suggests just how quickly Baraka had inserted himself into discussions among experimental poets, and how successfully he had managed to integrate *Yügen*, *The Floating Bear*, and *Kulchur* into a field that included experimental magazines like *Evergreen Review*, *Black Mountain Review*, and *Big Table*. "I received Bears 14 and 15 yesterday, but no recent Kulchurs," Ginsberg writes to Baraka from India in March 1962. In a 1961 letter to Henry Wenning, a publisher and manuscript collector, Ginsberg urges him to get in touch with Baraka, "a key person in younger literary scene & in contact with almost everybody." Ginsberg continues: "his magazine Yügen is historically rare & valuable, and also he puts out a mimeographed sheet 'The Floating Bear' which is a gas."[23]

Baraka's magazines benefited from his evident talent for correspondence and collaboration, his skill at integrating himself into the scene, and his genuine commitment to the aesthetic principles—openness, spontaneity, immediacy, an emphasis on process over final product—his magazines defended. They also appeared on the scene at an unusually propitious moment. The new poets emerging from World War II moved deftly to define themselves against the New Criticism, a figure of poetic authority so predictable and institutionally powerful that it had become increasingly vulnerable. New Critical paradigms, then dominant in colleges, universities, and academic quarterlies like the *Kenyon* and *Sewanee Reviews*, offered a remarkably portable model of poetic engagement and critique, of how one might go about defining a set of aesthetic criteria and then writing poems that embodied them. These criteria, however, and the social positions and cultural attitudes they implied, were narrow enough to invite criticism, if not outright revolt. Even little magazines of the 1950s that were relatively vague about their aesthetic positions generated a sense of vanguard momentum by embracing previously unacceptable content (sexual, excessively spiritual, left political, drugged-out, absurdist) and by claiming to resist the "academicism . . . sapping the vitality of most . . . university magazines and of the literary reviews in general," as New Mexico–based poet and publisher Judson Crews, another of Baraka's correspondents, did in advertising his own small magazines.[24]

Baraka's little magazines thus situated themselves explicitly within a larger cultural and literary historical effort to shape an alternative canon in mid-century American poetry. This was an effort, as Alan Golding has argued, consolidated by the publication of Donald Allen's *The New American Poetry* in 1960 but already well underway in the 1950s in little magazines such as *Origin* and *Black Mountain Review*.[25] Though some of these magazines—*Origin*, for instance—survived long enough to be called institutions, most of them, including those Baraka helped publish, had a much more provisional character. They presented themselves as avant-garde and anti-institutional: loose organizational structures devoted to a shared aesthetic and set explicitly in opposition to those universally recognized institutions—colleges and universities, corporations, branches of the military—whose self-perpetuating hierarchies Baraka's bohemian cohort hoped to escape.

This resistance to so-called academic poetry, however, did not constitute an anti-institutional stance so much as an insistence on founding and supporting alternative institutions, such as jazz clubs, bookstores, or avant-garde theaters. Little magazines like *Yūgen* and *The Floating Bear* necessarily lacked the stability and long-term trajectory of literary quarterlies with broader subscription bases and the financial support of a college or university. Laid out in apartments and mimeographed or printed cheaply in the neighborhood, they were distributed in alternative bookstores or through the mail, allowing artistic communities to coalesce immediately and achieve cultural impact without making long-term investments in infrastructure, organizational structure, or reputation. They could be shut down just as quickly as they started up and react to political and cultural events just as swiftly as they could issue statements on poetry and poetics. Like Olson, they were "involved in speed, in communication."

Just as urgently for Baraka, the poetry magazines to which he committed himself seemed to offer the possibility of writing himself actively into literary history. As he narrates in his *Autobiography*, his growing attachment to literature while serving in the Air Force (from 1954 to 1957) was matched by his feeling of alienation from the tone, form, and content of the poems he read during those years in magazines like *Partisan Review* and *The New Yorker*. Reading a poem from *The New Yorker* while stationed in Puerto Rico, Baraka begins to cry, realizing he "could never write like that writer," and that the subtle formalism of the verse, full of "lawns and trees and dew and birds" and "jingling rhymes . . . spoke of a world almost completely alien to [him]." Reading Ginsberg's "Howl" after arriving in the Village, by contrast, Baraka writes: "I was moved by this poem so much because it talked about a world I could identify with and relate to. His language and his rhythms and the poem's contents were real to me. Unlike the cold edges and exclusiveness of the *New Yorker* poem that had made me cry, Ginsberg talked of a different world, much closer to my own."[26]

Baraka's narrative remains useful for my argument for a number of reasons, not least in its demonstration of the emotional logic Baraka employs to advance his case. Here as elsewhere, affect anticipates analysis. Feelings of sadness and exclusion brought on by his encounter with the poem in *The New Yorker* lead first to confusion and inaction and, eventually, to criticism of the aesthetic and ideological positions he associates with the magazine and its audience. Feelings of attachment to Ginsberg's "Howl," on the other hand, deepen Baraka's engagement with the kinds of small magazines and presses that would publish the work of a poet like Ginsberg—one of which, Judson Crews's *Naked Ear*, had just published Baraka's first poem. Beginning with the work of what Jonathan Flatley would call "affective mapping," wherein we register "the affective values of the various sites and situations that constitute our social worlds,"[27] Baraka begins to imagine himself as a poet with an audience. He begins to think of himself as an active participant in literary debates whose wider cultural and sociological implications resonate for him as well as for his readers. By the early 1960s, as demonstrated by Ginsberg's comments in letters to and about him, by the success of *Yügen*, and by his appearance in Allen's *New American Poetry*, Baraka's influence in these debates was already considerable. The affective maps he had drawn of midcentury American poetry began to change, and to extend themselves beyond the literary and into a cultural realm that was being more and more broadly defined.

* * *

Kulchur magazine, lasting twenty issues and published from the spring of 1960 to the winter of 1965, stands as the least provisional of the three magazines Baraka helped edit in the late 1950s and early 1960s. It was by far the most expensive to produce, and it was the publishing venture over which he had the least control. Baraka produced *Yügen* at home with his first wife, Hettie Jones, and with help from the various friends and fellow poets who tended to live with them for the weekend, if not for weeks at a time; he coedited the mimeographed newsletter *The Floating Bear* with di Prima from 1961 to 1963, when Baraka resigned as editor and left the magazine to di Prima, who kept publishing it until 1969. Accounts by di Prima and Jones of the collective work of editing, typing, laying out, collating, and stapling *Yügen* and the early issues of *The Floating Bear*—with Cecil Taylor running the mimeograph machine, no less—have often been cited in celebration of the shared labor of putting together the mimeographed magazines of the era.[28] With contributions from various combinations of Beat, Black Mountain, New York School, and West Coast experimental poets, *Yügen* and *The Floating Bear* already had an improvised, collaborative feel. Baraka placed himself at the center of the collaboration, investing enormous personal energy in both magazines and imbuing them with his own distinctive sense of the cultural landscape. Di Prima remembers that "LeRoi . . . could read two manuscripts at a time, one with each eye. He would spread things out on the table while he was eating supper, and reject them all—listening to the news and a jazz record he was going to review, all at the same time."[29]

Kulchur had a different operational structure. Founded by the journalist Marc Schleifer, it secured financial support from Lita Hornick, a wealthy socialite whose financial backing and editorial influence gave the magazine a much neater, glossier feel than either *Yügen* or *The Floating Bear*. Hornick began holding editorial meetings in her apartment and took seriously her work as publisher and then as managing editor; by *Kulchur*'s fifth issue she had the magazine appearing on a tight quarterly schedule. In Baraka's *Autobiography*, *Kulchur* is associated with the fun and simultaneous irritation of the trips uptown undertaken by the "frayed-at-the-edges semi-bohemians" who gathered to make editorial decisions at Hornick's plush Park Avenue apartment.[30] In its most stable configuration in 1962 and 1963, the masthead featured Baraka as music editor, O'Hara as art editor, Bill Berkson as film editor, Joe LeSueur as theater editor, Gilbert Sorrentino as books editor, and Olson, di Prima, Spellman, and Donald Phelps as contributing editors.

If Baraka was never in charge of *Kulchur*, he was nonetheless the figure whose association with the magazine lasted the longest, from its first to its penultimate issue. Nor is there any doubt that *Yügen* had helped create the audience for *Kulchur*, just as it had helped both socially and intellectually to pull together some of its most important contributors, including O'Hara, di Prima, Spellman, and Sorrentino. Baraka characterizes *Kulchur* as "another vehicle for expression of our broad common aesthetic," and Sorrentino remembers it as "the critical wing of *Yügen*."[31] It thus began as an extension of the larger movement already underway in New York magazines like *Yügen*, Sorrentino's *Neon*, and Baraka and di Prima's *The Floating Bear*, whose first years of publication overlapped with those of *Kulchur*. Baraka helped shape *Kulchur*'s first two issues and helped position it in the publishing landscape; his involvement continued after Hornick signed on as publisher.

From the outset, *Kulchur* was less a poetry magazine than a magazine of criticism and cultural commentary, aspiring to become an edgy, avant-garde alternative to *Partisan Review*. It published essays on a wide range of topics, including poetry, jazz, ballet, modern dance, film, theater, television, comedy, sexuality, pornography, and drug culture. O'Hara's "Art Chronicles," though short lived, are well known; they sit on the pages of *Kulchur* alongside statements on poetry by Olson, George Oppen, and Louis Zukofsky; North African travel sketches by Paul Bowles; jazz reviews by Spellman and Baraka; the first of Burrough's "Yage Letters"; and a striking essay titled "Balanchine Choreographing" by Edwin Denby. Some of Baraka's best-known statements on race and music appeared for the first time in *Kulchur*, including an early version of "African Slaves/American Slaves: Their Music," later published in *Blues People*, and "Tokenism: 300 Years for 5 Cents," later collected in *Home: Social Essays* (1966). As the contentious title of this last essay would indicate, *Kulchur* was also known for a particularly combative, confrontational style, one that Sorrentino has described as "personal, colloquial, wry, mocking, and precisely vulgar when vulgarity seemed called for." "[N]othing was ever explained," he continues, "the writing was elliptical, casual, and obsessively conversational. We had wanted a flashing, brilliant magazine that had nothing to do with the academic world."[32]

This is a prose style—combative, elliptical, and vulgar when necessary—that many of *Kulchur*'s readers would have associated with Ezra Pound, just as they would have understood the magazine's title as a tribute to Pound's *Guide to Kulchur* (1938). Comparing the postwar magazine to Pound's *Guide*, however, only reinforces our sense that culture meant something different after World War II than it had to modernists. By the time *Kulchur* appeared, the work of orienting oneself historically had shifted from Pound's attempt to place himself within the full history of human civilization, charting its decline from "Attic grace" to "accelerated grimace," as he puts it in "Hugh Selwyn Mauberly," to the very different project of keeping pace with contemporary culture. Pound's *Guide* hopes to encompass all human art, thought, action, and civilization; it celebrates authentic "way[s] of life" (such as Confucianism) and instances of the most "human and high[est] state[s] of culture" (such as the *Iliad* and the *Odyssey*).[33] In *Kulchur*, by contrast, high art and popular entertainments overlap and cross-fertilize. Its writers and editors helped invent the criticism of any number of popular genres: stand-up comedy, Westerns, rhythm and blues. Authoritative judgments about works of literature and philosophy are intertwined with, and often displaced by, efforts to generate new frameworks for discussing cultural fields that remain both poorly understood and full of potential to reshape literature. Such is the case for the writings on black music that Baraka—along with critics like Spellman and Martin Williams—published in the early 1960s, in *Kulchur* and in jazz magazines like *DownBeat*, *Jazz Review*, and *Metronome*.[34]

Kulchur thus exemplifies the features Denning associates with the transformation of culture during the Cold War. New Left intellectuals, Denning argues, "redefined culture neither as arts and letters nor as manners and customs," as it had been thought of by previous generations, "but as the new means of communication," mass produced by culture industries and state apparatuses.[35] Though dedicated at the outset to cultivating its roots in poetry and poetry criticism, *Kulchur* begins more and more to focus on the expansion of culture in the United States, taking part in the ongoing project of inventing new vocabularies, modes of ideology critique, and intellectual frameworks capable of accommodating popular culture and its multiple audiences. It moves to rethink American politics in cultural terms, and in terms various or supple enough to accommodate *Gunsmoke*, modern dance, experimental poetry, film history, and the comedy routines of Ernie Kovacs and Lenny Bruce. At the same time, *Kulchur* registers the larger historical frame within which culture expands so dramatically, that of the Cold War, with its grand ideological clashes and tripartite geopolitical division between communism, capitalism, and the developing world—or, as Baraka puts it in 1960, the "*new peoples*" of Asia, Africa, and Latin America.[36]

* * *

Kulchur 3, which appeared in the spring of 1961, provides a striking demonstration of the magazine's historical self-consciousness and sense of its own internal tensions and unsettled relationship to contemporaneous political events. The cover photograph, by LeRoy McLucas, somewhat ambiguously invokes armed conflict and revolutionary upheaval, setting the stage for the issue's own internal disagreements over the Cuban Revolution and the Bay of Pigs invasion, the failed, CIA-orchestrated invasion of the island that April. A second photo by McLucas, contained within the issue, depicts Baraka and fellow poet George Stanley expressing their unspoken support for the revolution; Schleifer's editorial statements reinforce this position. As the issue makes clear, however, not all the magazine's editors and contributors were equally invested in Castro's Cuba, nor were they all as enthusiastic as Baraka was about documenting and defending political revolution.

Baraka, Schleifer, and McLucas weren't the only artists and intellectuals drawn to the Cuban Revolution. Mills, Lawrence Ferlinghetti, Harold Cruse, Maya Deren, Jean-Paul Sartre, and Simone de Beauvoir all visited Cuba during a brief, remarkably fertile period of cultural exchange inaugurated by Castro's triumph over Fulgencio Batista on January 1, 1959, and concluded in the aftermath of the Bay of Pigs invasion, when Castro became decidedly more culturally conservative and wary of outside influences. Ginsberg famously visited Cuba in 1965, after Castro, Che Guevara, and other Cuban leaders had begun to enforce increasingly repressive policies; he criticized Castro publicly for his mistreatment of homosexuals and was promptly put on a plane to Prague. As Todd Tietchen has argued, the "Cubalogues" produced by writers like Baraka, Ferlinghetti, Schleifer, Cruse, and Ginsberg in the early to mid-1960s remind us how powerfully the Cuban Revolution affected artists and intellectuals in the United States and began to shape political debates within the American left. These "rhetorical travelogues," of which Baraka's "Cuba Libre" was among the best known, constitute "a politically engaged form of literary reportage in which stock features of Beat writing—ranging from the celebration of spontaneity, to the veneration of musical culture, to the glorification of the street hustler and unconventional sexualities—were explicitly recast against the backdrop of early revolutionary events."[37] They garnered significant attention in the United States, displaying a different version of Beat political engagement and intercultural exchange than readers encountered in, for example, Kerouac's novels. Just as it did for Baraka, for many U.S. intellectuals the Cuban Revolution offered an initial, unforgettable image of liberation politics—of the active, global resistance to neocolonialism, racism, and economic exploitation by nation-states and international corporations. Jameson has described it as "the great event [that] announces the . . . 60s as a period of unexpected political innovation," and as a "palpable demonstration . . . that revolution was not merely a historical concept and a museum piece but real and achievable."[38]

As Baraka describes it in his "Cuba Libre" essay, an account of his 1960 visit to Cuba first published in *Evergreen Review* and reprinted in *Kulchur* 2, the Cuban Revolution served as a stunning example that "people still *can* move," and that revolutionary vitality might still be discovered outside the deadness and self-deception of U.S. intellectual life.[39] Castro's revolution, furthermore, struck Baraka as a desirable and entirely legitimate effort to wrest power from a corrupt regime in order to redistribute wealth and opportunity to the people. His essay transmits eloquently how moved he was to witness firsthand the massive educational and agrarian reforms underway in the first eighteen months of the Castro government. The new government's unquestioned commitment to racial equality, striking to Americans in the midst of the civil rights movement, impressed Baraka all the more for remaining unremarked upon by officials.

Not all of *Kulchur*'s contributors, however, shared his perspective. In his *Autobiography*, Baraka singles out Sorrentino as a vocal skeptic. "I hate guys in uniforms," Baraka remembers Sorrentino responding when asked to contribute a poem to a pamphlet Baraka planned to publish in support of the Cuban Revolution.[40] Sorrentino's comment, at once disapproving of military power and committed to poetry's autonomy from politics, bothers Baraka all the more because he comes to associate it with his own defense, when confronted while in Cuba by a group of Mexican poets, of poetry as an aesthetic activity, necessarily separate from politics. "I'm a poet," he finds himself saying when questioned about his political commitments. "[W]hat can I do? I write, that's all, I'm not even interested in politics."[41] And if the trip he recounts in "Cuba Libre" stands as a turning point for Baraka, not all his fellow poets and downtown intellectual cohort undergo this same personal transformation, thus generating notable tensions within the experimental communities that had supported Baraka's little magazines from the outset.

Kulchur 3 thus takes its place within both personal and larger cultural discussions. It begins with McLucas's cover and a brief editorial statement by Schleifer, expressing disappointment in the failed, CIA-sponsored invasion of Cuba and casting the Bay of Pigs as a statement on the decline of America's moral authority and progressive imagination. "It started April 15th," begins the issue's opening editorial. "An eyewitness in Havana who saw the B-26's coming in high over the sea reported that 'Militiamen on guard duty joined in defensive firing, emptying their submachine guns at the plane as it passed over residential areas.'"[42] As if to complete the frame, the issue concludes with a "Cuban Sampler" compiled by Schleifer and addressed to "some of my friends," presumably those same friends and intellectuals Baraka expresses such frustration toward in "Cuba Libre": those "rebels among us . . . who grow beards and will not participate in politics."[43] The "sampler" consists of a long list of suggested reading for those who call Castro a "tyrant," "demagogue," or "paranoiac," or for those who are sure that "nothing ever changes."[44]

Schleifer's statements in the magazine notwithstanding, the most arresting statement in *Kulchur* 3 of the magazine's contentious support for the Cuban Revolution appears in a photograph that appears without caption or commentary on an unnumbered page between pages 6 and 7. The photograph captures Baraka and Stanley in a second-floor window of the apartment Baraka and Hettie Jones rented on East 14th Street between 1st and 2nd Avenues.[45] Baraka and Stanley pose together silently, palms against window panes, staring out at the viewer. They seem to offer implicit support for the text stretching out below them, black letters hand-painted against the white metal sign that separates the brownstone's first floor from the second. The white streak of the sign and the white windows, both above and below, stand in contrast to the dark rectangles of the brick building; the active force of the words on the sign—at once revolutionary slogan and speech act—is juxtaposed with the passive stance of the two men behind the window, their forms echoed near the bottom of the picture by the forms of the two trash cans. As if they cannot speak, frozen behind the windows in the photograph, the sound and sentiment of their thoughts get represented for them by the hand-painted text.

"CUBA, SI, YANQUI, NO": the revolutionary slogan reverberates through Baraka's "Cuba Libre" essay and other Cubalogues of the period. In the photograph, the painted slogan bisects the page horizontally and serves as just one of a series of oppositions troped here, including black and white, above and below, yes and no, opaque and transparent, English and Spanish, inside and out. Behind these antinomies stand the overarching oppositions between U.S. imperialism and Latin American self-determination, and between poetic silence and political speech. The first opposition helps construct the second in the photograph, just as it had for Baraka while in Cuba, where the explicit commitments to revolution expressed by Latin American artists left him questioning his own commitment to aesthetic autonomy. The photograph thus manages to express support for Castro's Cuba while simultaneously underscoring the relative helplessness of American poets hoping to play an active role in social transformation. These poets, the image suggests, are trapped in their own interior worlds; they gaze out on the field of revolutionary speech and political action but fail to participate.

In Hettie Jones's account of this incident, part of the strangeness of Baraka's work of public art, which induces a brief shudder in everyday life and traffic along East 14th Street, has to do with the presence in the midst of this scene of a second, more permanent, slogan, also in Spanish. "LE DIRA TODO LO QUE DESEA SABER," promises Profesora Luz, the palm reader and advisor: "she will tell you everything you want to know." In support of Castro's first visit to the United Nations in September 1960, Baraka and a friend (Stanley, one assumes) had painted their own revolutionary slogan on the metal sheet affixed to the front of the building's "narrow, wrought-iron balcony." By the following evening, "an angry crowd had torn down the sign. Twisted, defaced, for a week it lay like a warning on the sidewalk."[46] As in the photograph, in Jones's account the fortune-teller's painted storefront, a shabby but still eye-catching trompe l'oeil, adds an unlikely, surrealist element to the

"Cuba, Si, Yanqui, No," *Kulchur* 3, spring 1961, photograph by LeRoy McLucas.
Kulchur Foundation Records, Rare Book & Manuscript Library, Columbia University,
New York.

scene. It suggests a potentially magical, prophetic relationship to revolution while also soliciting from us the skepticism that such promises to foretell the future can inspire. It adds an extra element to the scene, its language and imagery opening up new interpretive possibilities. Are the two men in the photo waving to us or trying to escape? Are they affirming their support for the revolution against American imperialism or meditating on the gap that separates the poet in his apartment from the world of potentially radical action outside? Or, one can't help asking, are they having their palms read?

* * *

In "Look for You Yesterday, Here You Come Today," Baraka describes the poet and little magazine editor alone in his New York apartment:

People saw metal all around the house of Saturdays. The Phone
rings

terrible poems come in the mail. Descriptions of celibate parties
torn trousers: Great poets dying
with their strophes on. & me
incapable of a simple straightforward
anger.
(*T*, 17)

Alone with his own poems and faced with the task of reading the other poems that arrive, Baraka's speaker feels trapped, blocked in his attempts at active engagement—whether social or emotional—with either the world outside his apartment or the poems inside, which strike him as flat, conventional, out of tune. This scene will reappear frequently in Baraka's first three published volumes, in poems such as "Political Poem" or "A Poem Some People Will Have to Understand," where Baraka's speakers "read a little," "scratch against silence slow spring / afternoons," and are frustrated by their attempts to write disruptive poems ("the poem undone / undone by my station"; *T*, 107, 122).

In this sense, Baraka's poems from the late 1950s and early 1960s echo and reinforce McLucas's photograph. As in the photograph, external events in the poems exert pressure on the emotional states of their speakers, often situated in New York apartments and confronted with the difficult work of writing poetry. Even as, over the course of the early 1960s, Baraka begins to sharpen the political edges of his poems, dedicating himself more and more intensively to the work of identifying and critiquing various forms of American power and hypocrisy, the emotional atmosphere they project is frequently one of prolonged stasis and dissatisfaction. The poems dramatize this emotional state by way of halting, discontinuous argument, and by fragments of imagery meant to transmit emotional disruption as cultural critique.

"Poetry aims at difficult meanings," Baraka writes in "Gatsby's Theory of Aesthetics," "[m]eanings not already catered to" (*T*, 132). One of the difficulties of his poetry lies in his willingness to confront readers, even friends and fellow bohemians and artists, with his newly politicized positions. Another lies in the poems' fusions of critique and negative affect. Though in many cases this fusion makes intuitive sense and results in something very much like Mackey's "anti-reflective position . . . having been arrived at by way of reflection," in other instances it seems harder to square Baraka's critiques with his emotional performances. As in the photograph taken at East 14th Street, emotional and political elements coalesce in Baraka's poems and challenge readers directly. And yet the challenge they articulate is never entirely clear: the poet's political statements are redirected into self-criticism, or combined with additional figures whose significance—like that of Profesora Luz, the palm reader and advisor—we can never fully explain.

Indeed, Baraka's poems can be difficult to follow even before one starts to untangle their political positions, affective complexity, or penchant for self-criticism. They give themselves over to the disruptive logic of their own internal fragments, allowing these fragments to emerge in series, as non sequiturs, or as sound patterns that begin to pull away from connotative meaning to perform rhythmically instead. Consider, for example, the following excerpt from "Black Dada Nihilismus":

Black scream
and chant, scream,
and dull, un
earthly
hollering. Dada, bilious
what ugliness
(*T*, 99)

The argument and imagery of these lines remain relatively accessible, describing the black diasporic disruption of white, European privilege in all its "ugliness." Even so, the "scream" and "chant" invoked here slip away from rhetoric and rational argument and begin to take themselves literally. They become figures for sound itself, organized explosively within a series of one-, two-, and three-beat lines, heavily accented staccato bursts that trip down the page as if to reinforce the poem's critique of "a moral code, so cruel / it destroyed Byzantium, Tenochtitlan, Commanch" (*I*, 99). Among its multiple connotations, its play on Daddy and Dadaism, "Dada" becomes a nonsense word, setting up the play of sounds between "bilious" and "ugliness." Somewhat counterintuitively, "Black Dada Nihilismus" manages, like so many of Baraka's poems, to be forcefully and effectively polemical while also resisting easy interpretation. Such poems confront their audiences by challenging—even insulting—them, but also by refusing to issue the challenge in stable, accessible language.

Poems like these suggest Baraka's fragmented, nonnarrative approach to history, just as they document his poem's continual play between lyricism and social argument, a dialectical movement that persists well into Baraka's Black Arts period.[47] Lyric moments remain throughout the 1960s, even in poems from his third published volume, *Black Magic* (1969), known for its expressions of black nationalism and often assumed to contain little more than propaganda; likewise, even the most delicate lyrics from Baraka's first two volumes, *Preface* and *The Dead Lecturer*, demonstrate a trenchant awareness of the sociological pressures to which they respond. All three volumes include remarkable poems: process-oriented, contradictory, intensely experimental responses to Cold War–era conflicts and debates.

Along with the difficulties created by their cuts between sound and sense and sudden shifts in imagery or perspective, Baraka's poems make themselves difficult by expanding poetry's potential field of cultural allusion. Like *Kulchur* magazine, Baraka's poems began to reach more and more inventively beyond the previous field of literary allusion, limited, for instance, to those works of culture and religion (Greek myth and philosophy, Catholicism) one might encounter in W. B. Yeats's "Among School Children," or to the sternly biblical geographies of early poems by Robert Lowell. Numerous other postwar experimental poets—from Jack Spicer to John Ashbery, from Ginsberg to Edward Dorn—joined Baraka in this effort; O'Hara's "I do this I do that" poems are exemplary in their embrace of whatever cultural stimuli the speaker might encounter or daydream about as he moves through the Manhattan streets. Baraka's trick, however, is to insist, even more forcefully than O'Hara, that something vital is at stake in one's choice of James Brown over Steve McQueen, Bessie Smith over Elizabeth Taylor, Federico García Lorca over William Empson. Paintings, movie scenes, and cartoon characters are less likely to be set free to drift across the surface of Baraka's poems, as they so often are in Ashbery's, a fact that I illustrate in a final close reading.

Baraka's "Kenyatta Listening to Mozart," one of many underappreciated poems from *Black Magic*, has been celebrated for the complexity of its response to the global anticolonial movements we see Baraka engaging in essays like "Cuba Libre" and in forums like *Kulchur*. It has likewise been read as a meditation on Baraka's choice in the early 1960s between two different aesthetics—one Beat and the other politically engaged—or between aesthetics and politics in a more absolute sense.[48] But we also need to read "Kenyatta Listening to Mozart" as a searching meditation on cultural politics in the Cold War era. As the poem sees it, culture needs to open itself as broadly as possible, thus encompassing and taking seriously a whole range of previously marginalized people and practices. The African present, the poem suggests by its title, is just as vital as the European past—and more influential *in the present*. As culture expands, both globally and in the United States, it needs to do so without losing track of the politics involved in the choice of one object, artist, cultural form, or political figure over another.

I quote the poem in its entirety:

> on the back trails, in sun glasses
> and warm air blows cocaine from city
> to river, and through the brains of
> American poets in San Francisco.
>   Separate
>   and lose. Spats brush through
>   undergrowths of fiction. Mathematics
>   bird, undressed and in sympathy with absolute
>   stillness, and the neutrality of water. (We do not
>   write poems in the rainy season.) Light to light,
>   the weighted circumstance prowls like animals in the
> bush.
>   A zoo of consciousness,
>   cries and prowling
>   anywhere. Stillness,
>   motion,
>   beings that fly, beings
>   that swim
>   exchanging
>   in-
>   formation.
>   Choice, and
>   style,
>   avail
>   and are beautiful
>   categories
>   If you go
>   for that.[49]

In this poem, Baraka's mind wanders to Africa. In 1957, as he writes in his *Autobiography*, "Ghana's Kwame Nkrumah had hoisted the black star over the statehouse in Accra, and Nkrumah's pronouncements and word of his deeds were glowing encouragement to colored people all over the world."[50] Still inspired by his trip to Cuba and impatient with the pace of racial progress in the United States—and with the integrationist, nonviolent tactics of the civil rights movement—Baraka writes in tribute to a black leader now negotiating for his country's independence from Great Britain.

Baraka does not, however, present a choice in this poem between the racially conscious and historically progressive Jomo Kenyatta, recently imprisoned and soon to become prime minister of an independent Kenya, and Wolfgang Amadeus Mozart, who might fairly be taken to represent the sort of abstract, rational, putatively neutral position that Baraka in the 1960s often associates with European culture and American liberalism. Behind the language and imagery of the poem, rather, is Baraka's debate with other black writers and intellectuals who, at least from Baraka's perspective, long for their own autonomy from a racial struggle in which they have no choice but to engage.[51] "Separate / and lose," he writes, echoing an attack on the South African writer Peter Abrahams that he published the same year, 1963, that "Kenyatta Listening to Mozart" first appeared in *Matter*, a little magazine edited by Robert Kelly.[52] In "Brief Reflections on Two Hot Shots," originally published in *Kulchur* and later collected in *Home*, Baraka condemns both Abrahams and James Baldwin, taking them to task (more than a little unfairly, as even Baraka would later admit) for their "overly passionate declaration[s] of 'individuality.'" The primary example Baraka adduces during his attack on Abrahams has to do with Abrahams's visit with Kenyatta some years earlier. "[F]aced with the decision of whether to stay with Jomo Kenyatta for a weekend or at a hotel which the British Government would provide," Abrahams hesitated, Baraka writes, offering his own summary of the events Abrahams describes in an article published in 1960 in Langston Hughes's *African Treasury*. Baraka quotes Abrahams with scorn: "It dawned on me that I had become, for the moment, the battlefield of that horrible animal, the racial struggle. I made up my mind, resenting both sides."[53] Baraka quotes Abrahams again near the conclusion of his essay, criticizing him for his naïve longing for racial harmony and acceptance: "When I had left South Africa in the dim and distant past, there were isolated islands where black and white could meet in neutral territory."[54]

Baraka's poem echoes Abrahams's essay in a number of places, situating Kenyatta in "the bush," where "the weighted circumstance" of racial tension indeed "prowls like animals" and where "neutrality," as Baraka sees it, becomes impossible. "Choice, and / style, / avail / and are beautiful / categories," he writes, seemingly with Abrahams in mind. "If you go for that," he concludes, stating what would have to be read as an unqualified commitment to the racial struggle if it weren't for all the unmistakable elements of style on display throughout the poem. Indeed, "Kenyatta Listening to Mozart" sings of cocaine and sunglasses and then changes shape as it proceeds, using a fragmented lineation fairly common among midcentury experimental poems. Does the poem not indicate its own investments in style and choice, not least when it begins to disperse across the page at the end of the second stanza? The contradiction this poem circles around is that style is both necessary, a form and sign of historical intervention, and insufficient. Like the poet trapped in his apartment while associating himself with the language of political engagement and change, the speaker in "Kenyatta Listening to Mozart" signifies stylistically while also expressing anxiety over whether such gestures can ever respond fully to the weight of "circumstance."

"Kenyatta Listening to Mozart" offers us another complex but extraordinarily vivid example of negative affect, vivid in part because Baraka's resentment toward those who choose style over circumstance, independence over collective struggle, is so much subtler and harder to discern than the anger or frustration he expresses in other poems. Baraka's efforts in his little magazines and essays from the 1960s to describe his own contemporary historical position, and to relate it to the long history of U.S. race relations and class tensions, are refracted in his poems through tones and images of anxiety, confusion, and discontent.[55] Already in the years leading up to the controversial statements of his Black Nationalist period, Baraka had developed a combative, publicly aggressive, and politically incisive style, one as evident in his editorial work as it is in his poetry. It is a style often described as rhythmic and ideological, but it might just as accurately be characterized by the emotional atmospheres it projects, in which dissatisfaction continually verges on antagonism, and antagonism then strains to transform itself into some new form of solidarity.

We need to imagine the negative affects circulating through Baraka's poems not just as expressions of frustration—with former friends, fellow bohemian poets, or intellectual rivals, for instance—but also as an index of his ongoing commitment to working and thinking collectively. This commitment never wavered for Baraka, even if, like a difficult musician, his artistic vision changed over time, as did the personnel with whom he chose to collaborate. As suggested by his long involvement with little magazines, an involvement that continued even after Baraka left the Village for Harlem and then Newark, Baraka always insisted on imagining a shared, historical context for his work, even when that meant criticizing his current community or framing his work in relation to some anticipated, as-yet-unrealized social formation. When Baraka, in poems, essays, and editorials, adopts a voice at once hip and quick to critique hipsterism, he does so not just to express frustration with the hypocrisies of one avant-garde community. Rather, such critiques simultaneously restate his commitment to the larger project of consolidating vanguard structures of feeling; they predict his migration toward the collectivities and collaborations still to come.

Di Prima's Hipsters

Experimental Poetry and the Birth of the Cool

So here I am the coolest in New York
what dont swing I dont push

—Diane di Prima, "Three Laments"

"Sweetheart / when you break thru," begins one of Diane di Prima's earliest poems, "you'll find / a poet here." "Not quite what one would choose," she adds, a note of tough, ironic realism that offsets the term of endearment with which she begins. For who would choose a poet in an era of businessmen and housewives; soldiers, scientists, and Hollywood stars? The situation only gets worse. The next stanza reads,

I won't promise
you'll never go hungry
or that you won't be sad
on this gutted
breaking
globe

What should the sweethearts of poets expect but poverty, and with it the likelihood of going hungry now and then, even in an era of historic economic prosperity and growth? Widening the angle, di Prima sets daily challenges like finding food (or perhaps, as in another early poem, scrounging up enough money to pay the gas bill) in the context of world wars and atomic bombs. The world has been "gutted"; the planet is "breaking." Di Prima's line breaks slow readers down and invite them to linger over the damage.

She concludes on a note of (not unqualified) compensation:

but I can show you
baby
enough to love
to break your heart
forever[.][1]

In its vernacular address and pose of sentimental knowingness, these final lines of "Song for Baby-O, Unborn" capture something like the ironic, critical ethos Lee Konstantinou associates with the hipster. Di Prima understands all too well human vulnerability and desire but remains detached enough from them to tell us the truth. She remembers the feeling of a broken heart but can stand back and "dig" it as she does, as Billie Holiday might if she were telling you about it in a song. And yet, unlike Norman Mailer, Ralph Ellison, or Thomas Pynchon, central characters in Konstantinou's engaging portrait of "the hipster as critic," di Prima never pretends to fashion a single, canonical story of hipness or a fully formulated theory of postwar irony.[2] Her early writings can be classified as experimental, rather, inasmuch as they remain stubbornly tentative and preliminary. They gain force when read not just individually but as a group, and when heard in dialogue not just with the newly "open" and spontaneous free-verse forms of the New American Poetry but also with vernacular practices of New York bohemian communities of the late 1950s and early 1960s. Further, as "Song for Baby-O, Unborn" suggests in its address not to a lover but to a child, di Prima's writings should be read in relation to her everyday life and responsibilities as a woman. These include, as Maria Damon puts it, the work of childbearing and raising kids, cooking "vast meals for extended families of aesthetic *confrères* and *soeurs*," and a whole range of other "domestic 'duties'" male authors of her generation most often managed to avoid.[3]

This chapter is about the birth of the cool in U.S. poetry, and about how postwar experimental poets embraced subcultural styles as models of historical orientation and lyric address. As a way of making my case, I examine hipsterism in the early writings of Diane di Prima, particularly those collected in *Dinners and Nightmares*, first published in 1961. Like Mailer's writings of the period, which I invoke here by way of comparison, the poems and prose sketches in *Dinners and Nightmares* represent hipsterism as an emergent structure of feeling: a social and aesthetic style carrying an undeniable charge and yet hard to categorize or define. Striving to document the lived, improvised, and emotionally complicated stances hip subcultures fashioned in response to the insults and pleasures of urban life, di Prima's early writings provide an especially vivid example of the pose. They call our attention to the subcultural energies that helped reshape American literature after World War II and underscore the widespread cultural influence that hipness—as an affective stance, an argument about originality, and a new fusion of art and life—exerted in the postwar United States.

They call our attention as well to internal differences within this subcultural and affective field, and to the ways women like di Prima went about reinventing hipness for their own ends. If women were doing all the work of childbearing, why shouldn't they give birth to the cool? Making di Prima central to the story of hip's emergence allows us to reimagine a now-familiar subculture in relation to a wider set of gendered identities and experiences. From her perspective, this inchoate vernacular style was even more capacious than was suggested by the masculine performances of the era.

Few subcultures have had the potential hipsterism did in the 1950s and early 1960s to generate avant-garde buzz and electricity. Camp, as I touched on in my readings of O'Hara, provided postwar poets and everyday subjects alike a set of vernacular and affective strategies for negotiating cultural authority and categories of taste in a world transformed by mass culture.[4] Though camp has been criticized for reinforcing the very norms it pretends to subvert (as in the exaggerated femininity of drag queens or the poor kid putting on the expensive clothes and speech patterns of the rich), my reading insists on what Eve Sedgwick describes as its "reparative," "additive," and "accretive" aspects. Camp's expressions of enthusiasm, identification, and expertise—about even the trashiest or most antiquated aspects of culture—have long served to shore up vulnerable subjects and communities.[5] For di Prima and her cohort, hipness offered something comparable: a vernacular style that few understood but that anyone in the know could inhabit; a performance of toughness and wit that might help protect one's emotional attachments. It held out the promise of alternative lifestyles and communities—artistic, sexual, bohemian, interracial—at a moment when Cold War anxieties were meant to be assuaged with good jobs, consumer goods, and the security of traditional families. It was, as Joel Dinerstein characterizes it in his voluminous *The Origins of Cool in Postwar America* (2017), "a public mode of covert resistance"; an existentialist, "post-Christian" response to the traumas and geopolitical crises of modernity; a refusal of patriotic materialism; a "walking indictment of society" at a moment when its substantial transformation seemed unlikely; and an expression of solidarity with the destitute and oppressed.[6] As Scott Saul argues in his history of hard bop, the "figure of the hipster was a kind of cultural putty," put to different uses by different artists, intellectuals, and everyday-vernacular performers. Its uses remain impossible to understand, however, outside the double contexts of the literature of "conformity"—represented by books like David Riesman's *The Lonely Crowd* (1950), C. Wright Mills's *White Collar* (1951), and William Whyte's *The Organization Man* (1956)—and "the public acts of defiance that galvanized the civil rights movement."[7] At its sharpest, hipsterism constituted a serious reflection on the limits of U.S. freedom at the end of the Jim Crow era and the beginning of the postindustrial era.

Any serious reflection on hipsterism needs to acknowledge its critics, who have had almost as charismatic a history as the figure of the hipster himself. As Konstantinou points out, the hipster had hardly appeared before he was being parodied, commodified, and deconstructed. Insider guides to the "hep" slang of jazz subcultures began appearing as early as the late 1930s; Anatole Broyard's influential "A Portrait of the Hipster" was published in *Partisan Review* in 1948.[8] Would beatniks and hipsters continue to signify as resistant or original once they were identified by the wider public, tagged by advertisers, emulated by hangers-on? This is a familiar question, one that critics of the hipster helped originate and that has since been asked of every significant youth cultural aesthetic of the intervening years, from hippie to punk to hip hop.

Konstantinou goes even further, however, arguing that the hipster was never resistant in the first place. He managed to reproduce instead, in everyday vernacular form, the dominant intellectual position of the era. Like the New Critic or New York intellectual, the hipster was at home with irony and ambiguity in all its forms, able to sit back coolly and analyze both the tightly structured antinomies of great works of literature and the two great dangers of the era: that of unchecked consumer capitalism in the "first" world and of Soviet totalitarianism in the "second."[9] Great poems, as Cleanth Brooks suggested in a famous essay on Yeats, "are shot through . . . with a recognition of . . . problem[s] . . . the reflective human being can never escape." Unable to find a solution, the poem "comes to terms with the situation"; it "develops an attitude . . . which everywhere witnesses to the insolubility of the problem."[10] Di Prima's speaker in "Song for Baby-O, Unborn," one might say, comes to a similar conclusion about the insoluble problems of heartbreak and love, or about the inevitability of sadness on "this gutted / breaking / globe." She is left to project "an attitude" and in so doing to shield her own hopes and attachments, just as other hipsters did when confronted with seemingly insoluble problems like racial and economic inequality, dead-end jobs, the threat of nuclear war. Whether analyzed at the level of intellectual ideology or everyday consumer choice, hipsterism remained vulnerable to the charges leveled at what Herbert Marcuse called "affirmative culture."[11] It offered the satisfaction of ironic knowingness to intellectuals, just as it offered hipper forms of music or clothing to white- and blue-collar workers. From this perspective, it was not, in fact, inconsistent with much of postwar professional life. The pleasure of creative self-fashioning—of superior attitude and style—was one of the compensations one earned when one worked all day, played by the rules, and accepted the status quo.

These criticisms of the hipster echo and overlap with the recent criticisms of the New American Poetry outlined in my introduction. Rebelling against stodgy academics and cataloging the revolutionary exploits and alternative lifestyles of their generation, New American poets captured cultural logics that by now seem all too familiar. They played their own modest part in what Thomas Frank, in his influential history of postwar business culture, describes as "bohemian cultural style's trajectory from adversarial to hegemonic"; that is, "hip's mutation" over the course of the 1960s "from native language of the alienated to that of advertising."[12] The lyric strategies of O'Hara's uncannily popular "Having a Coke with You," once so novel—even shocking—when the poem was written in 1960, seem from our twenty-first-century vantage point like the best ad copy you've ever read, a spontaneous expression of precisely the sort of intimacy and fullness of experience the Coca-Cola corporation would like consumers to associate with their signature product.[13] The typographic and rhythmic innovations of U.S. experimental poets of the 1950s and 1960s, their experiments with tone, the idea that free verse might finally be free: all these investments in the creative self-fashioning of poets and, through them, their readers ("MY POETRY is whatever I think I am," LeRoi Jones/Amiri Baraka proclaims) are in some cases hardly distinguishable from the cleverly defiant poses of the hipster.[14] The aesthetic autonomy promised by these midcentury experiments, furthermore, was often assumed to be connected to a more progressive vision of politics than the movement itself managed to deliver. How was it possible, if poetry could be whatever it wanted, that the anthology in which Baraka's statement first appeared, Donald Allen's signal *The New American Poetry* (1960), included only one poet of color (Baraka) and four women?

Though undeniably persuasive, such criticisms can hardly be expected to end our attachment to literary movements or texts—or to subcultural styles—that have long held our attention, and whose value to us in the present may well reside in insights altogether different from those they initially emphasized. To dismiss the hipster altogether would be to dismiss the efforts and imaginations of countless texts and performances, from James Baldwin's short stories to Simone de Beauvoir's meditations on race. Why, if so many significant artists and intellectuals, not to mention countless anonymous subjects, were attracted to hipsterism as an everyday and avant-garde practice, a mode of commentary on the standard schedule of work, sleep, and pleasure in the decades following World War II, would we dismiss it as ineffective—as nothing more than a fad or a form of manipulation? One could ask similar questions, in the context of literary criticism or of contemporary poetry and poetics, about Beat, Black Mountain, San Francisco Renaissance, and New York School poetries, which have their flaws and yet undoubtedly contain resources we have yet to discover, insights that will reveal themselves when we are ready to consider them.[15] Moreover, global capitalism's success in commodifying various forms of pleasure, refusal, or dissent should not lead us to underestimate the historical importance of these forms, any more than it should blind us to their experimental qualities. In the particular case at issue here, the rapidity with which hipsters were parodied in the popular press or made infamous on television should hardly outweigh hipsterism's initial force as a lived and aesthetically sophisticated commentary on many of the culture's most pressing concerns.[16]

Nor, di Prima's writings urge us to consider, should we let our present skepticism about the emergent movements of the past lead us to overlook the criticisms that were directed at those movements at the time, perhaps especially from participants. Indeed, di Prima's tense but influential relationships to both hipsterism and the New American Poetry ask us to revisit them, and to think again about the roles women played in the midcentury avant-garde.[17] As is illuminated in the scholarship of critics like Damon, Michael Davidson, Rachel Blau DuPlessis, Lynn Keller, Maggie Nelson, and Libbie Rifkin, the originality of women's contributions to postwar experimental poetry has too often been overlooked, their contributions minimized (or elided altogether) in the interest of male poets and their self-reinforcing narratives of masculine influence, achievement, and succession.[18] Similarly, both champions and critics of cool have portrayed it as an essentially masculine stance, one based on a disdain for sentimental attachments and committed to moving continually through streets, shops, bars, clubs, and crash pads and avoiding the more stable—and inevitably feminized—space of the home and the nuclear family. This basic profile, and the gendered assumptions it entails, underwrote the failures of early and influential subcultural theorists to consider the role played by women in the groups they studied; it lives on in critical and theoretical approaches that, as Susan Fraiman points out, make critique, opposition, and originality feel like "masculine" activities while associating oppression, domination, and traditional thinking with women, mothers, and domesticity.[19]

Cool genealogies placing di Prima next to male literary hipsters like Mailer and Kerouac might offer us a different set of possibilities, not to mention a more expansive account of the relationship between gendered affects and experimental aesthetics. *Dinners and Nightmares* manages quite cleverly to celebrate the vitality of the new bohemianism while also rewriting it to accommodate women. Urban, jazz-inflected, and sexually liberated, di Prima's hipsterism nonetheless thinks regularly about cooking, cleaning, and shopping for dinner. It takes seriously the possibility, rarely considered in

Kerouac or Mailer, that sex could lead to pregnancy, and that pregnancy could leave one with children to look after. Moreover, di Prima reimagines the affective procedures of hipsterism so that its dance between pleasure and detachment—attraction and indifference—might be performed by women as well as men. In di Prima's recoding of cool, we encounter a repetition that is also a difference.

Finally, as I suggested in my introduction, reading hipsterism in the late 1950s and early 1960s as an emergent "structure of feeling" allows one to emphasize how unmistakably this term depends on "feeling," a word Raymond Williams employs suggestively but never really theorizes in his influential account of the phrase. Williams writes:

> We are talking about characteristic elements of impulse, restraint, and tone; specifically affective elements of consciousness and relationships: not feeling against thought, but thought as felt and feeling as thought: practical consciousness of a present kind, in living and interrelating continuity. We are then defining these elements as a 'structure': as a set, with specific internal relations, at once inter-locking and in tension. Yet we are also defining a social experience which is still in *process*, often indeed not yet recognized as social but taken to be private, idiosyncratic, and even isolating, but which in analysis . . . has its emergent, connecting, and dominant characteristics, indeed its specific hierarchies.[20]

Feeling, Williams suggests perceptively, helps give shape and substance to those "characteristic elements of impulse, restraint, and tone" that remain a fundamental part of social experience, though they are often overlooked in favor of fixed and explicit institutions, social formations, and ideologies. It does so, furthermore, both at the moment an experience is in process, "in living and interrelated continuity," and after the fact, as a matter of theory and analysis. As I hope to suggest in my readings of di Prima's hipsterism as a departure from hipsterism in Mailer, subcultures are related to yet never precisely synonymous with structures of feeling. Critics call upon both terms to describe the continual inventiveness and political charge of style, or to capture the collective improvisations of social groups not yet recognized as such. And yet subcultures tend to contain multiple and even contradictory structures of feeling, as is the case with hipsterism in the late 1950s. One might go so far as to argue that affect becomes a primary point of interest and sign of discord among hipsters, who define themselves through their everyday emotional postures.

* * *

For avant-garde poets and their contemporaries in the 1950s and early 1960s, popular hipster figures like James Dean and Miles Davis captured something larger and more dispersed than the various subcultures and social identities with which these poets identified. Davis and Dean represented a generalized search for stylistic innovation in a culture of conformity, for the invention of a style that would signify not just for an elite group of artists and intellectuals but for anyone on the street hip enough to recognize this new, more popular form of genius. "Alone / in the empty streets of New York / I am its dirty feet and head / and he is dead," O'Hara writes in "For James Dean," an elegiac tribute to Dean's "unnatural vigor" and the "invention of his nerves."[21] "And yet, where would we be without . . . / Bye bye blackbird, as Miles plays it, in the 50's?" (*SP*, 153), di Prima asks in "Goodbye Nkrumah," looking back on the postwar hipster from the early 1970s. One could describe Miles's muted tones in "Bye Bye Blackbird"—in which hesitations and slurs are as expressive as moments of clear, bright sound—as elegant versions of James Dean's weighted silences and mumbled, nonverbal articulations of dissatisfaction and desire in *Rebel Without a Cause*, released the same year, 1955. Dean's and Davis's performances—at once fierce and guarded, brash and distant—embody a contradictory structure of feeling that runs through so many of the modes of hipster rebellion that flourished among the mass-cultural products and mass-marketed poses of the postwar era. There is always something vague about hipness, a fact exemplified brilliantly by the album title of Davis's *Birth of the Cool* (1957). The title manages at once to seem apt and mysterious and to imply the revolutionary, epochal force of Davis's art and personality without defining explicitly the style, state of being, or attitude to which his new post-bop ensemble was supposedly giving birth.[22]

No postwar poet rang changes on the affective performance of hip with more dedication than di Prima, whose notorious *Memoirs of a Beatnik* (1969) offers commentary on the game of "cool" as it defined social and sexual interaction in bohemian New York of the 1950s, and whose early poetry takes both its voice and its subject matter from this same milieu. Her early works are sprinkled with precisely the sorts of slang phrases, unmistakable characters, and distinctive settings that made these new bohemian subcultures so unforgettable and culturally influential. Here are jazz musicians hooked on heroin, roach-infested apartments, injured ballet dancers, painters reading up on Picasso while standing in line at the cafeteria, French lovers and love triangles. Here are lines so succinctly resonant as to explain why Hollywood moved quickly to adopt the beatnik as a standard type: "Shit man I said nearly everybody's bisexual"; "No I said I guess we don't know 31 people who work"; "I like Pollock said Betty."[23]

And yet di Prima's bohemian sketches refuse to be read as one-dimensional or flatly affirmative portrayals of hipsterism. Di Prima chooses rather to mix a genuine faith in the freedoms promised by new bohemian lifestyles with moments of trenchant criticism of her own hip stances and coolly utopian investments. She stands out as both a clever, creative representative of the hipster and a proto-feminist critic of hipsterism as embodied in the writings of other postwar artists and commentators. Both her incipient feminism and her hipsterism, furthermore, can be read as other names for her avant-gardism, an avant-gardism without a specific political program and yet decidedly anti-bourgeois, dedicated to crashing art into life and to privileging creative processes over the works that result—to doing "what will *not* work / in living / as in poems" (*SP*, 65). Her writing can seem unashamedly sloppy, awkward, multigeneric, and inconsistent, set against ideals of formal precision and careful construction of the poetic artifact and invested instead in the constant and spontaneous record of daily life, thought, conversation, emotion. At their best, di Prima's early writings seem to be hunting down those words, images, and rhetorical occasions that might manage to allegorize a particular affective experience.

In early poems and prose, and particularly in *Dinners and Nightmares*, di Prima reproduces an affective stance with genealogical links to the nineteenth-century dandy, who exhibits what Baudelaire describes as an "unshakeable determination to remain unmoved."[24] Like other mid-twentieth-century hipsters, however, she reconfigures slightly the dandy's stylish, cosmopolitan distance: his technique of remaining emotionally disengaged from the social confusions and endless exchanges of modern urban life by being, or affecting to be, blasé. Hipsters in postwar U.S. cities replace the dandy's aristocratic identifications with a jazz-inspired, racially inflected version of populist elitism that nonetheless serves the same function as the dandy's aristocratic pose: it allows one to protect profound attachments by maintaining an emotional distance from the shocks of both rivalry and competition among lovers and friends and the endless and anonymous confrontations entailed in moving through urban space. "In case you put me down," she writes in "More or Less Love Poems," "I got it figured,"

how there are better mouths than yours
more swinging bodies
wilder scenes than this.
(*DN*, 114)

Like the dandy, the hipster's overarching need "to combat and destroy triviality" and "to create a personal form of originality" takes precedence over any particular encounter or disappointment. Di Prima's hipster, like Baudelaire's dandy, savors "the pleasure of causing surprise in others, and the proud satisfaction of never showing any oneself."[25] For di Prima in the late 1950s and early 1960s, the potential advantages and particular challenges of playing it "cool," both in print and in person, reside in the general assumption that such play—from the dandy to the hipster, from Mezz Mezzrow to Miles—was largely the province and artistic property of men.

* * *

Case in point: in the late 1950s, no spokesperson for hipsterism was more infamous, at least in New York intellectual circles, than Norman Mailer, whose "White Negro" was first published in *Dissent* in 1957. His six-part essay, subtitled "Superficial Reflections on the Hipster," begins with an overwhelmingly pessimistic evaluation of the historical mood in the shadow of World War II, whose twin spectacles of state-sponsored genocide—by concentration camp and atomic bomb—have wreaked "psychic havoc . . . upon the unconscious mind of almost everyone alive in these years."[26] Mailer goes on to describe what he identifies as a new, avant-garde cultural response to a repressive and desperately repressed historical moment: a rebellious, violent, creative, orgasmic, and individualistic response that at once clashes with and substantiates di Prima's hipsterism.

"In such places as Greenwich Village," Mailer famously asserts, "a ménage-à-trois was completed—the bohemian and the juvenile delinquent came face-to-face with the Negro, and the hipster was a fact in American life" (*AM*, 340). The Negro, as suggested by Mailer's title, becomes the central figure in this transaction, a "sexual outlaw" (*AM*, 348) and primitive pleasure-seeker whom Mailer invents and then reinterprets by way of his own idiosyncratic combination of existentialism and psychopathic hedonism. These characteristic romanticizations of black masculinity have been critiqued since Mailer's essay first appeared, with a deftness and complexity inaugurated by James Baldwin's initial response, "The Black Boy Looks at the White Boy." They have been dismissed as racist and then reclaimed (though never quite rehabilitated) as influential articulations of a long tradition of imitation and homosocial attraction, in which white men, from the mid-nineteenth century forward, have projected social and sexual fantasies onto black male bodies and styles of performance.[27]

Such responses underscore the extent to which hipness as a vernacular practice was invented within African American communities and then reinvented continually as it was taken up by white writers such as Mailer, di Prima, Kerouac, Pynchon, and Robert Creeley, to say nothing of white performers from

Elvis Presley to the Stones. White hipsters of the 1950s thus play their part in what Andrew Ross describes as "that long transactional history of white responses to black culture, of black counter-responses, and of further countless and often traceless negotiations, tradings, raids, and compromises."[28] This history became further complicated over the course of the 1960s, as corporations embraced hipness as a marketing strategy and began to tie advertising campaigns to the newest version of countercultural chic. As hipness attached itself to a seemingly endless series of cool poses and consumer products, it became more and more difficult to remember the moment during which the idea of cool itself seemed like an emergent structure of feeling—"visibly alternative," potentially "oppositional" (*ML*, 124), and racially explosive.

"The White Negro" in fact invokes something very close to Williams's "structure of feeling," what Mailer refers to once as "abstract states of feeling" and another time as "the curious community of feeling in the world of the hipster" (*AM*, 340, 342). Like Williams, Mailer implies that this structure is only tenuously and imperfectly available to us. As is clear from his general emphasis on "feeling" and his specific emphasis on the psychopathic emotional profile of the hipster, Mailer turns to affect as one way of approaching this state, structure, or community that he designates "Hip." Another, overlapping, strategy he uses as he attempts to describe this community is that of cataloging—or of simply invoking and repeating—hip slang. As he works to construct his new, instinctively critical, sexually charged identity, he becomes obsessed with "the language of Hip." He seems desperate to own, categorize, and stabilize hip slang, an undertaking that contradicts his emphasis elsewhere on process, growth, and constant movement. "But let us see," writes Mailer tentatively. "I have jotted down perhaps a dozen words, the Hip perhaps most in use and most likely to last with the minimum of variation. The words are man, go, put down, make, beat, cool, swing, with it, crazy, dig, flip, creep, hip, square" (*AM*, 349).

All of Mailer's hip vocabulary words appear in di Prima's early writings, along with a number he fails to register, such as "goof," "drag," and "chick." "So here I am the coolest in New York / what dont swing I dont push" (*DN*, 119), she writes, giving credence to the idea that, without employing a specific argot, it remains impossible to give expression to the "abstract state of feeling" that constitutes hipness. Though cognizant of the African American roots of hipness, di Prima is less invested than Mailer in its continued association with black criminality and more willing to let it float free and attach itself to white bohemian collectivities. Like Mailer, as I have already suggested, di Prima starts in her early poems with the assumption that the postwar hipster lives in an atmosphere of generalized institutional oppression and state-enforced conformity. She would have agreed, one assumes, with Mailer's emphasis on "the general anxiety" of living in "a partially totalitarian society" (*AM*, 339), though she tends to approach this anxiety with at once a deeper sadness and a greater sense of irony.

Such is the case with her sequence of thirteen "Nightmares," in which the everyday alienation of dealing with state or corporate bureaucracies (the post office, the unemployment office, the power company, the public health clinic) is presented in dreamlike, mock-paranoid tones. Likewise, the public harassment of various bohemian characters is dealt with in the self-ironizing form of faux conspiracy theory, allowing di Prima to make her point about state-sanctioned violence while simultaneously implying that she mistrusts or feels slightly detached from her own critique. "I saw it man, I read it in one of their god damned trade journals," she writes in "Nightmare 10":

> "Open season on people over 21 in dungarees or ancient sneakers,
> men with lipstick,
> women with crew cuts,
> actors out of work,
> poets of all descriptions. Bounty for heads ten dollars.
> Junkies and jazz musicians five dollars extra."
> (*DN*, 49)

Di Prima's early poems often revolve around melancholy or cartoonish psychological profiles; they tend to represent rhetorical and interpersonal exchanges that will allow her to outline something as vague and mesmerizing as the hipster's emotional procedures. Like Mailer, she defines hipsterism by way of affect and slang, but there are wide disparities between the hipsters that result.

Indeed, di Prima's early writings undercut Mailer's hipster mythology more frequently than they reinforce it. Mailer's hipster is inordinately sensitive and ready to respond to the slightest provocation with violence, a readiness for which Mailer provides lengthy justifications. "Hip," he writes, "which would return us to ourselves, at no matter what price in individual violence . . . requires a primitive passion about human nature to believe that individual acts of violence are always to be preferred to the collective violence of the State; it takes literal faith in the creative possibilities of the human being to envisage acts of violence as the catharsis which prepares growth" (*AM*, 355). This emphasis on the psychopathic emotional state and immediately violent engagements of the hipster is directly contradicted by di Prima's hipster stance, with its preference for performed indifference and blasé impassivity. Instead of imagining individualized and creative acts of violence as the catharsis necessary for more widespread growth and emancipation, di Prima again and again assumes a pose of disengagement that, paradoxically, allows her to protect and maintain emotional attachments.

While sometimes this disengagement takes the form of exaggerated paranoia, as in the "Nightmare" poems, it can also take the form of a dreamlike, exaggerated revolutionary desire. "The day I kissed you . . . / The UN abolished prisons," she writes in one of her "More or Less Love Poems," "and the Pope / appointed Jean Genet to the College of Cardinals." "The day we made it," she continues, "Pan returned; / Ike gave up golf; / the A&P sold pot" (*SP*, 16). In this and similar moments in her early work, ironic humor is deployed in support of a deeply felt but vulnerable devotion to utopic longing. Di Prima's insistence on including dreamy and comedic elements in her poems expands the hipster's aesthetic and emotional procedures along lines set forth by the surrealists, for whom, as Benjamin reminds us, non-literary genres ("demonstrations, watchwords, documents, bluffs, forgeries") provided illuminating textual models, and for whom "the threshold between waking and sleeping was worn away."[29] Yet di Prima's integration of longings and fantasies into her writing never implies a confidence in either revolutionary transformation or the immediate success of impassioned action. While Mailer's hipster strives for total revolt and liberation and favors direct, immediate, and violent expressions of frustration and desire, di Prima's hipster operates at a slight but perceptible distance from emotional events and urban stimuli that seem potentially debilitating, even when those events and stimuli promise something like joy, sexual pleasure, or hope. Among the potentially debilitating events di Prima evokes in her early writing are the disappointed dreams of a love that once felt like social transformation, the state-sponsored acts of violence that Mailer despises, and the individual acts of violence he celebrates.

* * *

A violent and potentially debilitating event comes immediately into focus in di Prima's "The Poet," which appeared first in *Dinners and Nightmares* and was republished soon after in *The Moderns* (1963), Baraka's decidedly hip anthology of new experimental prose. In clipped, conversational textures, "The Poet" sketches a brief scene in which a male poet pressures di Prima's female narrator to endorse his stated commitments to love and empathy while they stand together, "watching this cat beat up his chick in the street" (*DN*, 76). Creating an abrupt, back-and-forth structure that juxtaposes the poet's impassioned address with the narrator's passive responses, di Prima's sketch undermines the poet's creative ideology and lazy idealism. Throughout the piece, he reiterates his devotion to the emotional labor of being sad—and of loving and weeping for "the lost children"—while never once commenting upon (much less intervening in) the scene of violence he witnesses. But what good, the narrator seems to suggest, are vague gestures toward "the lost children" in response to domestic abuse as it spills out onto the streets? More broadly, what use is old-fashioned sincerity when the constant shock and confrontation of urban life threaten to destroy our receptiveness to the world around us? With a hipness suggested by her vocabulary, the narrator meets the male poet's active statements and insistence that she accede to his emotional posture with passive resistance, responding to his prodding with "sure man" and "great," and breaking away from their conversation in order to narrate the street scene that plays out over the course of their exchange.

While di Prima's representation of physical abuse in "The Poet," in its seeming pointlessness and misogyny, can thus be read as an indirect critique of Mailer's psychopath, there is more at stake here than being for or against individual acts of violence. In this bohemian sketch, as in other early works, di Prima seems to offer something like a different representational approach to the mundane yet sometimes violent shocks of urban experience. For Mailer, the experience of living in a modern, technologically mediated, partially totalitarian society feels violent in a way that invites immediate passion and active participation. Violence in *Dinners and Nightmares*, on the other hand, is both less predictable and more difficult to respond to directly. It tends to be threatened but then deferred indefinitely, or, when it does happen, to be witnessed passively and at an emotional remove. Further, even while embracing irony and emotional detachment, di Prima's hipster seems somewhat self-critical in "The Poet" and unsettled by her own practice of disengagement. As "the fuzz . . . pull[s] up to dig the scene" (*DN*, 77), the quasi-hip detachment of the police officers and the crowd starts to suggest a critique of disengagement, a critique that touches the speaker herself, who seems to identify with the assaulted chick and yet does nothing to help her.

Such complications recur throughout *Dinners and Nightmares*, in which characters and poetic speakers perform myriad versions of cool or "uncool." Taken together, these performances might be said to constitute what Williams describes as "thought as felt and feeling as thought: practical consciousness of a present kind, in living and interrelated continuity" (*ML*, 132). Speakers comment incisively on "the affective elements" of their "consciousness and relationships," on those shared elements of style and philosophy that draw them together, and on the larger historical conditions shaping their choices (*ML*, 132). Sketch after bohemian sketch in *Dinners and Nightmares* represents something like felt reflection on a city full of opportunities for sex and friendship, the gift of cheap apartments and enough sporadic employment to scrape by on rent and food, the frequent shocks of violent confrontation or romantic disappointment, and the ubiquitous spur and confusion of a world in which art and experience are increasingly mediated by technology (the record player, the telephone, the movie projector). Di Prima's poems and prose are shot through with a sense of collectivity, combined with the understanding that the "structures of feeling" shared here are still in process, tense and contradictory, just barely taking on the aspects of a social formation.

As she has outlined in her memoirs, di Prima's early work recalls a mid-1950s moment just before white, bohemian hipness was articulated publicly in texts such as Mailer's "White Negro" and Ginsberg's "Howl" (1956). "As far as we knew," she writes about the months before Ginsberg's poem appeared in print, "there were only a small handful of us—perhaps forty or fifty in the city—who knew what we knew: who raced about in Levis and work shirts, made art, smoked dope, dug the new jazz, and spoke a bastardization of the black argot. We surmised that there might be another fifty living in San Francisco, and perhaps a hundred more scattered throughout the country."[30] The vanguard collectivity di Prima describes is distinguished by its shared style of dress, language, and social practices. Central to these practices is the shared intellectual work of defining a "cool" stance toward the dominant culture, that "terrifying indifference and sentimentality" that surrounds them.[31] This work remains a process rather than a task that one might complete, a practice of charged but nonviolent conflict and of ironic reversals. Characters in *Dinners and Nightmares* willing to describe themselves as "uncool" are invariably much cooler than those who perform hipness too aggressively and thus reveal themselves as having misunderstood the specific tones and forms of restraint that, for di Prima and others, insinuate hipsterism as a collective style.

These tones are captured brilliantly in "A Couple of Weekends," the final prose piece in later editions of *Dinners and Nightmares*.[32] "A Couple of Weekends" represents a milieu that Mailer too will plumb a few years later in *American Dream* (1964). Both texts portray late-night intersections between writers, gangsters, drug users, jazz musicians, and minor celebrities; both create narrative momentum by way of sexual tensions and the threat of violence, though di Prima avoids Mailer's infatuation with the most extreme and sensational plot elements.[33] Indeed, violence never erupts in "A Couple of Weekends," a fact that, as I have already suggested, is not inconsistent with hipsterism as di Prima imagines it. Being "cool" here, as elsewhere in *Dinners and Nightmares*, implies an awareness of harm and harassment as a constant threat, yet it depends equally on one's capacity to live with this threat without losing interest or responding with violent acts of one's own. In this sense, hipsterism for di Prima remains an art of suspension and passive resistance, of refusing indifference without succumbing to sentimentality. Less obviously in "A Couple of Weekends," the structure of feeling di Prima's narrator occupies entails a wary, quizzical relationship to new technologies and discourses of publicity.

All this is suggested in the story's opening paragraph, which reads as follows (eschewing capitalization):

> we were working for some kind of publicity man, when somebody asked us if we wanted to go to a jam session. actually, i was the one who was working, lynn olsen just sat on the couch and knitted afghan squares. she sat with her legs crossed and her toes sticking out of her sneakers, and we both looked very tough and inseparable and nobody ever asked what she was doing there. (*DN*, 154)

These three casual sentences capture the tone and central themes of the sixteen paragraphs to follow. Among other things, they address the exciting and vaguely sinister qualities of publicity, the bohemian ambivalence about working for a living, and the need to perform toughness as a means of masking vulnerability. The narrator is working for "some kind of publicity man," and the curious details that emerge about this employer and his home office are as engaging as anything in the story.[34] "[H]e stayed in bed a lot," di Prima's narrator tells us, "while all his guests got drunk, and listened to them over the rigged intercom system" (*DN*, 155). The intercom—still a relatively new term and suddenly a widespread technology in the early 1960s—is used along with "pocket wire recorders" to record the conversations of the publicity man's guests in order to blackmail them for money or favors.[35] Later in the story, there is suddenly "too much traffic with wire recorders back and forth to some private detective's office," a technological bad omen that leads the narrator to decide to quit her job and hang out elsewhere. The "investor types and the showgirls" who once frequented the home office now are outnumbered by "gangster types," whose "menacing" attitude helps explain the "very tough and inseparable" demeanor that the narrator and her friend and lover "lynn olsen" have assumed from the outset (*DN*, 156). "A Couple of Weekends" thus extends di Prima's meditations on mundane decisions and practices, and on the attitudes one projects in order to avoid serious confrontation while retaining one's enthusiasm for moving through the streets, going to work, and spending time with lovers. All of these activities make art possible for the hipster-poet, just as they become art's primary subject matter.

But "A Couple of Weekends" is also about the jam session the narrator and her partner are invited to in the story's first sentence, and about the little world of unpublicized scenes and underground practices that, like hipster slang, help produce and consolidate a sense of shared subcultural belonging:

> when we got to the session it was friday night and nobody was playing. they had all stopped to drink and I think to turn on but they did that someplace else and didn't invite us. after a while they started and it was like all young white jazz of the early fifties with just the trappings of bebop and nothing happened. but we liked being there, and watching the people, and we sat and listened or talked and drank tumblers of gin. when it got to be light some people went to sleep. we went to sleep around noon on saturday and when we got up there was still the music. A girl had come who sang and she was singing, and there was a new guy playing alto sax. (*DN*, 156)

There are resonances in this scene of so many studies of subcultures, with their emphasis on extended evenings and weekends—on living, as Dick Hebdige writes of British mods, "in the pockets of free time which alone made work meaningful."[36] The narrator and her partner arrive on Friday night and slip into a seemingly different temporality, affected by drug use (heroin for the musicians and alcohol all around), lack of sleep, and extended attention to the music and its many lulls and shifts in mood or quality, which are in turn affected by changes in personnel—the girl who starts singing, for instance, or the "new guy playing alto sax." They have also slipped into a different model of publicity, joining a romanticized counterpublic sphere advertised only by word of mouth and special invitation. Indeed, even more finely differentiated levels of invitation are at issue here: the narrator and her partner have been invited to the session, for instance, but not to "turn on" with the musicians.

By way of intentional subtlety and restraint—hipsterism at the level of narrative tone and technique—"A Couple of Weekends" circles around the sexual politics of "the sessions" and the melancholy drift of the characters we meet there. Repetitions at the beginning of paragraphs create an understated narrative arc, a sense of time passing and characters drifting together and apart with great feeling but without much fanfare: "we went to a lot of sessions and sometimes they showed up"; "we went to a lot of sessions and then we stopped"; "one day i heard of a session somewhere and I went" (*DN*, 156, 158). New characters are introduced—the girl singing, the new guy on saxophone, the drummer—who form a love triangle that parallels the narrator's own tense involvement with "lynn olsen" and "cliff callanan." A complicated yet never spectacular love story emerges from di Prima's sketch of a particular milieu, one which culminates not with the ultimate confrontations with death and courage that conclude Mailer's *American Dream,* but rather with a final, melancholy coupling after the last session. With "lynn olsen" suddenly absent, the narrator attends a final session alone, after which she makes love with the young saxophonist on the floor of the loft he once shared with the singer.

* * *

Mailer and di Prima, then, both embrace hipsterism and situate themselves within the same bohemian subcultures: bisexual, interracial, resistant, dedicated to social and artistic experimentation. Reading *Dinners and Nightmares* and "The White Negro," one feels again the intensity with which artists and intellectuals embraced hipsterism as a figure of resistance to the larger systems that seemed to hover behind and motivate everyday forms of conformity and oppression. And yet the structures of feeling we discover in Mailer and di Prima are not just different but in fact strongly contradictory. Mailer's vision of hipness is immediately active, reactive, rebellious, and violent. Di Prima's hipster draws back rather than reacting immediately, responds to both violence and pleasure with detachment, and expresses both rebellion and critique ironically. Mailer's individualized, violent resistance seems self-indulgent (personally aggressive rather than collectively ambitious), while di Prima's attempts to stay engaged through blasé disengagement seem to be more about survival (the survival of emotional attachments, the survival of utopic longing, the survival of direct abuse) than they are about social transformation.

One could also say that di Prima approaches hipsterism as both a structure of feeling and a resulting subculture, whereas Mailer works to characterize the structure of feeling without caring so much about the specific collectivities it might produce. Though his version of cool begins with a set of subgroups (racial, criminal, musical, and narcotic), it moves quickly to delineate an existential conundrum that everyone will face and most will fail to master. "One is Hip or one is Square," Mailer writes, "(the alternative which each new generation coming into American life is beginning to feel), one is a rebel or one conforms, one is a frontiersman in the Wild West of American night life, or else a Square cell, trapped in the totalitarian tissues of American society, doomed willy-nilly to conform if one is to succeed." "No matter what its horrors," he adds, "the twentieth century is a vastly exciting century for its tendency is to reduce all of life to its ultimate alternatives" (*AM*, 339, 357). Di Prima, on the other hand, resists Mailer's turn toward individualism and "ultimate alternatives"; she remains in the realm of everyday social life and continually invested in collectivity. Her approach manages to chart more intimately than Mailer's the beginnings of a shared, neo-bohemian approach to life and art, focused on illuminating the everyday and maintaining open and insistently creative attachments in a world full of rigged intercoms, spo-radic violence, and coercive ideology. To the extent that di Prima represents hipness as a structure of feeling rather than a specific subculture, she never presents it as an emotion per se, but rather as a specific modulation of strong feeling. Hipness anticipates and reacts to the potentially powerful emotional reactions—of desire, disappointment, discomfort, intense annoyance—that might emerge from a specific encounter. In managing such feelings, di Prima renders identifiable a strategy and structure, a recognizable pattern and ver-nacular philosophy of "impulse" and "restraint," a specific disposition.

A more complete story of subcultural influences on U.S. experimental poet-ry in the 1950s and 1960s would need to expand well beyond the comparison I have offered here between Mailer and di Prima. It would need to consid-er other views of hipness in midcentury verse, other affective poses, and a broader range of literary subcultures. It would need to leave New York City to survey black experimentalism in Cleveland, Chicago, Detroit; the Beat communal circles of Lenore Kandel; the gnostic anticapitalism of the Jack Spicer and Robert Duncan group in Berkeley and San Francisco; the Bud-dhist circuits of Joanne Kyger and Gary Snyder. Di Prima herself would move west by the end of the 1960s, weary of the New York scene and hungry for fresh and expansive visions of community.[37] Like Baraka, whose increasingly revolutionary activities after he moved to Harlem and then Newark in 1965 she followed closely, di Prima left New York throwing shade on those who stayed behind. She addresses "Magick in Theory & Practice"

> to all you with gaunt cheeks who sit
> glamourized by the sounds of art in the
> last remaining lofts, shining like gold in ore
> in the sleek grime of NYC under the shadow
> of MOMA

and in doing so says good-bye to New York, "oh home / I may never see again" (*SP*, 220).

Hipsterism, in nearly every account, has only one potential future: as an increasingly ubiquitous feature of marketing and design, a soundtrack for advertisers desperate to distinguish one product from another. And yet for di Prima the immediate future felt different, less a matter of individual con-sumer decisions than of arranging one's life to avoid them. She moved even farther underground and into the collective; she had even less interest in saving money, buying a house, or keeping track of any product that could be mass-produced or marketed for profit. "No to canned corn & instant / mashed potatoes," she admonishes; "No to rice krispies. / No to special K"

(*SP*, 213). The proto-feminist hipster of *Dinners and Nightmares* became the countercultural anarchist of *Revolutionary Letters* (1971), still raising children and cooking dinner for anyone who happened to wander through, still writing daily and distributing poems on the fly. The hipster detachment of the early 1960s gave way to the increasing revolutionary commitments of the decade's end, including a taste for violence—and for the rhetoric of antistate violence in particular—that she had previously attempted to ironize or resist. Yet di Prima was no less a poet of subcultural practice, her emotional poses and modes of address refashioned in an attempt to capture and consolidate the emergent communities she embraced as her own, living communally, supporting political dissidents, delivering food to communes or distributing it on the streets.[38] "[L]et no one work for another / except for love," she writes in the ninth letter of *Revolutionary Letters*, "and what you make / above your needs be given to the tribe" (*SP*, 205). Her poetry continued to wrap itself in the messy details of specific times and places and to register the hopes and frustrations that oriented her at the time, no doubt hoping they would be given new life in the future.

"Howl" and Other Poems

Is There Old Left in These New Beats?

> As flowers turn toward the sun, by dint of a secret heliotropism the past strives to turn toward that sun which is rising in the sky of history. A historical materialist must be aware of this most inconspicuous of all transformations.
> —Walter Benjamin, "Theses on the Philosophy of History"

> The job would be beyond my means, for the present, however there is always hope for the Future. . . . I am the Trotsky with no dogma in your party.
> —Allen Ginsberg, *Journals: Mid-Fifties*

It is difficult to resist the pull of the future. It is difficult, in the case I will discuss in this final chapter, not to place Allen Ginsberg's poems of the 1950s within overwhelmingly forward-moving, future-oriented cultural narratives. According to such narratives, Ginsberg's first published poems remain notable above all because of what they announced for the future, or, to put it another way, because of the influence they had on what we now call the past. Literary historians often refer to "Howl" as the most important poem since *The Waste Land*, arguing that it helped free American poetry from New Critical hegemony by proclaiming loudly and abruptly that free verse, the personal, and the political belonged again in the poetic vernacular. Similarly, social histories of the 1960s often cite "Howl" (and the Beat movement more generally) as the most famous embodiment of a structure of feeling—youthful, dissatisfied, rebellious—that would soon coalesce into the explicitly political cultures and practices of the New Left. In such cultural and literary-historical accounts, Ginsberg's poems earn their place of importance because of their undeniable connection to the emergent. These poems announce the emergence of both a new American poetry and a number of overlapping new social movements—gay liberation and the antiwar movement, in particular—that gain momentum in the United States in the 1960s and early 1970s.[1]

Without denying the force of such narratives, I want in this essay to gaze backward as I think forward, emphasizing Ginsberg's longing for an Old Left past that seems as insistent in his early poems as do his dreams of new freedoms present or future. Focusing on *"Howl" and Other Poems* (1956), Ginsberg's first published volume, I argue for a newly historicized and melancholic reading of a poet whose important but complicated position in U.S. literary and cultural history we have only just begun to understand, and whose nostalgic affinities for the prewar left have been mostly ignored by Ginsberg scholars, scholars of postwar U.S. culture, and critics of postwar American poetry.[2] From Wobblies to American socialists, Young Socialists, communists, Yiddish communists, and Trotskyites, Ginsberg's work in the 1950s is shot through with references to political identities supposedly antiquated and actively discredited by intellectuals on both the left and the right during the Cold War moment.[3] His hopes for the future, as my epigraphs suggest, are bound up in his capacity to call up past figures of freedom and resistance, figures who, like Trotsky, manage to signify revolutionary hope while refusing the (Stalinist) violence and discipline that had tainted revolution by the 1950s. To the extent that Ginsberg's great poems of the 1950s, "Howl" above all, are prophecies of emergent movements and collectivities, they are also elegies for cherished pasts at risk of receding irretrievably, of being inconspicuously transformed and finally erased by narratives of progress that manage—by dint of historical victories—to limit the possibilities of the future. Like Benjamin's image of the flowers of the past striving constantly to reorient themselves in relation to that sun that is rising in the sky of history, the flowers we find scattered throughout Ginsberg's *"Howl" and Other Poems* retain their own undeniable agency and attraction. We can only understand them as fully as Benjamin suggests we might, however, if we manage to read against the unidirectional, categorically progressive heliotropisms that have too long oriented our approach to them. We need instead to reassert Ginsberg's tendency to commemorate the resources of the past, to infuse them with the poetic energies of the present, to reconfigure them in the face of shifting historical circumstance.

Narratives of postwar American verse frequently begin with economic prosperity, bureaucratization, and conformity, and with the "closed" poetic forms that seem both to echo and to help produce these more widespread social attributes. These "closed" forms are self-contained rhetorical structures, traditionally rhymed and metered, animated by tightly constructed tonal or metaphorical tensions. They come complete with their own bureaucratico-educational practice (close reading), their own managers (the New Critics), and their own white-collar "workforce" (instructors of literature in American high schools, colleges, and universities). Against this backdrop, narratives of postwar American poetry introduce the "open" forms and the infusion of personal and social content represented by the poets and movements—Beat, Black Mountain, New York School—set forth in Donald Allen's landmark *The New Amer-*

ican Poetry (1960). Allen's anthology quite rightly stands as synecdoche for this literary-historical watershed. It clarifies and consolidates for poets and critics alike the full strength and diversity of this movement toward free verse and apparent spontaneity of composition. It serves as a fulcrum that propels us forward in literary history, toward the dominant poetic statements (confessional, experimental, openly political) and countercultural movements of the 1960s and 1970s.

In Ginsberg's case, there is real cultural momentum behind narratives founded on some version of the following chronology: Ginsberg reading "Howl" for the first time at the Six Gallery in 1955, when the Beat movement began to gain public acclaim; at early antiwar protests in 1963; on the planning committee for the quintessentially "hippie" Human Be-In in Golden Gate Park in 1967; chanting mantras to calm Yippies and police outside the 1968 Democratic Convention in Chicago; and giving his famous *Gay Sunshine* interview in 1972, in which he speaks about his homosexuality more openly, some have suggested, than any public or literary figure had previously.[4] It seems important, however, to wonder about the narrative possibilities this neatly progressive cultural and literary chronology shuts down. For all such stories of forward movement—from Beat poetry to social criticism, from rebellious aesthetics to organized mass demonstrations, from gay poetry to gay liberation—lose something in the telling. In particular, the chronology manages to elide Ginsberg's attachments to the left-collective cultures that had thrived in the years preceding World War II, cultures he endowed with a strange, anachronistic afterlife during the vehemently anticommunist years of the Cold War.

Focusing on the anachronisms, repetitions, and potentially fruitful revisions Ginsberg's generational vision folds within itself, one discovers an alternative to the progressive-generational model most often called upon to define postwar culture. Such models tend to lose sight of melancholic attachments to past ideals or failed movements, lost objects of identification that are never fully mourned or forgotten and that continue to animate the texts of the present. They ignore those identifications alternately concealed and exposed, built into and constantly revised by social subjects in the face of unstable local and historical contexts. They ignore those disjunctions we experience when social identities assumed to belong to previous generations resurface to disrupt our confident notions of the contemporary.[5] From the perspective of Benjamin's historical materialist, progressive histories ignore the insight that progress is neither neat nor decisively future-oriented. Benjamin's angel of history, while he is driven "irresistibly . . . into the future," has "his face . . . turned toward the past." If not for the storm propelling him forward, "the angel would like to stay, awaken the dead, and make whole what has been smashed."[6]

Without trying to make too much of the coincident imagery in Ginsberg's "Howl" and Benjamin's short meditation from "Theses on the Philosophy of History"—two texts in which angels are defined by the wreckage and violence that surround them—I want to found my readings of Ginsberg's political identifications on Benjamin's vision of melancholic progress, of history moving forward while gazing backward, longing to recuperate that which has been damaged. This vision helps illuminate the historical disjunctions of U.S. culture during the 1950s, a decade during which Allen Ginsberg might long for the politics and poetics of a communist youth while embracing a postwar culture of unapologetic homosexuality and dreamlike nonconformity. Such disjunctions are reproduced and reconfigured in "Howl," Ginsberg's great and indelible statement of postwar political upheaval, and in a whole series of images and thematic juxtapositions from Ginsberg's poems of the 1950s. "America I'm putting my queer shoulder to the wheel" he promises at the conclusion of "America," forging an image that typifies the divided nature of his politics and poetics during this period.[7] The image is at once industrial and identitarian, anachronistic and prescient. It performs its melancholic attachment to the working-class collectives of the past even while it strives onward, toward the queer liberations and new collectivities of the future. It suggests that the pull of the future—the storm that propels Benjamin's angel forward, or "that sun which is rising in the sky of history"—is no more insistent than the continued strivings of the past, and that the two can only be redeemed together.

* * *

Throughout his life, Ginsberg maintained a deep attachment to the ideals and organizations of the prewar left. His mother, Naomi, was a dedicated communist who took her young sons to party meetings in Paterson, New Jersey, and vacationed with them at a Yiddish-American summer camp where "the adults debated ideology" and "[p]ictures of the enemy—capitalists and socialists with exaggerated features, blood dripping from their hands—lined the walls of the mess halls."[8] Allen's father, Louis, was a well-known poet and lifelong socialist who named Allen's older brother after Eugene Debs, whom he had often heard speak as a child. Louis, at constant odds with Naomi over left political questions and frequently taken to task by her for his overly "bourgeois" perspective on both poetry and politics, would recite Dickinson, Poe, Shelley, Keats, and Milton as he moved around the house. Naomi, as Ginsberg recalled for a biographer, countered Louis's recitations by improvising fables for her children in which "the king or prince went out and saw the condition of the workers and helped them out and everyone lived happily ever after."[9] "Naomi reading patiently," Ginsberg remembers in "Kaddish," "story out of a Communist fairy book—Tale of the Sudden Sweetness of the Dictator—Forgiveness of Warlocks—Armies Kissing— / . . . The King & the Workers" (*CP*, 214).

Neither Ginsberg's passion for political debates and fairy tales nor his connections to left organizations ended with childhood. In 1943 he enrolled at Columbia University with the support of a partial scholarship from the New Jersey CIO, and in 1950 he took an early postgraduate job with the *Labor Herald*, the newspaper of the New Jersey AFL. Both during and after college Ginsberg's devotion to literature overwhelmed his initial plan to study labor law or economics and to devote himself to the struggle against poverty and exploitation. Nevertheless, he retained throughout his life a stated affective and philosophical affinity with left organizations and political activities, an affinity that distinguished him from such Beat fellow travelers as Jack Kerouac and William S. Burroughs. While Kerouac and Burroughs may have subscribed to many of Ginsberg's criticisms of American life, they would never have found themselves defending the foreign policy of the Soviet Union in the late 1950s, as Ginsberg did in letters to his father. Despite negative encounters with communist governments in Havana and Prague, and a growing lack of faith in all Cold War governments, Ginsberg never gave up the hope that the spirit of the radical left might be reanimated.[10]

We gain further insight into Ginsberg's political identifications around the time he composed "Howl," and into the strangely haunted and interstitial historical position this poem articulates, by considering his relationship with Carl Solomon. While *"Howl" and Other Poems* as a volume is dedicated to Kerouac, Burroughs, and Neal Cassady, "Howl" itself is dedicated to Solomon, whom Ginsberg met in a psychiatric institute in 1949. Unlike Kerouac and Burroughs, Solomon shared Ginsberg's Jewish and New York–New Jersey childhood and his memories of pre–Cold War idealism and collectivity. His "I Was a Communist Youth," published in 1961 by Amiri Baraka (then, LeRoi Jones) and Diane di Prima in *The Floating Bear*, offers a fascinating portrait of the fate of New York student radicalism as World War II ended and the Cold War began. Solomon writes,

> It was during the war. Red movements were flourishing everywhere. On the City College campus in 1944, when I began college, there were at least five hundred supporters of the American Communist Party out of a student body of a couple of thousand. Such was the educational environment of the war generation. We were raised under these slogans: Win the war, destroy fascism. After the war: full employment and the "century of the common man."

Fascism was the most hated philosophy of all time. Hitler and Mussolini and Tojo were seen as the most significant tyrants of history.

Moods have changed and time has brought about a difference in us all. After the war, America was to break with her wartime allies and they were to grapple on the battlefields of Korea. The great disillusionment was to come.

[. . .]

My travels brought me to Europe and to the West Indies and I had a glimpse of the world that the war against fascism had created.

[. . .]

What I saw in Cuba in 1945 was a preview of what was to come in the late fifties.

What I saw in Yugoslavia in 1945 was the Partisans, wearing red stars on their arms.

[. . .]

Only in America and from America came the slogan: Freedom. The slogan freedom meant white supremacy and the suppression of every movement for human hope on the face of the planet. So the cold war began.

The men, like Franco of Spain, whom we had been taught to hate we were now told were our allies in a struggle against the "Eastern Bloc."

Men like Dimitrov of Bulgaria who had had the courage to defy fascism during the Thirties, we were now told were our enemies, a group of cowardly tyrants.

Who knows what his opinions are amid such nonsense.[11]

Solomon's clipped narrative hints at a history more widespread than is typically acknowledged in accounts of the postwar avant-garde. In memoirs of the period, this history surfaces insistently as a previous kind of bohemian posture quickly forgotten once Beat, bebop, and post-bop culture displace the political investments, styles of dress, and proletarian folk songs that still echoed around Washington and Union Squares in the 1950s. On the one hand, the avant-garde tends to depict these proletarian styles and political investments as unquestionably obsolete and unworthy of serious consideration. On the other hand, the ideological force of these styles and investments still haunts the "new" American artists and erupts stubbornly in their poems, memoirs, and magazines.[12]

Solomon's narrative represents both these positions at once—Old Left obsolescence and haunting, irrelevance and longing—without adding to this dialectic Ginsberg's performances of faith in the eventual return of left collectivity. "I Was a Communist Youth" reads as much like a parable as it does an accurate log of Solomon's teenage travels, moving paratactically and in a deadpan-cynical tone through a list of concrete historical references arranged to tell a tale of state-sponsored hypocrisy and generational disillusionment. In what one might call a "catalogue as generational parable" (a phrase one could also apply to "Howl") Solomon begins with youthful idealism, proceeds by geopolitical observation, and culminates in existentialist cynicism. "Who knows what his opinions are amid such nonsense," Solomon concludes, occupying a final rhetorical position far removed from such optimistic slogans as "full employment and the 'century of the common man.'"

The cynicism and points of critical emphasis that shape Solomon's brief political autobiography echo the postwar works of sociology and social theory often named as the intellectual guidebooks of the New Left. Just before and into the Eisenhower era, left intellectuals such as Herbert Marcuse and C. Wright Mills developed critical positions that began with dire assessments of social and political life in the United States and other advanced industrial nations. Diagnosing "the troubles that confront . . . all men and women living in the twentieth century" by way of the "white-collar people" who best represent the state of work, entertainment, and social relations under advanced industry, Mills in 1951 comes to a pessimistic conclusion. He portrays an international middle class increasingly dominant both in sheer numbers and in the prevalence of its social experiences, yet with no enabling or critically and politically empowering sense of its own social position.[13] Similarly, in *One-Dimensional Man* Marcuse takes as his point of departure the new modes of economic and ideological organization that have come to dominate advanced industrial society. Whether communist, fascist, or capitalist, advanced industrial societies with the sudden potential to meet the basic material needs of their citizens have begun to realize this potential using technological and organizational means that also increase "the scope of society's domination over the individual." As this domination of the individual morphs inevitably into collective control, "[c]ontemporary society," Marcuse writes, "seems to be capable of containing social change."[14]

Yet Solomon's melancholic longing for the Communist Party and the Popular Front against fascism creates a kind of tension between his generational parable and the arguments of Mills and Marcuse as I have summarized them. While these New Left intellectuals situate hope and resistance within critical analysis or in the space of properly dialectical thought, Solomon's hope appears precisely in his invocation of lost hope, of an Old Left faith now untenable, of a belief in political agency that no longer seems viable. Even as this lost faith structures his cynicism, it designates a potential alternative to his current political affect. It creates a temporal disjunction, calling up a past social identity at once buried under cynicism and exposed to justify it, but which cannot be exposed without simultaneously underscoring a position of resistance both to that cynicism and to the post-Fordist, Cold War forces that produce it. In Ginsberg's poems of the 1950s, such melancholic attachments to the Old Left generate even greater rhetorical energy. They come to symbolize the continued possibility of questioning prosperity and resisting the sophisticated social controls of advanced industrial society. They act to disrupt dominant postwar logics of present political consensus and future compromise, invoking "the old" as the sign of "the new," inviting past generations to haunt the present, troubling the notion that some contemporary dominance will necessarily structure the future.

* * *

"Howl" and Other Poems is full of expressions of longing, expressions layered one on top of the other and certainly not all melancholic gestures toward a former faith in left collectivity and political agency. There are longings here for love (often a trope for longing itself), for male-male sexual relations or camaraderie, for the means to express a self that thinks itself infinite, and for the public acknowledgment of this capacious, godlike self and its capacity for poetry. "I want people to bow as they see me and say he is gifted with poetry, he has seen the presence of the Creator," Ginsberg submits to the reader in "Transcription of Organ Music." "And the Creator gave me a shot of his presence to gratify my wish, so as not to cheat me of my yearning for him" (*CP*, 141). Few poets manage to be so consumed by and yet so optimistic about want, wish, and yearning as does Allen Ginsberg in the 1950s.

As infinite or transhistorical as these expressions of longing can seem, one soon notices them winding themselves around invocations of a lost past with a particular historical profile. Often this lost past emerges through images of automobiles and trains, images that connect industrial production and working-class employment with Beat romanticizations of American machinery in endless motion along the roads and tracks of town and country. These machines are stationary or inaccessible as often as they move freely; they signal failure or anticipation as frequently as they signal successful movements and happy deliveries. "[S]o lonely growing up among / the imaginary automobiles / and dead souls of Tarrytown" (*CP*, 78), Ginsberg writes in "Wild Orphan." "I walked on the banks of the tincan banana dock and sat down under the huge shade of a Southern Pacific locomotive to look at the sunset over the box house hills and cry," he remembers in the opening sentence of "Sunflower Sutra," a poem that works to rehabilitate both the sunflower he discovers on that dock and "the specter and shade of a once powerful mad American locomotive" (*CP*, 138–39). These imaginary automobiles and once powerful locomotives help create the impression of a past mourned because it cannot be recaptured, but celebrated because of what it continues to represent: solidarity and collectivity, shared purpose and freedom, the beauty of production, the promise that stationary machines and imaginations might be set in motion again.

These are potential energies that Ginsberg repeatedly associates with the working classes. He attacks white-collar culture without hesitation and, not surprisingly for a poet who self-identified as bohemian, he seeds his Beat poems with heroic images of the lumpenproletariat: musicians, bums, junkies, and other "angels" of Skid Row. Yet just as frequently as Ginsberg's work of the 1950s attacks the middle class or sings the praises of the lumpenproletariat, it strives to imagine the proletariat. It fetishizes, celebrates, and sanctifies the working classes, placing them at the imaginative center of poems like "In back of the real," "In the Baggage Room at Greyhound," and "Sunflower Sutra." In these and other poems from the 1950s, the proletariat is sometimes present, often absent, but longed for consistently. The poet searches for workers on the docks and in "the old red Wobbly Hall" in "Afternoon Seattle" and among the silk-strikers of his own memory in "America." He gestures toward the absent railroad switchman in "In back of the real" and dreams of grocery boys in "A Supermarket in California." In Denver in 1947, Ginsberg wrote "The Bricklayer's Lunch Hour," a poem unabashedly romantic about both laborers and manual labor and his first poem that friend and mentor William Carlos Williams considered truly promising. In 1951, he began "A Poem on America" with the following observation: "America is like Russia. / . . . / We have the proletariat too" (*CP*, 64).

In his poems of the 1950s, Ginsberg continues to remember and hopes to reimagine an Old Left culture in which "work and art, labor and beauty" remain in constant dialogue, workers supporting artists who in turn celebrate the beauty of labor.[15] His poems struggle to depict alliances between workers and his own coterie of avant-garde artists, in the absence of a contemporary political or organizational space to support such alliances. Unions were not inviting Ginsberg to conduct poetry readings in their halls, and in the postwar moment the work/art dialectic of the 1930s and 1940s lacked viable sites in which it might develop. Visiting Seattle's Wobbly Hall with Gary Snyder in 1956, Ginsberg finds "bleareyed dusty cardplayers dreaming behind the counter," with little faith in either themselves or their visitors: "but these young fellers can't see ahead and we nothing to offer" (*CP*, 150). Structured by their own elegiac insistence on failed communication and organizational absence, Ginsberg's proletarian images most often coalesce as expressions of longing, spiritual abstractions struggling to preserve a time when different forms of political culture seemed possible. They become invocations of a moment when art might somehow engage with and reconstitute its relationship to conditions of labor, when poems might still represent an expansive left collectivity.

Ginsberg's "In back of the real" presents something like a parable of this hope for strategically anachronistic resistance. The poem expands the melancholy of Old Left identification articulated in Solomon's "I Was a Communist Youth" into a metaphysical poetics of industry that might sustain itself even without the organizational spaces and supports of the 1930s and 1940s:

> railroad yard in San Jose
>   I wandered desolate
> in front of a tank factory
>   and sat on a bench
> near the switchman's shack.
>
> A flower lay on the hay on
>   the asphalt highway
> —the dread hay flower
>   I thought—It had a
> brittle black stem and
>   corolla of yellowish dirty
> spikes like Jesus' inchlong
>   crown, and a soiled
> dry center cotton tuft
>   like a used shaving brush
> that's been lying under
>   the garage for a year.
>
> Yellow, yellow flower, and
>   flower of industry,
> tough spiky ugly flower,
>   flower nonetheless,
> with the form of the great yellow
>   Rose in your brain!
> This is the flower of the World
> (*CP*, 113)

Ginsberg moves in this poem from a series of physical juxtapositions rendered in prepositional phrases to a series of imaginative, idealized relationships represented through metaphor. In so doing, he moves the reader from the initial desolation of the industrial space emptied out and militarized to a Blakean vision of the blessed and beautiful form within all creatures. The (absent) labor that defines this space as the poem begins—referred to obliquely as the speaker situates himself "in back of the . . . railroad yard," "in front of a . . . factory," and "near the switchman's shack"—is transfigured over the course of the poem and finally resituated within a poetico-spiritual realm in which industrial setting, flower, and workers can be at once symbolically merged and endowed with a sacred, eternal form. In back of the real, one might say, Marx and Engels's workers of the world are imaginatively transformed into the flowers of the world, each a little ugly and dusty but holding "the form of the great yellow / Rose in [its] brain."

The difficulty and the potential of such an interpretation lie in two places. They lie first in the absence of the workers themselves, of even the switchman, whose shack is nearby but who neither shows himself nor communicates with the poet. Second, such an interpretation must justify itself in relation to the tropes that take the place of absent workers in this poem: first the hay flower, then similes comparing the flower to Jesus and to a used shaving brush, and finally the great yellow rose. Like the "gray Sunflower" in "Sunflower Sutra," "crackly bleak and dusty with the smut and smog and smoke of olden loco-motives in its eye" (*CP*, 138), the hay flower in "In back of the real" might be said to represent the "perfect beauty" of all human souls in the often alienat-ing and degrading struggles over labor, profit, and industrial production. Yet all the marks of left collectivity we find in other poems from the 1950s—for instance, the "class consciousness" and the poignant "We have the proletar-iat too" of "A Poem on America"—have been evacuated from the desolate, first-person-singular wandering of "In back of the real." In its place are met-aphors, a series of figures the poet offers up and yokes together as a way of continuing to imagine, to remember, or to believe in an ideal form he can no longer see, even in those spaces where he thinks he should find it. Jesus appears here as a figure of faith, of the Christian belief in redemption: a uto-pian future that could suddenly enter and transform the present. Likewise, the poet's hopes for working-class collectivity and artist-worker connections reside in tropes and in the very act of troping, of generating figures of faith to counter the symbolic emptiness of postwar industrial space.

Ginsberg's engagement in "In back of the real" with lost forms of left collec-tivity and culture are echoed by the poem's engagement with a long tradition of romantic imagery and political idealism. In both its specific metaphors and its activation of these tropes as symbols of some deeper, fuller life with-in modern, urban, industrial culture, Ginsberg's poem recalls Blake's "Lon-don" and "Ah Sunflower," Wordsworth's "I Wandered Lonely as a Cloud," and Yeats's "The Rose of the World," to name only a few. The "I wandered" of "In back of the real" echoes Blake's "London" and Wordsworth's tale of "golden daffodils," though unlike the wandering "I" in these famous lyrics, which speaks to us from their first to their last stanzas, Ginsberg's "I" recedes over the course of the poem. Standing forth long enough to begin producing metaphors, Ginsberg's "I" blends into them once this production begins, thus compromising slightly the narrative control Blake's and Wordsworth's speakers maintain throughout "London" and "I Wandered."

This integration of speaker and imagery suggests that agency functions somewhat differently in "In back of the real" than it does in this lyric's famous predecessors. Agency in "In back of the real" is displaced slightly from the speaker and partially relocated in "the brain" of the poem's "flower of industry" (itself a trope, of course, for the speaker). As the poem ends, it is somewhere in the imaginative space between the speaker and the flower that we discover the power to hold on to and reactivate emotional attachments and images of self that seem to promise transformation. Without factory and railroad workers to wander through, transfiguring the "real railroad yard" with their collective presence, Ginsberg's speaker is left celebrating a flower, while the flower, in turn, is left remembering the ideal forms in its own brain, a seemingly endless loop of idealization that threatens to collapse under its own metaphorical weight. Stationary and solitary, Ginsberg's "flower of industry" lacks the collectivity and capacity for movement implicit in Benjamin's image of the flowers of the past, which, though they may at times stand in the grip of a simplistically progressive heliotropism, are nonetheless full of the very play between past and present that makes redemption possible. Ginsberg's flower stands alone, hinting at a sort of overly romantic melancholy—what Benjamin called "left wing melancholy"—that risks reproducing itself endlessly, oblivious to other flowers or to the potential for a different sun to rise one day in the sky of history.[16]

It is no accident that during the 1950s Ginsberg's invocations of the ideal collectivity of the proletariat reside in metaphorical circuits and melancholic gestures toward a prewar past, rather than residing in gestures of support for the postwar initiatives of the labor movement. Though radical segments of the labor movement still existed in the 1950s, the CIO's 1949 purge of all unions who refused to embrace policies of anticommunism signaled what Stanley Aronowitz has called "an unprecedented era of conformity" within the trade union movement.[17] A few notable exceptions notwithstanding, unions participated willingly in the Cold War consolidation of power in the hands of those Mills named "the power elite," in the crusade against any and all "un-American" expressions of political dissent, and in the increasing migration of the best industrial jobs and wages into whites-only suburbs or rural areas. Labor's complicity during the Cold War era with even the most egregious corporate and governmental initiatives was an undeniable sign for Ginsberg's contemporaries that U.S. political discourses in the 1950s would spend less time working through Depression-era class conflicts than they would interpreting the unequal distribution of mass-produced prosperity, consumer opportunity, and political influence. "Mass society," Aronowitz writes of the 1950s, "had replaced class society as the overarching spirit of the times," and the challenge for many on the left was to fashion a critique of "deprivations . . . [that] were not material in the old sense" but "appeared postindustrial," the product of an economy that now had the capacity to provide all of its workers with full-time employment and fulfilling social lives but refused to do so.[18]

While many postwar artists and intellectuals eagerly embraced this notion that an epochal shift had rendered prewar forms of art and politics obsolete, Ginsberg's poetic and political imaginary retains its investment in Popular Front–style assertions of working-class beauty and the cultural centrality of the work-art dialectic. Though poems like "In back of the real" and "Sunflower Sutra" suggest that the poet's connection with the proletariat becomes more and more a function of memory and metaphor, they nonetheless concern themselves with industrial rather than white-collar work. These poems mark the increasing difficulty of imagining a resistant proletariat in consumer culture, and thus register the shift from an industrial to a postindustrial economy, by substituting commodities for workers as the figures of industrial production. It is through discarded commodities—"a used shaving brush / . . . lying under / the garage" (*CP*, 113), "dead baby carriages, black treadless tires forgotten and unretreaded, . . . condoms and pots" (*CP*, 138)—rather than exploited workers that Ginsberg manages to allegorize the productive and social relations he seeks to redeem. And though it is true, furthermore, that these relations finally assume an abstract, spiritual form in "Sunflower Sutra" and "In back of the real," I would argue that this form grows out of and contains within itself (within its "brain" or memory) a specifically melancholic vision of collectivity, one based on factory economies and on the class consciousness structuring and structured by industrial social relations. Ginsberg's difficulty in the 1950s stems from his desire to continue to represent past forms of left collectivity and artist-worker solidarity now that the historical bloc that once sustained these forms no longer exists. In reaction to this difficulty, he substitutes figures of faith for a political faith difficult to maintain in the railroad yards of the 1950s, an act of substitution that both holds open a space for left collective resistance and runs the risks of dwelling endlessly on the past. In "Howl," we see how a potentially debilitating attachment to prewar configurations of political resistance begins to rearticulate itself as a new form of oppositional collectivity, a new form, "Howl" suggests through its prophetic repetitions, that would be impossible to imagine without the cultural resources of the past.

* * *

"I saw the best minds of my generation destroyed by madness," proclaims the first line of "Howl," prefiguring a generational rhetoric that would soon structure, among other notable statements, John F. Kennedy's inaugural address and an obscure but influential manifesto of student activism, the *Port Huron Statement*.[19] Explicitly, the minds America has driven to madness are those of the male, mostly homosexual, drug-using members of Ginsberg's own Beat-bohemian coterie. These are the

> angelheaded hipsters burning for the ancient heavenly connection to the
> starry dynamo in the machinery of night,
> who poverty and tatters and hollow-eyed and high sat up smoking in the
> supernatural darkness of cold-water flats floating across the tops of
> cities contemplating jazz,
> (*CP*, 126)

and who are often references to Ginsberg himself. Marjorie Perloff recounts that, as Frank O'Hara listened to Ginsberg begin a reading of "Howl" by invoking the most inspired intellects of his generation, O'Hara is said to have turned to his neighbor and quietly deadpanned, "I wonder who Allen has in mind?"[20]

As O'Hara's joke suggests and as Perloff argues at greater length, "Howl" unquestionably solicits our attention as an autobiographical work. In keeping with my approach in earlier sections of this chapter, however, here I want to place the biographical movements of "Howl" within a larger cultural frame, one that focuses on the complex temporality of the poem's claims to political identity. During a postwar moment when the left is caught, as Ginsberg later described it, "between the Scylla of Stalinism and the Charybdis of anti-Stalinism," "Howl" speaks for a generation doomed, exhausted, institutionalized, yet nonetheless possessing a compelling vision of left collectivity, a vision both haunted by the past and predictive of political futures.[21] As "Howl" imagines it, Ginsberg's "generation destroyed by madness" is actually double: a postwar Beat illuminati inhabited (or energized) by a prewar generation dedicated to communist or socialist transformations.

The rhetorical and poetic techniques Ginsberg employs to give shape to his (multi)generational parable reproduce the strange and contradictory historical condition "Howl" sees itself occupying—at once repressive and liberating, paralyzed and animated, full of forward momentum and doubling back end-lessly. Generating momentum in each of its three sections by returning insistently to the same root word and syntactical structure, the poem stacks one image or anecdote of Beat illumination onto another to create an impression of expansive yet publicly unacknowledged collectivity, a new "holy" collectivity through which the Old Left might bid for a return to social influence in a new form. "Howl" fuses the proletarian nostalgia of a poem like "In back of the real" with anticipation, reviving with a difference the literary references of the Popular Front and reimagining America's industrial landscapes from the perspective of neon supernatural hipness.

In its very structure, "Howl" signifies Ginsberg's desire to merge his own generation of angelheaded hipsters with his parents' generation of dedicated socialists and impassioned communists. Again and again in its famous first section, "Howl" returns to "who," the relative pronoun that inaugurates long line after long line and propels the poem forward through catalogs of the poet's actions and those of his likeminded brethren,

> who bared their brains to Heaven under the El and saw Mohammedan angels
>   staggering on tenement roofs illuminated,
> who passed through universities with radiant cool eyes hallucinating Arkan-
>   sas and Blake-light tragedy among the scholars of war,
>   [. . .]
> who disappeared into the volcanoes of Mexico leaving behind nothing but
>   the shadow of dungarees and the lava and ash of poetry scattered in
>   fireplace Chicago,
> who reappeared on the West Coast investigating the FBI in beards and shorts
>   with big pacifist eyes sexy in their dark skin passing out incompre-
>   hensible leaflets,
> (*CP*, 126–27)

and so forth. From these short excerpts one gets a clear sense of the poetic structure without which "Howl" could not exist, the parallel syntactic structure and anaphoric return to "who" that leaves readers anticipating the next predicate: "wept at the romance of the streets," "scribbled all night rocking and rolling," "jumped off the Brooklyn Bridge," "sang out of their windows in despair," "barreled down the highways of the past" (*CP*, 129).

As a poetic device, anaphora helps Ginsberg create rhythm and generate prophetic momentum from line to line. But the device also becomes a powerful trope in its own right, a figure of return that troubles linear progression and confuses origins by insisting on starting over, again and again, seemingly at the same place (the "who") but always with a difference (the predicate). Though "Howl" begins by announcing itself as a generational manifesto and proceeds to catalog the actions, attitudes, and suffering of a certain group at a certain historical moment, the form of the poem leads us to wonder when exactly—and with whom—these actions and attitudes originate. Through force of repetition, one might say, the relative pronoun "who" becomes interrogative, and the form of Ginsberg's poem subtly undermines the notion that generations break away cleanly, defining themselves through their clear difference from the past.

"Howl" reinforces its tendency to trouble origins and generational logic by collapsing its primary objects of identification: the poet's dedicatee and contemporary, Carl Solomon, and the poet's mother. Already near the end of Part I, we find the poet's addresses to Solomon merge perceptibly with descriptions of Naomi Ginsberg:

> Pilgrim State's Rockland's and Greystone's foetid halls, bickering with the
>   echoes of the soul, rocking and rolling in the midnight solitude-bench
>   dolmen-realms of love, dream of life a nightmare, bodies turned to
>   stone as heavy as the moon,
> With mother finally * * * * * *, and the last fantastic book flung out of the
>   tenement window, and the last door closed at 4 A.M. and the last
>   telephone slammed at the wall in reply [. . .]
> ah, Carl, while you are not safe I am not safe, and now you're really in the
>   total animal soup of time—
>   (CP, 130)

In 1955, just before Ginsberg composed "Howl," he was shaken by news that Solomon, who had been faring well for a period outside mental hospitals, had again been institutionalized. He had been sent to Pilgrim State Hospital, where Ginsberg's mother was also a mental patient and where in 1947 she had been lobotomized with her sons' written consent.[22] Pilgrim State, Rockland, and Greystone all name New York–area hospitals where Solomon and/or Naomi Ginsberg were institutionalized at one time or another. As Ginsberg evokes the "foetid halls" of these hospitals, where dreams turn to nightmares and bodies to stone, the biographies of mother and contemporary begin to merge, joining together in solidarity "in the total animal soup of time." Just as Ginsberg's use of anaphora forces us to question the historical origins of both social afflictions and collective resistance in "Howl," this blurring of the poet's central objects of identification implies that his lamentation for the madness of his own generation is also a lamentation for the blighted hopes and wasted intellects of their precursors. As in Benjamin's "Theses," one discovers in "Howl" the conviction that the spirit of both struggle and possibility in the present should be nourished by memories of past suffering, oppression, "courage, humor, cunning, and fortitude."[23]

Again in Part III, the poet's statements of solidarity with his contemporary become imbricated with expressions of sympathy for his communist mother:

Carl Solomon! I'm with you in Rockland
        where you're madder than I am
[. . .]
I'm with you in Rockland
        where you imitate the shade of my mother
[. . .]
I'm with you in Rockland
        where fifty more shocks will never return your soul to its body again
        from its pilgrimage to a cross in the void
I'm with you in Rockland
        where you accuse your doctors of insanity and plot the Hebrew
        socialist revolution against the fascist national Golgotha
[. . .]
I'm with you in Rockland
        where there are twentyfive thousand mad comrades all together sing-
        ing the final stanzas of the Internationale
        (CP, 132–33)

Madness in "Howl" functions as an effective trope for acts of social resistance that are almost futile yet still somehow inspiring, or, to put it another way, for the fate of the revolutionary imagination during a decidedly nonrevolutionary era. This figure is not, however, limited to a single generation. Is it Solomon or Naomi who plots "the Hebrew / socialist revolution against the fascist national Golgotha"? Is it his generation or hers that, in its socially produced madness, hears "twentyfive thousand . . . comrades all together sing- / ing the final stanzas of the Internationale"? By the end of the poem, these two figures, and through them their generations, have become almost indistinguishable, Solomon imitating the shade of Naomi so that the poet can swear his simultaneous devotion to them both. Images of a mental patient dreaming of revolution, or of the institutionalized joining together to sing the Communist Party anthem, are composites. They are meant to suggest that the cultural resources of the prewar left have not disappeared in the postwar moment, that the costs of a fervent belief in social transformation are high in either case, and that the past and present can only be redeemed together.

Since its composition, political interpretations of "Howl" have thought of the poem as an early sign of a new American counterculture invested in a wide range of social issues, and, more specifically, as a harbinger of gay liberation. During the 1960s, New Left movements—such as those against the Vietnam War, in support of civil rights, for the reform of U.S. universities—

departed (as "Howl" does) from liberal optimism about American institutions and from liberalism's Cold War–era foreign policy as it manifests itself both abroad and as strategy for enforcing political consensus and justifying repressive police actions within the United States.[24] These movements were also historically united because they have come unhinged (as "Howl" has) from the Old Left requirement that various issues and movements be subordinated to the larger effort to replace capitalism with an economic system of, for, and by the working class. One hears rumblings in "Howl" of organized movements that, in Nancy Fraser's terms, will demand "recognition" for identity groups culturally and discursively excluded from full democratic participation without claiming that such exclusions can be remedied only through complete economic transformation.[25]

Throughout this chapter, however, I have tried to suggest that the articulations of collective action and political identity that energized the 1960s and 1970s, insofar as we can see them connected to, or predicted by, the models of resistant collectivity represented in Ginsberg's work of the 1950s, were not as new as they seemed. In memoirs and manifestos, postwar formations like the Beat generation and the New Left reveal their deep though ambivalent attachments to a set of supposedly antiquated cultural resources: a class consciousness that can activate critique and collective resistance, the integration of art into the collective struggle, the art of demanding social transformation even when it seems uncertain. Unquestionably reconstructed in the face of new historical conditions, these resources nonetheless helped galvanize the statements and stances of movements too often thought of as having created themselves spontaneously—rising forth in rebellion against a dominant formation, such as the New Criticism or Cold War consensus, that has long rendered obsolete the left formations of the past. My point is not to argue that the New Left is only the Old Left in new clothing, but rather to remind us that "the new" can only be constructed by exaggerating the decline of "the old." Ginsberg's poems of the 1950s mark the presence within the New American Poetry of Old Left political identifications that continue to agitate even as they are defined as outmoded. As we think through the political and cultural movements and identifications of the postwar moment, his poems remind us that old forms can always be reconstituted in the face of new conditions. These forms are never as distant as they might seem, and the trick is to recognize them among us, to identify them to one another, and to rearticulate them as figures of historical agency.

Epilogue

Meditations in an Emergency, Catastrophes of the Present

Postmodernism, Andrew Hoberek suggests in his conclusion to *The Twilight of the Middle Class* (2005), "is the universalized worldview not just of the white-collar middle class, but of this class during the specific period when the postwar boom seemed to sever the traditional Marxist connection between capital and class."[1] Hoberek has Thomas Pynchon's *The Crying of Lot 49* (1965) and Don DeLillo's *White Noise* (1985) in mind, as well as Fredric Jameson's *Postmodernism, or, The Cultural Logic of Late Capitalism* (1991). All three works, Hoberek argues, reflect to a significant extent the "characteristic postmodern turn from consumption to production . . . underwritten . . . by the ambiguous position of the postwar middle class, structurally proletarianized but not (yet) subject to the loss of income or status."[2] As the workplace during the economic boom of the postwar becomes a site of increasing standardization and conformity, postmodernism turns its attention to consumption: to the emotional charge one might experience during a lunchtime shopping excursion in Manhattan, or while wandering through a supermarket in California. More broadly, postmodernism casts the world as an all-powerful but mysterious system, a set of organizations and social relations one can never quite grasp. For Hoberek, the aesthetic of "cognitive mapping" orienting the "affective maps" I have returned to throughout *Poetics of Emergence* disguises a truth about class revealed to us at the end of the twentieth century, when the precarity of the middle class became increasingly visible. Over the course of the century, the U.S. middle class gave up on owning property and had gone to work instead for corporations or for some other increasingly corporatized entity, trading small businesses, stores, and farms for jobs at IBM, General Motors, or Apple, or at one or another university, art museum, or national laboratory. As the century ended, it discovered that when the economy slows, the mental labor it was hired to provide is just as expendable as the manual labor traditionally associated with the working class. All the many adventures it had set out on—on the road or just in its bohemian wanderings across the city—were sponsored by a postwar economic prosperity that seemed eternal but was not.

To make matters worse, poets of the postwar middle class might be said to have been complicit in their own decline, offering forms of imaginative compensation to distract readers from the situation at hand. John Ashbery, in Chris Nealon's illuminating reading of his poetry of the 1970s, continually registers but then "wanders away" from the crises that descend on New York as the postwar boom ends in recession.[3] In Jasper Bernes's survey of poetry and labor in the era of deindustrialization, the Ashbery of the 1970s acquiesces to the restructuring of the economy and "cultivat[es] [an] ironic attitude towards the experience of struggle," while Frank O'Hara's poems of the 1950s and 1960s speaks in the language of advertising, in the tones of the service sector, with "the charisma of the salesperson."[4] Baraka gets a pass in both, his lyrics redeemed by an implicit Marxism that becomes more and more explicit over time. And yet critiques of Baraka's writings throughout the 1960s are equally available to us, since they feature so prominently in the assessments he himself offers, over the course of his career, of his own previously articulated positions. The same might be said of di Prima's bohemian aesthetics, or of a political nostalgia in Ginsberg that longs to reanimate the laboring cultures of the past yet also seems willing to accept his own intimate cohort of "angelheaded hipsters" as an equivalent substitute. Can it still be considered subversive, as it clearly felt at the time, to refuse respectable employment and live by your wits, publishing whatever you could and securing whatever funding you could find? Or were Ginsberg, Baraka, and di Prima more like the freelance writers and online magazine editors of their era, crowdsourcing when they could or hustling to secure funding from wealthy investors? The whole bohemian-countercultural house of cards threatens to collapse if we view it only as a brief digression in the story of our own deepening precarity.

And yet to characterize postwar experimental poems as, from our twenty-first-century perspective, less resistant or transformative than they might once have seemed fails to explain why they seemed so in the first place. Nor does it mean we shouldn't continue to read and take pleasure in them, let ourselves grow attached to them, or take them up as lyric resources in the present. For lyric poems speak to us of the present: in the rhythms of their line breaks and individual lines as well as in their forms of address. As Jonathan Culler and others have insisted, they speak words to an addressee we then imagine overhearing as we read, thus offering us—at least those of us who have grown fond of poetry—another mode of engagement with the world. It's a mode of engagement that Baraka, Ginsberg, di Prima, O'Hara, and other New American poets helped to keep alive, if imperfectly, passing it from little magazines and apartments to public readings and anthologies, and from more widely circulated publications like *Poetry* or *The Nation* to public television or *The*

Dick Cavett Show. Part of what it meant to keep the lyric alive after World War II, I have been arguing, was to invent subgenres (the hipster sketch, the "I do this I do that poem," the postindustrial jeremiad, the lyric of black bourgeois dissatisfaction and critique) that might then be revised and reapplied in different circumstances. More broadly, it meant calling our attention to the new emotional atmospheres that emanate from and supplement the discursive and musical patterns of the poem. Indeed, it meant taking seriously the poem's efforts to map the feelings of frustration or historical belonging emerging in the present, to conceive of these feelings as collective rather than simply private, and to give them a form to which others might respond.

A final close reading might demonstrate the strengths of this approach and give readers one last opportunity to see it applied to a poem. O'Hara wrote "Present" in early January of 1960; it was first published in *The Nation* in December 1964 and then included by Donald Allen in *The Collected Poems of Frank O'Hara* (1971). Like so many of the poems I discuss, "Present" is a poem that describes concrete movements through the city, projects a mood or set of affective tensions, and then links this mood to structural pressures it struggles to characterize. Why is it, the poem asks, that we so often feel distant from those to whom we would like to feel connected, and what is it that keeps us apart? What attachments continue to sustain us and to give us hope? These are recurring questions in O'Hara's poetry, related but not identical to his investments in love and friendship. We might think of the mood or affective atmosphere of the poem, as I argued in my introduction, as mediating between the different levels of meaning in the poem: the intimate and the public, the personal and the impersonal, the immediately perceptual and the more distantly political. By turns tender, utopic, and preemptively melancholic, the tone of the poem hovers between and attempts to connect elements of contemporary experience that more often remain separate. "[I]t survives," as W. H. Auden once put it, "[a] way of happening, a mouth."[5]

"Present" is undoubtedly a love poem, part of that famous outpouring of lyrics O'Hara wrote for Vincent Warren between 1959 and 1961, worrying over the lovers' fate as a couple and trying to counter this worry with repeated expressions of romantic enthusiasm and desire.[6] As in other poems, in "Present" O'Hara fuses questions about human connection in general with statements of romantic longing for a specific lover. He conjures for us an overarching perspective, here a cosmic or celestial one, from which the lovers' fate might be made clear and the joining or separation of persons might begin to make sense. This perspective, described in the poem's final line as "some peculiar insight / of the heavens" (*CP*, 353), is never required to reveal why it would choose to unite some lovers and separate others. It exists, rather, as a trope for forces one acknowledges but then folds back into the ongoing, affectively mediated experience of the present.

"The stranded gulch, / below Grand Central," the poem begins, "the gentle purr of cab tires in snow / and hidden stars" (CP, 352). We are pulled into the darkness of an evening commute, one O'Hara would have made on his way home from the Museum of Modern Art to his apartment on East 9th Street, passing by Grand Central Station and through Union Square. He feels gloomy at first, as indicated by the "stranded gulch" in which he finds himself at the outset, "the hidden stars" he senses but can't see, and the "dark thoughts which surround neon" as he rides home. Yet he remains attentive, poetically engaged, poised to catch a glimpse of something that might shift his mood. The shift comes when the speaker sees his lover across Union Square, "head bent to the wind / wet and frowning" on the walk to some destination known to the speaker but never revealed to us. Both lovers are wrapped in melancholy, isolated by their own working lives and obligations, and the poem imagines transforming this loneliness into something different, beginning with the promise that "we'll meet / . . . later and will be warm." Beyond this immediate promise, the speaker wants to reassure himself and his lover—whom he addresses throughout the poem—that "nothing pushes us away / from each other." He imagines leaning "across the square" to greet him, shedding as he does the "dark thoughts" of the gulch and "the quarrels and vices of / estranged companions" (CP, 353) in order to generate a new mood, in which loneliness and workaday conflict will be banished and the lovers held together by fate. He continues to generate feelings of optimism and attachment, one might say, even while acknowledging the lingering doubts and social antagonisms that would seem to warrant pessimism.

Reading the poem's final lines, one wants to ask what it means for someone

> to become a way of feeling
> that is not painful casual or diffuse
> and seems to explore some peculiar insight
> of the heavens for its favorite bodies
> in the mixed-up air
> (CP, 353)

These lines show us how O'Hara's poetry operates by proposing states of feeling it presents, quite self-consciously in this case, as mediating atmospheres. The appearance of the speaker's lover both creates a new emotional atmosphere—defined negatively as "not painful casual or diffuse"—and presses him to ask why the heavens seem to favor some bodies over others, allowing them to navigate the air to be together. Why are some people allowed to be happy, "to

remember life's marvelous" (*CP*, 341), while others are discouraged from do-
ing so? O'Hara returns here to a metaphor established midway through the
poem, comparing persons to "celestial bodies" and claiming for lucky people
the capacity to meet more often than their gravitational rotations would allow,
since "nothing pushes us away / from each other." As the line breaks suggest
throughout the poem, however, pushing us continually from one syntactical
unit—or from one image, metaphor, or perceptual investment—to the next,
"Present" expresses just as powerfully the anxiety that something will indeed
pull O'Hara away from his lover.[7] Perhaps love won't redeem the loneliness of
workaday life, and the fantasies of the good life, as Lauren Berlant suggests,
wear us down even as they sustain us. Perhaps these larger forces will not favor
us after all, and we will drift apart instead and into the "mixed-up air."

The reading I am proposing here is not that "Present" takes an explicit
ideological position, but rather, as I argued in chapter 1, that O'Hara's poems,
particularly in the late 1950s and early 1960s, spin continually away from the
stresses of his professional life at the Museum of Modern Art and scan the
city in search of some enabling vision of affection or solidarity. As they do so,
they rely on mood or tone to mediate for them, cataloging the speaker's likes,
dislikes, and everyday movements and then linking them to a set of larger
structures, allegorized in this case as a set of heavenly or celestial powers.
The poem concludes by proposing a novel "way of feeling" that we might,
following José Esteban Muñoz, describe as an image of the queer future. Here
O'Hara and his male lover become "favorite bodies," and the frustrations of
the white-collar worker—O'Hara was then an assistant curator at the Mu-
seum of Modern Art—are brushed away by his lover's hand.[8] As in Muñoz's
utopian reading of postwar texts, however, this way of feeling remains hypo-
thetical; it can only be negatively defined, and it only leads to further spec-
ulation. It "*seems* to explore some peculiar insight" (my emphasis), O'Hara
concludes, into forces over which we have no control.

In this respect, it seems fair as well to read "Present" in relation to what Mi-
chael Davidson has described as O'Hara's insistent meditations on the Cold
War's politicization of lyric tropes, including the Sputnik-era "idea that heav-
enly bodies were now the province of sublunary political agencies."[9] While
O'Hara builds other poems around one readily identifiable historical event—
Khrushchev's visit to the United States in September 1959 or the landing, that
same month, of an unmanned Soviet spacecraft on the moon—the absence
of such an event in "Present" only serves to underscore the everyday qualities
of historicity that pulse continuously beneath events we later come to think
of as significant. Everyday life in "Present" remains affectively mediated and
made up of the continual filtering of public and personal events—the space

race, the glimpse of a lover, the hope one invests in a romantic relationship, the sense of being constrained by one's working life and social position, the encounter with city lights and traffic on the way home from work—that O'Hara's poems attempt to sort through on the fly. And since the form he takes up with such skill, the improvised free-verse poem in which each line seems poised to veer off suddenly in pursuit of a different thought, echoes and reinforces this impression of ongoing, imaginative movement, O'Hara's poems convey with particular force the idea that the long-term implications of events remain unsettled at the moment we experience them. We feel them, his poems suggest, and then we try to figure them out.

NOTES

Introduction

1. On Donald Allen's *The New American Poetry, 1945–1960* (Berkeley: University of California Press, 1960), see Marjorie Perloff, "Whose New American Poetry? Anthologizing in the Nineties," *Diacritics* 26.3–4 (1996): 104–23, and Alan Golding, "*The New American Poetry* Revisited, Again," *Contemporary Literature* 39.2 (Summer 1998): 180–211.

2. Marjorie Perloff, *21st-Century Modernism: The "New" Poetics* (Malden: Blackwell, 2002), 2–3.

3. In Christopher Nealon's subtle analysis of John Ashbery's poems from the 1970s, the queer poetics attributed to Ashbery in John Shoptaw's *On the Outside Looking Out: John Ashbery's Poetry* (Cambridge: Harvard University Press, 1995) and John Emil Vincent's *John Ashbery and You* (Athens: University of Georgia Press, 2008) get reframed in relation to Ashbery's overriding tendency to conjure the "great events, . . . the looming catastrophes and conflicts" of late capitalism before "turning to face the other way." Ashbery's "posture of minority," Nealon continues, "encodes a wish not to be party to violence, which shades into a wish not to be responsible for it, which shades into a wish not to know about it" (78). See Nealon's *The Matter of Capital: Poetry and Crisis in the American Century* (Cambridge: Harvard University Press, 2011), 73–106.

4. Consider, for example, how the myriad cultural implications packed into a single Frank O'Hara poem in Andrew Ross's "The Death of Lady Day," in *Frank O'Hara: To Be True to a City*, ed. Jim Elledge (Ann Arbor: University of Michigan Press, 1990), 380–91, get overwritten in recent economic readings of O'Hara by Jasper Bernes, *The Work of Art in the Age of Deindustrialization* (Stanford: Stanford University Press, 2017), 37–63, and Michael Clune, *American Literature and the Free Market, 1945–2000* (New York: Cambridge University Press, 2010), 53–76.

5. Serge Guilbaut's *How New York Stole the Idea of Modern Art: Abstract Expressionism, Freedom, and the Cold War*, trans. Arthur Goldhammer (Chicago: University of Chicago Press, 1983), continues to influence critiques of abstract expressionism and affiliated art forms as ideologically complicit in U.S. economic and foreign policy. Guilbaut reads abstract expressionism as a "political apoliticism" in line with the dominant liberal ideologies of the era and responsive to "the cultural needs of the new United States that emerged from World War II" (2–3).

6. Juliana Spahr, *DuBois's Telegram: Literary Resistance and State Containment* (Cambridge: Harvard University Press, 2018), 110–15.

7. My argument here sets poems in relation to the era in which they were produced but also assumes literary texts reach beyond that era to resonate with texts and audiences across time. This is perhaps clearest in my readings of Ginsberg's backward glances in chapter 4; it is also implied by my own investment in poems written five or six decades ago. For important critiques of the narrow periodization of literary texts, see Rita Felski, "'Context Stinks!,'" in *The Limits of Critique* (Chicago: University of Chicago Press, 2015), 151–85, and Eric Hayot, *On Literary Worlds* (New York: Oxford University Press, 2012). See also Bruno Latour, *Reassembling the Social: An Introduction to Actor-Network-Theory* (Oxford: Oxford University Press, 2005).

8. Jonathan Culler, *Theory of the Lyric* (Cambridge: Harvard University Press, 2015), 286–87.

9. Olson's famous "Projective Verse" essay opposes "open" to "closed" verse. It imagines process-oriented, free-verse poems, influenced by Williams and Pound, in which a series of "perceptions" take shape organically, not in any preestablished metrical pattern but according to the rhythms of the poet's breath and ear as he composes the poem: "COMPOSITION BY FIELD, as opposed to inherited line, stanza, over-all form, . . . the 'old' base of the non-projective" (387). See Charles Olson, "Projective Verse," in Allen, *The New American Poetry*, 386–97. On the exaggerated, socially and editorially constructed masculinity of Olson's essay and of the poetic genealogies it helped produce, see Rachel Blau DuPlessis, *Purple Passages: Pound, Eliot, Zukofsky, Olson, Creeley, and the Ends of Patriarchal Poetry* (Iowa City: University of Iowa Press, 2012), 89–168 and especially 138–41.

10. Quoted in Marjorie Perloff, *Frank O'Hara: Poet among Painters* (1977; Chicago: University of Chicago Press, 1998), 141, emphasis in original.

11. Jonathan Flatley, *Like Andy Warhol* (Chicago: University of Chicago Press, 2017), 4.

12. Walter Benjamin, "On Some Motifs in Baudelaire," in *Selected Writings, 4: 1938–1940* Hereafter cited parenthetically in text as *CP*. (Cambridge: Belknap Press, 2006), 313.

13. Benjamin, *SW4*, 343.

14. See Frank O'Hara, *The Collected Poems of Frank O'Hara*, ed. Donald Allen (1971; Berkeley: University of California Press, 1995), 257. Hereafter cited parenthetically in text as *CP*. We call on art to perform another, related, task as well, that of freezing and rendering static and external those things we can "no longer contain." See Brian Glavey's illuminating meditations on movement and stasis in O'Hara, and particularly in "In Memory of My Feelings," in *The Wallflower Avant-Garde: Modernism, Sexuality, and Queer Ekphrasis* (New York: Oxford University Press, 2016), 103–30. Other important readings of the poem include James E. B. Breslin, *From Modern to Contemporary: American Poetry, 1945–1960* (Chicago: University of Chicago Press, 1984), 240–49; Perloff, *Frank O'Hara*, 141–46; and Lytle Shaw, *Frank O'Hara: The Poetics of Coterie* (Iowa City: University of Iowa Press, 2006), 81–114.

15. "I am mainly preoccupied with the world as I experience it," O'Hara begins his statement on poetics for *The New American Poetry*. "What is happening to me, allowing for lies or exaggerations which I try to avoid, goes into my poems." His

subsequent claim, that "I don't think my experiences are clarified or made beautiful for myself or anyone else, they are just there in whatever form I can find them," I read as somewhat misleading, since I think O'Hara's poems convey their own investments in both beauty and in the idea that they might clarify, for himself or for readers, any number of feelings or experiences. As I take it, what he means to resist here, as elsewhere in his short statement, is not clarification per se but rather explicit moralization about beauty or experience (i.e., what precisely we *should* want or feel, or what beauty *should* teach us about beyond our own capacity to experience it). See Allen, *The New American Poetry*, 419–20; see also *CP*, 500.

16. Lauren Berlant, *Cruel Optimism* (Durham: Duke University Press, 2011), 4.

17. Jonathan Flatley, *Affective Mapping: Melancholia and the Politics of Modernism* (Cambridge: Harvard University Press, 2008), 4.

18. Berlant, *Cruel Optimism*, 15.

19. Flatley, *Affective Mapping*, 79, 81.

20. Sianne Ngai, *Ugly Feelings* (Cambridge: Harvard University Press, 2005), 353. See also 1–37.

21. Raymond Williams, *Marxism and Literature* (Oxford: Oxford University Press, 1977), 132, 133.

22. Berlant, *Cruel Optimism*, 5.

23. Williams, *Marxism and Literature*, 132, 134.

24. Ngai, *Ugly Feelings*, 25.

25. Flatley, *Affective Mapping*, 26. Berlant makes a similar point when she argues that "affect theory is another phase in the history of ideology theory," *Cruel Optimism*, 53, as does Ngai, who quotes Lawrence Grossberg's suggestion that "[a]ffect is the missing term in an adequate understanding of ideology," *Ugly Feelings*, 46. See Grossberg, "Mapping Popular Culture," in *We Gotta Get Out of This Place: Popular Conservatism and Postmodern Culture* (New York: Routledge, 1992), 83.

26. One such mediating structure would be that range of "antidepressive melancholias" through which, in Flatley's account, modernist writers transform loss into the capacity to remain interested in a world marked by widespread cruelty. Another would be what Berlant calls "intuition" and describes as "the most acute mediator of the ways affect can take form in a crisis-intensified historical present." See Flatley, *Affective Mapping*, 26, and Berlant, *Cruel Optimism*, 53.

27. Berlant offers the term "cruel optimism" to describe such situations, in which "something you desire is actually an obstacle to your flourishing" (1).

28. C. Wright Mills, *The Sociological Imagination* (New York: Oxford University Press, 1959). See also my description in chapter 2 of Baraka's music criticism as a theory of affect and history.

29. Diane di Prima, *Selected Poems: 1956–1976* (Plainfield: North Atlantic Books, 1977), 197.

30. Amiri Baraka, *Transbluesency: The Selected Poetry of Amiri Baraka/LeRoi Jones (1961–1995)* (New York: Marsilio, 1995), 58.

31. I quote here from Donne's sonnet, which is widely available, and from T. V. F.

Brogan's short entry on the volta in *The New Princeton Encyclopedia of Poetry and Poetics*, ed. Alex Preminger and T. V. F. Brogan (Princeton: Princeton University Press, 1993), 1367.

32. Charles Altieri, "Surrealism as a Living Modernism: What the New York Poets Learned from Two Generations of New York Painting," *The Cambridge Companion to American Poetry since 1945* (New York: Cambridge University Press, 2013), 47.

33. Altieri, "Surrealism as a Living Modernism," 47, 56. Elsewhere in his work, Altieri elaborates explicitly affective descriptions of these "sites of being" and "strange conjunctions and states." See, for example, *The Particulars of Rapture: An Aesthetics of the Affects* (Ithaca: Cornell University Press, 2003).

34. Culler, *Theory of the Lyric*, 350.

35. Culler, *Theory of the Lyric*, 347. Adalaide Morris, *How to Live/What to Do: H.D.'s Cultural Poetics* (Urbana: University of Illinois Press, 2003), 2.

36. Di Prima, *Selected Poems*, 16.

37. James Schuyler, *Collected Poems* (New York: Farrar, Straus, and Giroux, 1993), 3–4.

38. Perceptive readings of "Freely Espousing" include Maude Emerson, "James Schuyler's 'Freely Espousing,'" *Jacket2* (30 June 2012), http://jacket2.org/article/james-schuylers-freely-espousing; Andrew Epstein, "'Building a nest out of torn up letters': James Schuyler, Trash, and the Poetics of Collage," *Jacket2* (30 June 2012), http://jacket2.org/article/building-nest-out-torn-letters; Timothy Gray, "New Windows on New York: The Figurative Vision of James Schuyler and Jane Freilicher," in *Urban Pastoral: Natural Currents in the New York School* (Iowa City: University of Iowa Press, 2010), 100–20; and David Herd, "Relishing: James Schuyler," in *Enthusiast! Essays on Modern American Literature* (New York: Manchester University Press, 2007), 168–96. See also Epstein's expanded discussion of Schuyler and collage, "'Each Day So Different, Yet Still Alike': James Schuyler and the Elusive Everyday," in *Attention Equals Life: The Pursuit of the Everyday in Contemporary Poetry and Culture* (New York: Oxford University Press, 2016), 70–109.

39. My reading of Schuyler's circuitous performances of sexuality, at once open and disguised, is echoed in other criticism on New York School poets, including Glavey's chapters on Ashbery and O'Hara in *The Wallflower Avant-Garde*, 103–65; Terrell Scott Herring, "Frank O'Hara's Open Closet," *PMLA* 117.3 (2002): 414–27; and Shoptaw's *On the Outside Looking Out*.

40. T. S. Eliot, "Ulysses, Order, and Myth," in *Selected Prose of T. S. Eliot*, ed. Frank Kermode (New York: Harcourt Brace, 1975), 177. On history in Pound and Eliot, see James Longenbach, *Modernist Poetics of History: Pound, Eliot, and the Sense of the Past* (Princeton: Princeton University Press, 1987).

41. O'Hara, Baraka, and di Prima all engaged politics and recent historical events explicitly in their poems yet did so in ways that feel preliminary and improvised, as if they were inching toward overarching political approaches or ideology they had yet to confirm. Ashbery famously described O'Hara as "too hip for the squares and

too square for the hips" and his poetry as one with "no program" that "therefore cannot be joined" (see John Ashbery, "Writers and Issues: Frank O'Hara's Question," *Selected Prose*, ed. Eugene Richie [Ann Arbor: University of Michigan Press, 2004], 81). This hardly stopped O'Hara, however, from meditating on his own revolutionary belatedness or seeding his poems with sudden bursts of collectivity. The 1960s, as I underscore in chapters 2 and 3, was a period of transition for both Baraka and di Prima, during which their poems began by articulating bohemian-aesthetic critiques of U.S. culture and politics but then angled toward increasingly revolutionary positions: Baraka's black nationalism and incipient Marxism; di Prima's radical, countercultural anarchism.

42. Paul Jaussen's *Writing in Real Time: Emergent Poetics from Whitman to the Digital* (Cambridge: Cambridge University Press, 2017) draws systems theory to offer an account of poetic emergence that differs from but resonates with my own.

43. Walter Benjamin, *Illuminations*, ed. Hannah Arendt, trans. Harry Zohn (New York: Schocken Books, 1968), 158.

44. Benjamin, *Illuminations*, 163, 165; this final quotation is translated in *SW4* as "the experience of giant cities, . . . the intersecting of their myriad relations" (320). On Baudelaire and experience, see Flatley, *Affective Mapping*, 16–19, 68–70; Martin Jay, *Songs of Experience: Modern American and European Variations on a Universal Theme* (Berkeley: University of California Press, 2005), 312–60; and Miriam Bratu Hansen, "Benjamin and Cinema: Not a One-Way Street," *Critical Inquiry* 25.2 (Winter 1999): 306–43. On Frank O'Hara and the position of the flâneur as reimagined in postwar New York, see Susan Rosenbaum, "O'Hara, Flâneur of New York," in *The Scene of My Selves: New Work on New York School Poets*, ed. Terence Diggory and Stephen Paul Miller (Orono: National Poetry Foundation, 2001), 143–73.

45. Robert A. Caro, *The Power Broker: Robert Moses and the Fall of New York* (1974; New York: Vintage Books, 1975), 12.

46. Amiri Baraka, *The Autobiography of LeRoi Jones* (New York: Freundlich Books, 1984), 124–201; Allen Ginsberg, *Journals: Early Fifties Early Sixties*, edited by Gordon Ball (New York: Grove Press, 1977); Brad Gooch, *City Poet: The Life and Times of Frank O'Hara* (1993; New York: HarperPerennial, 1994), 189–240; Diane di Prima, *Memoirs of a Beatnik* (1969; New York: Penguin Books, 1998) and *Recollections of My Life as a Woman: The New York Years* (New York: Viking, 2001); Hettie Jones, *How I Became Hettie Jones* (New York: Penguin Books, 1990); Barry Miles, *Ginsberg: A Biography* (London: Virgin Publishing, 2000), 133; Marjorie Perloff, "'A Step Away from Them': Poetry 1956," *Poetry On & Off the Page: Essays for Emergent Occasions* (Evanston: Northwestern University Press, 1998), 83–115; Jed Perl, *New Art City: Manhattan at Mid-Century* (2005; New York: Vintage Books, 2007).

47. Andrew Hoberek, *The Twilight of the Middle Class: Post–World War II American Fiction and White-Collar Work* (Princeton: Princeton University Press, 2005), 1–32.

48. Alan Nadel, *Containment Culture: American Narratives, Postmodernism, and the Atomic Age* (Durham: Duke University Press, 1995), 1–9 and elsewhere. See also

Elaine Tyler May, *Homeward Bound: American Families in the Cold War Era* (New York: Basic Books, 1988), and Michael Davidson, *Guys Like Us: Citing Masculinity in Cold War Poetics* (Chicago: University of Chicago Press, 2004).

49. Baraka, *Autobiography*, 170. Di Prima was also charged, though only Baraka testified at the grand jury hearing; see her account in *Recollections*, 269–71, 277.

50. Carl Solomon, "I Was a Communist Youth," in *The Floating Bear: A Newsletter: Numbers 1–37, 1961–1969*, ed. Diane di Prima and LeRoi Jones (La Jolla: Laurence McGilvery, 1973), 129. See my extended discussion of Solomon's essay in chapter 4.

51. William H. Whyte, *The Organization Man* (New York: Simon and Schuster, 1956), 394.

52. Mills, *The Sociological Imagination*, 4.

53. Mills, *The Power Elite* (1956; New York: Oxford University Press, 1980), 3.

54. Mills, *The Sociological Imagination*, 4.

55. Mills, *The Sociological Imagination*, 4.

56. Mills, *The Sociological Imagination*, 100–118.

57. C. Wright Mills, "The Decline of the Left," in *Power, Politics, and People: The Collected Essays of C. Wright Mills* (1963; New York: Oxford University Press, 1972), 225.

58. Mills, "The Decline of the Left," 222, 226.

59. Mills, "The Decline of the Left," 222.

60. Mills, "The Decline of the Left," 221.

61. DeKoven devotes the first chapter of *Utopia Limited: The Sixties and the Emergence of the Postmodern* (Durham: Duke University Press, 2004) to a discussion of Herbert Marcuse's *One-Dimensional Man* (1964). In Fredric Jameson's *A Singular Modernity: Essays on the Ontology of the Present* (New York: Verso, 2002), Greenberg becomes "that theoretician who more than any other can be credited as having invented the ideology of modernism full-blown" during the Cold War (169). Arendt's philosophical arguments shape Richard H. King's influential presentations of the civil rights movement as an active, participatory struggle; see his *Civil Rights and the Idea of Freedom* (New York: Oxford University Press, 1992).

62. Fredric Jameson, *Postmodernism, or, The Cultural Logic of Late Capitalism* (Durham: Duke University Press, 1991), 1–54.

63. Hoberek, *The Twilight of the Middle Class*, 113–30. "[T]he middle class lost its historical agency," Hoberek argues, "when, at mid-century, its members become white-collar workers" (129). "[T]he discovery of this state," however, "is a belated one"; it becomes clearer in the final decades of twentieth century, an era of downsizing that forces the middle class to begin grappling with its own increasing precarity (129). "Jameson's account of postmodernism," Hoberek suggests, "is . . . problematically totalizing insofar as it projects on the world at large the experience of the postwar middle class in transition" (117). It manages to elide "the crucial dimension of class" and in particular "the transformation of the American middle class into proletarianized white-collar workers" (117). With the benefit of hindsight, "we can now re-

turn and read postmodernism dialectically, as the worldview not only of middle-class privilege but of the hollowness of this privilege" (129).

64. Hannah Arendt, *The Origins of Totalitarianism* (1951; New York: Harcourt Brace, 1966), xxix.

65. Perl, *New Art City*.

66. Shoptaw, *On the Outside Looking Out*, 4. Jonathan D. Katz, quoted in Glavey, *The Wallflower Avant-Garde*, 106.

67. This quote from Ashbery appears in Richard Kostelanetz's 1976 *New York Times Magazine* profile of the poet; see Kostelanetz, "How to Be a Difficult Poet," *New York Times Magazine* 23 May 1976: 20. It appears as well in Gooch, *City Poet*, 190.

68. John Ashbery, "The Invisible Avant-Garde," in *Reported Sightings: Art Chronicles 1957–1987* (New York: Knopf, 1989), 390.

69. Baraka, *Autobiography*, 128. Historian Howard Brick offers a similar account of the shifts in mood falling across the postwar period: "Heady hopes for a 'new world' had flared briefly at the end of the war, just before a conservative mood settled in like a long postwar hangover; when its pall lifted, after the mid-1950s, the world again seemed fresh with possibility." See Brick's *Age of Contradiction: American Thought and Culture in the 1960s* (1998; Ithaca: Cornell University Press, 2000), xii.

Chapter 1

1. Frank O'Hara, *The Collected Poems of Frank O'Hara*, ed. Donald Allen (1971; Berkeley: University of California Press, 1995), 338. Hereafter cited parenthetically in text as *CP*.

2. References to everyday life and objects are nearly ubiquitous in O'Hara criticism. Representative examples include Marjorie Perloff's initial characterization, in her influential *Frank O'Hara: Poet among Painters* (1977; Chicago: University of Chicago Press, 1998), of O'Hara's *Lunch Poems* (San Francisco: City Lights Books, 1964), as "confound[ing]" the postwar literary public "with their recreation of everyday experience" (12), and the discussion of O'Hara that opens Andrew Epstein's *Attention Equals Life: The Pursuit of the Everyday in Contemporary Poetry and Culture* (New York: Oxford University Press, 2016), 1–3. Readings of the micropolitical in O'Hara begin with Andrew Ross, "The Death of Lady Day," in *Frank O'Hara: To Be True to a City*, ed. Jim Elledge (Ann Arbor: University of Michigan Press, 1990), 380–91.

3. Lauren Berlant, *Cruel Optimism* (Durham: Duke University Press, 2011), 4.

4. Fredric Jameson, *Postmodernism, or, The Cultural Logic of Late Capitalism* (Durham: Duke University Press, 1991), 51.

5. Kevin Lynch, *The Image of the City* (1960; Cambridge: MIT Press, 1992), 2–5.

6. Jameson, *Postmodernism*, 54.

7. Along with the relevant passages in *Postmodernism*, particularly in the opening chapter (44–45, 51–54) and conclusion (409–18), see also Jameson's essay "Cogni-

118 NOTES TO PAGES 24-29

tive Mapping" in *The Jameson Reader*, ed. Michael Hardt and Kathi Weeks (Oxford: Blackwell, 2000), 277–87.

8. Jonathan Flatley, *Affective Mapping: Melancholia and the Politics of Modernism* (Cambridge: Harvard University Press, 2008), 76–84.

9. Flatley, *Affective Mapping*, 79.

10. Flatley, *Affective Mapping*, 79.

11. Christopher Nealon, *Foundlings: Lesbian and Gay Historical Emotion before Stonewall* (Durham: Duke University Press, 2001), 8, 8–19.

12. As Gordon McVay recounts, Esenin made no secret of his distaste for America, which in one letter he called "the most frightening trash," and whose artistic culture he felt had been "cramped" by the "power of ferro-concrete," though such dismissals hardly kept him from expressing a competing fascination with the speed and scale of American industrialization. See McVay, *Esenin: A Life* (Ann Arbor: Ardis, 1976), 203–04 and elsewhere. O'Hara wrote other poems in tribute to or in dialogue with Russian poets, including "Mayakovsky," "Fantasia (on Russian Verses) for Alfred Leslie," "A True Account of Talking to the Sun at Fire Island," "Two Russian Exiles: An Ode," "Political Poem on a Last Line of Pasternak's," and "Answer to Voznesensky & Evtushenko," not to mention a whole series of birthday poems for Sergei Rachmaninoff, his favorite composer and longtime Russian exile in the United States. For an invaluable discussion of O'Hara's long-standing interest in Russian literature, see Lytle Shaw, "Combative Names: Mayakovsky and Pasternak in the American 1950s," in *Frank O'Hara: The Poetics of Coterie* (Iowa City: University of Iowa Press, 2006), 115–50.

13. Susan Sontag, "Notes on Camp," in *Against Interpretation and Other Essays* (1966; New York: Picador, 2001), 275–92, and Andrew Ross, "Uses of Camp," in *No Respect: Intellectuals and Popular Culture* (New York: Routledge, 1989), 135–70.

14. Charles Bernstein, "Stray Straws and Straw Men," in *Content's Dream: Essays 1975–1984* (1986; Evanston: Northwestern University Press, 2001), 45–46.

15. O'Hara "commence[s] / to write one of [his] 'I do this I do that' / poems" in "Getting Up Ahead of Someone (Sun)" (*CP*, 341), thus coining the term. Among the other persona poems O'Hara wrote around the time he composed "Memoir of Sergei O. . . ." is "Mary Desti's Ass," another poem in the voice of an Isadora Duncan travel companion.

16. Perloff, *Frank O'Hara*, 22–23; Charles Altieri, "Surrealism as a Living Modernism: What the New York Poets Learned from Two Generations of New York Painting," in *The Cambridge Companion to American Poetry since 1945* (New York: Cambridge University Press, 2013), 47.

17. Useful summaries of economic and employment trends in the United States following World War II can be found in Jasper Bernes, *The Work of Art in the Age of Deindustrialization* (Stanford: Stanford University Press, 2017), 3–8, 64–66, and elsewhere; and Andrew Hoberek, *The Twilight of the Middle Class: Post–World War II American Fiction and White-Collar Work* (Princeton: Princeton University Press, 2005), 1–32.

18. James Schuyler, "Frank O'Hara: Poet among Painters (excerpts)," in *Homage to Frank O'Hara*, ed. Bill Berkson and Joe LeSueur (Bolinas: Big Sky, 1988), 83. Accounts of O'Hara's hiring by Porter McCray in the International Program refer to his published art reviews and, especially, to his close connection with New York painters as a primary qualification for the job. McCray hired O'Hara as a special assistant and then as an administrative assistant in 1955; he was promoted to assistant curator in 1960 and then to associate curator in 1965. See Waldo Rasmussen's "Frank O'Hara in the Museum," in Berkson and LeSueur, *Homage to Frank O'Hara*, 84–90, and Renée S. Neu, "With Frank at MoMA," in Berkson and LeSueur, *Homage to Frank O'Hara*, 91–92, as well as Donald Allen's "Short Chronology" in *The Collected Poems of Frank O'Hara*, which lists his promotions, a number of his art reviews and interviews with artists, the catalogs he worked on, the exhibitions he helped organize, and the trips he took for MoMA abroad (*CP*, xiii–xvi).

19. John Ashbery, "Introduction," *CP*, vii–xi.

20. Bernes, "Lyric and the Service Sector: Frank O'Hara at Work," in *The Work of Art*, 37–63.

21. Bernes, *The Work of Art*, 25. See Bernes's full chapter, "Lyric and the Service Sector: Frank O'Hara at Work," 37–63, as well as Michael Clune's chapter "Frank O'Hara and Free Choice" in *American Literature and the Free Market, 1945–2000* (New York: Cambridge University Press, 2010), 53–76.

22. Bernes, *The Work of Art*, 57, 60–61.

23. "O'Hara had other plans for his adaptations of lyric techniques to the service environment," Bernes writes. "He wanted to show how the lyric modalities that were presumed to require exit (or at least critical distance) from the mercenary exchanges and exacting labors of the workaday world could instead take place among and through them, allowing for meaningful human interaction, erotic or otherwise." And yet, Bernes concludes, "[t]the fact that the poem can only be overheard, . . . means it can also very easily be *misheard*" (Bernes, *The Work of Art*, 56, emphasis in original).

24. This not to say that communism didn't remain a live possibility for poets in the 1950s and early 1960s, as I argue in chapter 4, as James Smethurst has argued about black experimental poets of the 1960s, and as scholars such as Kevin Killian have argued about San Francisco Renaissance poet Jack Spicer. Such studies only further emphasize, however, how underground, vulnerable, and organizationally unstable communist and socialist groups were in the 1950s and early 1960s, and how impossibly risky it seemed at that moment to be openly anticapitalist—or, in the case of Spicer or O'Hara, openly queer. See Kevin Killian, "Spicer and the Mattachine," in *After Spicer: Critical Essays* (Middletown: Wesleyan University Press, 2011), 16–35, and James Smethurst, *The Black Arts Movement: Literary Nationalism in the 1960s and 1970s* (Chapel Hill: University of North Carolina Press, 2005).

25. Michael Clune, *American Literature and the Free Market, 1945–2000* (New York: Cambridge University Press, 2010), 76. Clune's "Frank O'Hara and Free Choice" (53–76) offers a competing economic reading of O'Hara's poetry and poetics. Oren Izenberg's "The Justice of My Feelings for Frank O'Hara" joins Clune in investigat-

ing categories of choice, particularity, and the personal in O'Hara, though Izenberg separates these categories from economic and historical contexts in order to consider O'Hara's investments in personhood itself and the act of valuing as such. See Izenberg, *Being Numerous: Poetry and the Ground of Social Life* (Princeton: Princeton University Press, 2011), 107–37.

26. Important queer theoretical readings of O'Hara include Chad Bennett, "'The Dish That's Art': Frank O'Hara's Self-Gossip," in *Word of Mouth: Gossip and American Poetry* (Baltimore: Johns Hopkins University Press, 2018), 126–67; Brian Glavey, "Frank O'Hara Nude with Boots," in *The Wallflower Avant-Garde: Modernism, Sexuality, and Queer Ekphrasis* (New York: Oxford University Press, 2016), 103–30; Terrell Scott Herring, "Frank O'Hara's Open Closet," *PMLA* 117.3 (2002): 414–27; José Esteban Muñoz, *Cruising Utopia: The Then and There of Queer Futurity* (New York: New York University Press, 2009), 5–7; Maggie Nelson, *Women, the New York School, and Other True Abstractions* (Iowa City: University of Iowa Press, 2007); and Shaw, *Frank O'Hara*.

27. Bennett, *Word of Mouth*, 162; Muñoz, *Cruising Utopia*, 6.

28. Perloff, *Frank O'Hara*, 120–25.

29. I take this to be an image of Augustus Saint-Gaudens's statue in Grand Army Plaza, representing the angel of peace leading General Sherman, who sits dignified on horseback.

30. For a fuller reading of "Poem (Lana Turner has collapsed!)," see Benjamin Lee, "Spontaneity and Improvisation in Postwar Experimental Poetry," in *The Routledge Companion to Experimental Literature*, ed. Joe Bray, Alison Gibbons, and Brian McHale (New York: Routledge, 2012), 75–88.

31. "Close to the fear of war and the stars which have disappeared" in line 5 calls to mind Ashbery's description of the period just before O'Hara wrote "Music," quoted in slightly different form in my introduction. "I couldn't write anything from about the summer of 1950 to the end of 1951," Ashbery remembers. "It was a terrible depressing period both in the world and in my life. . . . The Korean War was on and I was afraid I might be drafted. There were anti-homosexual campaigns. I was called up for the draft and I pleaded that as a reason not to be drafted. Of course this was recorded and I was afraid we'd all be sent to concentration camps if McCarthy had his own way. It was a very dangerous and scary period." Ashbery's comments, like Sedgwick's, describe homophobia as a disruption of poetic and imaginative capacities. As suggested by "Music," one form depression takes is the inability to form and express attachments to the world around us. His comments appear in Brad Gooch, *City Poet: The Life and Times of Frank O'Hara* (1993; New York: HarperPerennial, 1994), 190. See also Mark Goble's meditations on this line from "Music," and on "the omnipresence of war" in Goble, "'Our Country's Black and White Past': Film and the Figures of History in O'Hara," *American Literature* 71.1 (March 1999): 75–78.

32. Eve Kosofsky Sedgwick, "Queer and Now," *Wild Orchids and Trotsky*, ed. Mark Edmundson (New York: Penguin, 1993), 244.

33. O'Hara adopts a slightly different tone when writing about Christmas several

years later, in "Essay on Style": "where do you think I've / got to? the spectacle of a grown man / decorating / a Christmas tree disgusts me that's / where" (*CP*, 394).

34. See Eve Kosofsky Sedgwick, "Paranoid and Reparative Reading, or, You're So Paranoid, You Probably Think This Essay Is About You," in *Touching Feeling: Affect, Pedagogy, Performativity* (Durham: Duke University Press, 2003), 123–51.

35. Sedgwick, "Paranoid and Reparative Reading," 150.

36. Sedgwick, "Paranoid and Reparative Reading," 150.

37. See the notes on "Rhapsody" in *CP* (543).

38. C. Wright Mills, *White Collar: The American Middle Classes* (New York: Oxford University Press, 1951). See also Herbert Marcuse, *One-Dimensional Man: Studies in the Ideology of Advanced Industrial Society* (1964; Boston: Beacon Press, 1991).

39. Gooch discusses O'Hara's penchant for cruising black working men in *City Poet*, 195–96. Critical discussions of O'Hara's representations of race in his poems are by now fairly extensive. See, for example, Ross, "The Death of Lady Day," 385–87; Aldon Lynn Nielsen, *Reading Race: White American Poets and the Racial Discourse in the Twentieth Century* (Athens: University of Georgia Press, 1988), 155–57; Yusef Komanyakaa's "Troubling the Water" and the accompanying notes in *The Best American Poetry, 1995*, ed. Richard Howard (New York: Simon and Schuster, 1995); David Lehman, *The Last Avant-Garde: The Making of the New York School of Poets* (New York: Doubleday, 1998), 195–201; Hazel Smith, *Hyperscapes in the Poetry of Frank O'Hara: Difference/Homosexuality/Topography* (Liverpool: Liverpool University Press, 2000), 35–36; Benjamin Friedlander, "Strange Fruit: O'Hara, Race and the Color of Time," in *The Scenes of My Selves: New Work on New York School Poets*, ed. Terence Diggory and Stephen Paul Miller (Orono: National Poetry Foundation, 2001), 123–41; Goble, "'Our Country's Black and White Past,'" 57–92; and Fred Moten, *In the Break: The Aesthetics of the Black Radical Tradition* (Minneapolis: University of Minnesota Press, 2003), 149–69.

40. Friedlander's reading of the poem's opening lines, in which "the rope of [Billie Holiday's] 'Strange Fruit'" becomes "the elevator cable," is worth considering here. See Friedlander, "Strange Fruit," 139.

41. The poem's title is also a reference to a 1954 film starring Elizabeth Taylor and set in a Swiss music conservatory; see Joe LeSueur, *Digressions on Some Poems by Frank O'Hara* (New York: Farrar, Straus and Giroux, 2003), 205–06.

42. Michael Davidson, *Guys Like Us: Citing Masculinity in Cold War Poetics* (Chicago: University of Chicago Press, 2004), 70. Davidson's full reading of O'Hara's Cold War lyricism (65–70) is illuminating. For a sampling of American criticisms of the Chinese government's handling of Tibet, see "Trouble in Tibet," *New York Times* 22 Mar. 1959.

43. I quote from two articles here: "God-King of Tibet," *New York Times* 4 Apr. 1959; and "Tibet—ABC of a Remote Land," *New York Times* 29 Mar. 1959. These two articles give readers background on a political situation—the Tibetan uprising, China's crackdown, the Dalai Lama's flight from Tibet and exile in India—that the newspaper covered closely that spring and summer.

44. See Perloff, *Frank O'Hara*, for instance, 179–82.

45. Accounts of the poem's composition and of the everyday biographical details it plays with are featured in Gooch, *City Poet*, 327–28; Lehman, *The Last Avant-Garde*, 197–202; LeSueur, *Digressions*, 191–96.

46. "The problem of historical reference in O'Hara's poetry," Goble suggests in his perceptive essay on O'Hara and film, "is that reference itself is never taken for granted," but is rather "always mediated, refracted through other registers of signification and other means of representation"; see Goble, "'Our Country's Black and White Past,'" 77. There is little doubt that O'Hara, as sentimental as he can sometimes seem, thinks carefully about how historical events are framed for us by, for example, newspapers, photographs, and films. Indeed, "The Day Lady Died" is a tour de force of such careful thinking in the form of a poem. Fundamentally, it reflects on the moment history is announced to us as having happened, the form that announcement takes, the response it solicits from us.

47. Clune, *American Literature and the Free Market*, 4–5.

Chapter 2

1. See the essays collected in White's *The Content of the Form: Narrative Discourse and Historical Representation* (Baltimore: Johns Hopkins University Press, 1987), particularly "The Value of Narrativity in the Representation of Reality" (1–25) and "Getting Out of History: Jameson's Redemption of Narrative" (142–68).

2. Fred Moten, *In the Break: the Aesthetics of the Black Radical Tradition* (Minneapolis: University of Minnesota Press, 2003), 85.

3. Baraka's own account of his trajectory can be found in, among other places, his *Autobiography of LeRoi Jones* (New York: Freundlich Books, 1984) and his "Preface to the Reader" and William J. Harris's introduction, chronology, and editorial notes to the selections in *The LeRoi Jones/Amiri Baraka Reader* (New York: Thunder's Mouth Press, 1991), xi–xiv, xvii–xxxiii, and following.

4. Critics who have helped shape my understanding of the tense, sometimes contradictory nature of Baraka's thought include Moten; Nathaniel Mackey, *Discrepant Engagement: Dissonance, Cross-Culturality, and Experimental Writing* (New York: Cambridge University Press, 1993), 22–48; Aldon Lynn Nielsen, *Black Chant: Languages of African-American Postmodernism* (New York: Cambridge University Press, 1997) and *Integral Music: Languages of African American Innovation* (Tuscaloosa: University of Alabama Press, 2004), 98–147; Andrew Epstein, *Beautiful Enemies: Friendship and Postwar American Poetry* (New York: Oxford University Press, 2006), 166–232; and Lorenzo Thomas, *Extraordinary Measures: Afrocentric Modernism and Twentieth-Century American Poetry* (Tuscaloosa: University of Alabama Press, 2000), 145–61.

5. Reading at the Asilomar Negro Writers Conference in Pacific Grove, California, in 1964, Baraka described the two different kinds of poems included in *The Dead Lecturer* (1964), his second published collection. You can find his reading on

PennSound's Baraka page (http://writing.upenn.edu/pennsound/x/Baraka.php); the quote appears in his introduction to the reading.

6. Amiri Baraka (LeRoi Jones), *Black Music* (1968; New York: Da Capo Press, 1998), 210. Hereafter cited parenthetically as *BM*.

7. This vision, articulated most forcefully in the final essay in *Black Music*, "The Changing Same (R&B and New Black Music)," captures succinctly what Werner Sollors once described as Baraka's "quest for a populist modernism," though in his essay Baraka represents this quest not in primarily literary terms but rather as an attempt, on the part of the musicians he most admires, to combine small-audience experimentalism with the rhythms and lyrical content of popular forms like blues and soul. See Sollors, *Amiri Baraka/LeRoi Jones: The Quest for a "Populist Modernism"* (New York: Columbia University Press, 1978), 2.

8. The idea of the "structure of feeling" first appears in Raymond Williams's *Drama from Ibsen to Brecht* (New York: Oxford University Press, 1968); Williams returns to it in subsequent works, most famously in *Marxism and Literature* (Oxford: Oxford University Press, 1977), 128–35.

9. Baraka's editorial commitments continued throughout his Black Arts and Third-World Marxist periods. I can only gesture here toward the number of projects he had overseen or been involved with after resigning from *The Floating Bear* in 1963 and as music editor of *Kulchur* in 1964. The most well-known is *Black Fire* (1968), the influential Black Arts anthology he edited with Larry Neal. Other projects include the music magazine *The Cricket*, edited by Baraka, Neal, and A. B. Spellman in the late 1960s; *Journal of Black Poetry*, the influential Black Arts journal for which Baraka served as contributing editor in the late 1960s and early 1970s; and various serial publications from the 1970s and 1980s, including *Black NewArk* and *The Black Nation*. For discussions of Baraka as editor, see Aldon Lynn Nielsen, "A New York State of Mind," in *Black Chant*, 78–169, and Christopher Funkhouser, "LeRoi Jones, Larry Neal, and *The Cricket*: Jazz and Poets' Black Fire," *African American Review* 37.2–3 (Summer/Fall 2003): 237–44. To situate Baraka's midcareer editorial projects within the wider field of Black Arts publishing, see James Smethurst, *The Black Arts Movement: Literary Nationalism in the 1960s and 1970s* (Chapel Hill: University of North Carolina Press, 2005).

10. Amiri Baraka, *Transbluesency: The Selected Poetry of Amiri Baraka/LeRoi Jones (1961–1995)* (New York: Marsilio, 1995), 17–21. Hereafter cited in parenthetically in text as *T*.

11. Lytle Shaw, *Frank O'Hara: The Poetics of Coterie* (Iowa City: University of Iowa Press, 2006), 6. See also Andrew Epstein, *Beautiful Enemies*, 86–126.

12. See Marlon Ross's comments on the complicated origins of Baraka's combative style in his essays from the 1960s; Ross, "Camping the Dirty Dozens: The Queer Resources of Black Nationalist Invective," *Callaloo*, 23.1 (2000): 290–312.

13. Fredric Jameson, *Postmodernism, or, The Cultural Logic of Late Capitalism* (Durham: Duke University Press, 1991); Michael Denning, *Culture in the Age of Three Worlds* (New York: Verso, 2004).

14. Denning, *Culture in the Age of Three Worlds*, 1.

15. Allen Ginsberg, *Collected Poems: 1947–1980* (New York: Harper and Row, 1984), 146–47.

16. The message that most concerned Friedan, of course, was that women should seek fulfillment exclusively as wives, mothers, and homemakers. Betty Friedan, *The Feminine Mystique* (1963; New York: Laurel, 1984), 15 and elsewhere; Herbert Marcuse, *One-Dimensional Man: Studies in the Ideology of Advanced Industrial Society* (1964; Boston: Beacon Press, 1991); C. Wright Mills, "The Structure of Power in American Society," in *Power, Politics, and People: The Collected Essays of C. Wright Mills* (1963; New York: Oxford University Press, 1972), 23.

17. Amiri Baraka (LeRoi Jones), "Cuba Libre," in *Home: Social Essays* (New York: William Morrow, 1966), 61.

18. Jameson, *Postmodernism*, 44–45, 51–54, and 409–18. See also Jameson, "Cognitive Mapping," in *The Jameson Reader*, ed. Michael Hardt and Kathi Weeks (Oxford: Blackwell, 2000), 277–87.

19. Baraka (LeRoi Jones), "Milneburg Joys (or, Against 'Hipness' as Such)," *Kulchur* 3 (1961): 41.

20. Mackey, *Discrepant Engagement*, 42.

21. *Kulchur* 5 (1962): 104.

22. Diane di Prima, "Introduction," *The Floating Bear: A Newsletter: Numbers 1–37, 1961–1969* (La Jolla: Laurence McGilvery, 1973), x.

23. Both the letter from Ginsberg to Wenning and the postcard he sent to Baraka from India remain unpublished and are contained in the Allen Ginsberg Papers at the Harry Ransom Center.

24. The quote is from a letter that Crews sent to potential *Suck-Egg Mule* subscribers. Driving home his point, the letter concludes as follows: "We believe the present is a period of crisis in the development of American Poetry. The universities are entrenched but the battle is not completely lost." Undated letter from the Judson Crews papers, Harry Ransom Center.

25. See Golding's *From Outlaw to Classic: Canons in American Poetry* (Madison: University of Wisconsin Press, 1995) and in particular his chapter "Little Magazines and Alternative Canons: The Example of *Origin*," 114–43. See also Steven Clay and Rodney Phillips, *A Secret Location on the Lower East Side: Adventures in Writing, 1960–1980* (New York: The New York Public Library and Granary Books, 1998).

26. Baraka, *Autobiography*, 117–18, 150.

27. Jonathan Flatley, *Affective Mapping: Melancholia and the Politics of Modernism* (Cambridge: Harvard University Press, 2008), 78.

28. Hettie Jones, *How I Became Hettie Jones* (New York: Penguin Books, 1990); Diane di Prima, "Introduction," *The Floating Bear: A Newsletter: Numbers 1–37, 1961–1969* (La Jolla: Laurence McGilvery, 1973), vii–xviii; Gilbert Sorrentino, "*Neon, Kulchur*, Etc.," *The Little Magazine in America: A Modern Documentary History*, ed. Elliot Anderson and Mary Kinzie (Stamford: Pushcart Press, 1978), 298–316.

29. Diane di Prima, "Introduction," xi.

30. Baraka, *Autobiography*, 172.

31. Baraka, *Autobiography*, 172. Sorrentino, *"Neon, Kulchur, Etc.,"* 311.

32. Sorrentino, *"Neon, Kulchur, Etc.,"* 312.

33. Ezra Pound, *Guide to Kulchur* (New York: New Directions, 1938), 24.

34. On Baraka, Spellman, and the New Jazz Criticism, see Scott Saul, *Freedom Is, Freedom Ain't: Jazz and the Making of the Sixties* (Cambridge: Harvard University Press, 2003), 224–33.

35. Denning, *Culture in the Age of Three Worlds*, 150.

36. Baraka, *Home*, 62, emphasis in original.

37. Todd F. Tietchen, *The Cubalogues: Beat Writers in Revolutionary Havana* (Gainesville: University Press of Florida, 2010), 3. Tietchen's "Introduction: The 'Stranger Relations' of Beat" (1–21) is helpful for my argument, as are his subsequent readings of visits to Cuba during this period by Ginsberg, Baraka, Schleifer, Ferlinghetti, McLucas, and Robert Williams.

38. Fredric Jameson, "Periodizing the 60s," in *Ideologies of Theory: Essays 1971–1986*, vol. 2, *The Syntax of History* (Minneapolis: University of Minnesota Press, 1988), 182.

39. Baraka (Jones), "Cuba Libre," in *Home*, 43, emphasis in original.

40. Baraka, *Autobiography*, 161, 164. Baraka reproduces this line with some slight differences in "Cuba Libre," where an unidentified "New York poet," "a close friend of mine," is quoted as saying, "I don't trust guys in uniforms" (*Home*, 20).

41. Baraka, *Home*, 42.

42. "Editorial," *Kulchur* 3 (1961): 2.

43. Baraka, *Home*, 61.

44. As if to back up his published positions with active participation, Schleifer disappeared to Cuba soon after *Kulchur*'s third issue was finished, returning to New York a year later to resign from the magazine for good. See Lita Hornick, *"Kulchur: A Memoir,"* in *The Little Magazine in America: A Modern Documentary History*, ed. Elliot Anderson and Mary Kinzie (Stamford: Pushcart Press, 1978), 281–85. See also Tietchen, *The Cubalogues*, 100–01, and Hornick's *The Green Fuse* (New York: Giorno Poetry Systems, 1989), 24–25. Here Hornick, who calls Schleifer "a liar and a creep," suggests that he secured financial support from her by promising "to build *Kulchur* up to the circulation and influence of the prestigious quarterlies," whereas in fact "he only wanted backing for #3, which was to be an inflammatory issue, before disappearing into the Cuban Revolution."

45. Grateful thanks to Aldon Nielsen for helping me identify Stanley as the second poet in this photograph, and to Stanley for his permission to reproduce it.

46. Both Baraka's and Hettie Jones's autobiographies contain brief descriptions of the sign captured in the photo, though not of the photograph or of its appearance in *Kulchur*. Hettie Jones recounts that, as a demonstration of support for Castro's first visit to the United Nations in the fall of 1960, "Roi and a friend hung over the narrow wrought-iron balcony outside our front windows, and painted a sign in two-foot-high black letters." *How I Became Hettie Jones*, 127.

47. While introducing poems from *The Dead Lecturer* at the Asilomar Negro Writ-

ers Conference in August 1964, Baraka describes the combination in this collection between "pure lyrics" and poems that "take some kind of specific social attitude." Listen to just the introduction, or to the full reading, at PennSound's Baraka page (http://writing.upenn.edu/pennsound/x/Baraka.php).

48. Both of these potential readings of "Kenyatta Listening to Mozart" are put forth eloquently in the discussion of the poem on the podcast *PoemTalk*, featuring Al Filreis with Herman Beavers, Alan Loney, and Mecca Sullivan (episode 20, 30 July 2009, http://poemtalkatkwh.blogspot.com/2009/07/baraka.html).

49. Amiri Baraka (LeRoi Jones), *Black Magic: Collected Poetry, 1961–1967*. Indianapolis: Bobbs-Merrill, 1969), 14.

50. Baraka, *Autobiography*, 184.

51. My reading of "Kenyatta Listening to Mozart" echoes Phillip Brian Harper's continually insightful reading of Black Arts poetry in "Nationalism and Social Division in Black Arts Poetry of the 1960s," *Identities*, ed. Kwame Anthony Appiah and Henry Louis Gates Jr. (Chicago: University of Chicago Press, 1995), 220–41. In Harper's reading, the oppositional rhetoric in poems by Baraka, Sonia Sanchez, Nikki Giovanni, and others is "thematized . . . not in terms of the us vs. them dichotomy that we might expect, however, with *us* representing blacks and *them* whites; rather, it is played out along the inherent opposition between *I* and *you*, both these terms deriving their referents from within the collectivity of black subjects" (236).

52. On *Matter*, see Clay and Phillips, *A Secret Location on the Lower East Side*, 132–33.

53. Baraka, *Home*, 117–18. Baraka is quoting from Peter Abrahams, "The Blacks," in *An African Treasury*, ed. Langston Hughes (New York: Crown Publishers, 1960), 50.

54. Baraka, *Home*, 120. Abrahams, "The Blacks," 49.

55. Alongside Mackey's discussions of Baraka's negative affects in "The Changing Same," other recent discussions of affect as a response to both racial inequality and historical location are illuminating here. See Flatley's *Affective Mapping* and Sianne Ngai, *Ugly Feelings* (Cambridge: Harvard University Press, 2005), in particular Flatley's chapter on Du Bois, "'What a Mourning': Propaganda and Loss in W.E.B. Du Bois's *Souls of Black Folk*" (105–45), and Ngai's chapters "Animatedness" (89–125) and "Irritation" (174–208).

Chapter 3

1. Diane di Prima, *Selected Poems: 1956–1976* (Plainfield: North Atlantic Books, 1977), 24. Hereafter quoted parenthetically in text as *SP*.

2. Lee Konstantinou, *Cool Characters: Irony and American Fiction* (Cambridge: Harvard University Press, 2016), 49–102.

3. Maria Damon, "Victors of Catastrophe: Beat Occlusions," in *Beat Culture and the New America: 1950–1965*, ed. Lisa Phillips (New York: Whitney Museum/Flammarion, 1995), 145–46.

4. Susan Sontag, "Notes on Camp," in *Against Interpretation and Other Essays* (1966;

New York: Picador, 2001), 275–92, and Andrew Ross, "Uses of Camp," in *No Respect: Intellectuals and Popular Culture* (New York: Routledge, 1989), 135–70.

5. See Sedgwick's defense of camp and her characterization of its critics in Eve Kosofsky Sedgwick, "Paranoid and Reparative Reading, or, You're So Paranoid, You Probably Think This Essay Is About You," in *Touching Feeling: Affect, Pedagogy, Performativity* (Durham: Duke University Press, 2003), 149–50.

6. Joel Dinerstein, *The Origins of Cool in Postwar America* (Chicago: University of Chicago Press, 2017), 14, 16–19, 22–24, 26–34.

7. Scott Saul, *Freedom Is, Freedom Ain't: Jazz and the Making of the Sixties* (Cambridge: Harvard University Press, 2003), 31, 32–33.

8. Konstantinou, *Cool Characters*, 55–58; Saul, *Freedom Is*, 35–40, 51–54.

9. Konstantinou, *Cool Characters*, 52–55, 99–102, and elsewhere.

10. Cleanth Brooks, *The Well-Wrought Urn: Studies in the Structure of Poetry* (New York: Harcourt, Brace, 1947), 187.

11. Herbert Marcuse, "The Affirmative Character of Culture," in *Negations: Essays in Critical Theory*, trans. Jeremy J. Shapiro (Boston: Beacon Press, 1968), 88–133.

12. Thomas Frank, *The Conquest of Cool: Business Culture, Counterculture, and the Rise of Hip Consumerism* (Chicago: University of Chicago Press, 1997), 8.

13. On the similarity between O'Hara's lyric strategies in this poem and the tactics of advertising, see Jasper Bernes, *The Work of Art in the Age of Deindustrialization* (Stanford: Stanford University Press, 2017), 37–63. On the "relatability" and uncanny popularity of O'Hara's poem, see Brian Glavey, "Having a Coke with You Is Even More Fun Than Ideology Critique," *PMLA* 134.5 (2019): 996–1011.

14. Amiri Baraka (LeRoi Jones), "How You Sound??," originally published in *The New American Poetry, 1945–1960*, ed. Donald Allen (Berkeley: University of California Press, 1960), 424.

15. José Estaban Muñoz's chapter on di Prima's close friend, the dancer Freddie Herko, argues for the utopian potential of downtown New York's experimental subcultures as they overlapped and spurred one another on in the late 1950s and 1960s; it tempts us to imagine some of the different directions in which di Prima scholarship might expand. See Muñoz, "A Jeté Out the Window: Fred Herko's Incandescent Illumination," in *Cruising Utopia: The Then and There of Queer Futurity* (New York: New York University Press, 2009), 147–67.

16. These include debates over the extent and effects of American affluence, racial tensions and aspirations, threats of violence and calls for nonviolence, the continued expansion of consumer culture, and anxieties over new forms of social conformity; see Ross, "Hip, and the Long Front of Color," in *No Respect*, 65–101, and Saul, *Freedom Is*, 29–98. See also Howard Brick's *Age of Contradiction: American Thought and Culture in the 1960s* (1998; Ithaca: Cornell University Press, 2000).

17. As others have noted, di Prima was not included in *The New American Poetry* (1960), though Allen and George Butterick did include her when they revised their anthology in the early 1980s; see Donald Allen and George F. Butterick, eds., *The Postmoderns: The New American Poetry Revised* (New York: Grove Press, 1982).

18. Rifkin, Davidson, and DuPlessis are among the critics who have deconstructed most forcefully the masculinist poetics of the era. See Rifkin's *Career Moves: Olson, Creeley, Zukofsky, Berrigan, and the American Avant-Garde* (Madison: University of Wisconsin Press, 2000); Davidson's *Guys Like Us: Citing Masculinity in Cold War Poetics* (Chicago: University of Chicago Press, 2004) and his chapter "Appropriations: Women and the San Francisco Renaissance," in *The San Francisco Renaissance: Poetics and Community at Mid-century* (New York: Cambridge University Press, 1989), 172–99; and DuPlessis's *Purple Passages: Pound, Eliot, Zukofsky, Olson, Creeley, and the Ends of Patriarchal Poetry* (Iowa City: University of Iowa Press, 2012). Essential scholarship on the insight and originality of postwar experimental writing by women includes Lynn Keller, "'Just one of / the girls:— / normal in the extreme': Experimentalists-To-Be Starting Out in the 1960s," *differences*, 12.2 (2001): 47–69; Maggie Nelson's *Women, the New York School, and Other True Abstractions* (Iowa City: University of Iowa Press, 2007); Daniel Kane's *All Poets Welcome: The Lower East Side Poetry Scene in the 1960s* (Berkeley: University of California Press, 2003); Andrew Epstein's chapter on Bernadette Mayer in *Attention Equals Life: The Pursuit of the Everyday in Contemporary Poetry and Culture* (New York: Oxford University Press, 2016), 156–96; and the essays collected in Terence Diggory and Stephen Paul Miller, eds., *The Scenes of My Selves: New Work on New York School Poets* (Orono: National Poetry Foundation, 2001), among them Keller's "Becoming 'a Compleat Travel Agency': Barbara Guest's Negotiations with the Fifties Feminine Mystique" (215–27). Recent essays on di Prima include Timothy Gray, "The Place Where Your Nature Meets Mine: Diane di Prima in the West," in *Urban Pastoral: Natural Currents in the New York School* (Iowa City: University of Iowa Press, 2010), 151–74, and Anthony Libby, "Diane di Prima: 'Nothing Is Lost; It Shines In Our Eyes,'" in *Girls Who Wore Black: Women Writing the Beat Generation*, ed. Ronna C. Johnson and Nancy M. Grace (New Brunswick: Rutgers University Press, 2002), 45–68. These essays build on significant efforts on the part of scholars like Johnson, Grace, and Maria Damon to expand Beat scholarship beyond a few central figures and to consider Beat poems by women. See, for example, Damon's "Victors of Catastrophe: Beat Occlusions"; the essays collected in Johnson and Grace, *Girls Who Wore Black*, including Johnson's "'And then she went': Beat Departures and Feminine Transgressions in Joyce Johnson's *Come and Join the Dance*" (69–95), Damon's "Revelations of Compassionate Love; or, the Hurts of Women: Janine Pommy Vega's 'Poems to Fernando'" (205–26), and Barrett Watten's "What I See in *How I Became Hettie Jones*" (96–118); and Johnson's "Three Generations of Beat Poetics," in *The Cambridge Companion to American Poetry since 1945*, ed. Jennifer Ashton (New York: Cambridge University Press, 2013), 80–93.

19. Susan Fraiman, *Cool Men and the Second Sex* (New York: Columbia University Press, 2003). For early, influential critiques of the masculinist blind spots of subcultural theory, see the essays collected in Angela McRobbie's *Feminism and Youth Culture* (1991; New York: Routledge, 2000).

20. Raymond Williams, *Marxism and Literature* (Oxford: Oxford University Press, 1977), 132 (hereafter cited in text as *ML*).

21. Frank O'Hara, *The Collected Poems of Frank O'Hara*, ed. Donald Allen (1971; Berkeley: University of California Press, 1995), 228–29.

22. Scott Saul's juxtaposition between the different versions of "cool" exemplified in Kerouac's *On the Road* and Davis's *Birth of the Cool* is illuminating; see *Freedom Is, Freedom Ain't*, 55–60. On the distinction between "hip" and "cool," a distinction I do not adhere to in this essay, see Dinerstein, *The Origins of Cool*, 226–32, 352–53.

23. Di Prima, *Dinners and Nightmares* (1998; San Francisco: Last Gasp, 2003), 93, 66, 68. My citations are from the revised and expanded version of the original *Dinners and Nightmares*, published by Corinth Books in 1961 (hereafter cited in text as *DN*).

24. Charles Baudelaire, "The Painter of Modern Life," *Baudelaire: Selected Writings on Art and Literature*, trans. P. E. Charvet (1972; New York: Penguin, 1992), 422.

25. Baudelaire, "The Painter of Modern Life," 420–21.

26. Norman Mailer, *Advertisements for Myself* (New York: G.P. Putnam's Sons, 1959), 338 (hereafter cited in text as *AM*).

27. Saul nicely summarizes reactions to Mailer's essay by a range of artists and intellectuals, including Baldwin, Ralph Ellison, Albert Murray, and Lorraine Hansberry; *Freedom Is, Freedom Ain't*, 67–72. Dinerstein offers a detailed account of Hansberry's public debate with Mailer over "The White Negro" in *The Origins of Cool*, 424–29. Eric Lott's *Love and Theft: Blackface Minstrelsy and the American Working Class* (New York: Oxford University Press, 1993) helped consolidate our understanding of the deep tradition of racial fascination behind twentieth-century performances by "white negroes" from Mailer to Mick Jagger.

28. Ross, "Hip, and the Long Front of Color," in *No Respect*, 67.

29. Walter Benjamin, *Reflections*, ed. Peter Demetz (New York: Schocken, 1978), 178, 179.

30. Di Prima, *Memoirs of a Beatnik* (1969; New York: Penguin Books, 1998), 175; a similar impression is captured in di Prima's *Recollections of My Life as a Woman*, where she again recalls the sudden appearance of Ginsberg's "Howl" and her sense that it heralded the coming of a larger and much more public movement. See *Recollections of My Life as a Woman: The New York Years* (New York: Viking, 2001), 163–64.

31. Di Prima, *Memoirs of a Beatnik*, 175.

32. "A Couple of Weekends" is dated 1961 but was first published in the expanded 1998 edition of *Dinners and Nightmares*.

33. These include but are not limited to murder, incest, interracial conflict and desire embodied in the narrator's romantic rivalry and bloody fight with Harlem jazz singer Shago Martin, and the narrator's demonstration of courage in a death-defying walk around a parapet high above Park Avenue. Norman Mailer, *An American Dream* (New York: Henry Holt and Company, 1964).

34. Called "Johnnie" in "A Couple of Weekends," the same character is referred to in *Memoirs of a Beatnik* as "a public relations man named Ray Clarke" (154); the three jazz musicians from the jam session also appear in *Memoirs of a Beatnik*, 159–61.

35. Merriam-Webster dictionaries date the shortening of "intercommunication sys-

tem" to "intercom" at 1940. *Merriam-Webster's Collegiate Dictionary*, 11th ed. (Springfield: Merriam-Webster, 2003), 652.

36. Dick Hebdige, *Subculture: The Meaning of Style* (1979; New York: Routledge, 2001), 53.

37. On di Prima's Western movement and the poetry it produced, see Gray, "The Place Where Your Nature Meets Mine," in *Urban Pastoral*, 151–74.

38. In an interview with David Melzer, di Prima describes the time just after her arrival in San Francisco: "Our new VW van was used by the Diggers for food pickup and delivery. Our house did two vegetable runs and a fish run every week, and delivered to twenty or twenty-five communes. That was our gig. I wrote lots of *Revolutionary Letters*, and they were going out through Liberation News Service to all the underground newspapers in the country. It was nice because I always had the feeling that I could believe this stuff but there was no way I could ever actually *do* anything, because it was McCarthy time and the FBI was chasing some of my friends. . . . Everything was like that in the '50s. Suddenly to be able to be out in public and do anything, delivering food, having be-ins—it just took a weight off your heart about having kept your mouth shut too long." Diane di Prima, interview with David Melzer, *San Francisco Beat: Talking with the Poets*, ed. David Melzer (San Francisco: City Lights, 2001), 19–20.

Chapter 4

1. For representative literary-historical accounts of Ginsberg's influence, see James E. B. Breslin, *From Modern to Contemporary: American Poetry, 1945–1960* (Chicago: University of Chicago Press, 1984), 53–109; Marjorie Perloff, "A Lion in Our Living Room: Reading Allen Ginsberg in the Eighties," in *Poetic License: Essays on Modernist and Postmodernist Lyric* (Evanston: Northwestern University Press, 1990), 199–230; and David Perkins, *A History of Modern Poetry: Modernism and After* (Cambridge: Harvard University Press, 1987), 331–53, 528–52. For representative descriptions of the Beat movement as precursor to the new social movements of the 1960s, see Stanley Aronowitz, "When the New Left Was New," in *The 60s Without Apology*, ed. Sohnya Sayres, Anders Stephanson, Stanley Aronowitz, and Fredric Jameson (Minneapolis: University of Minnesota Press, 1984), 11–43, and Todd Gitlin, *The Sixties: Years of Hope, Days of Rage* (New York: Bantam, 1987), 45–54.

2. In refocusing our attention on Ginsberg's attachments to the prewar left, I hope to contribute to a larger effort, begun by critics like Cary Nelson and Michael Denning, to help us overcome the "deep cultural amnesia" that has worked to erase from our collective memory the names and details of a U.S. radical past; see Denning, *The Cultural Front: The Laboring of American Culture in the Twentieth Century* (New York: Verso, 1996), 425. See also Nelson, *Repression and Recovery: Modern American Poetry and the Politics of Cultural Memory, 1910–1945* (Madison: University of Wisconsin Press, 1989) and *Revolutionary Memory: Recovering the Poetry of the American Left* (New York: Routledge, 2001). For a detailed and compelling assessment of Old

Left influences on Ginsberg, the New American Poetry, Black Arts, and other black experimental writers of the 1960s and 1970s, see James Smethurst, *The Black Arts Movement: Literary Nationalism in the 1960s and 1970s* (Chapel Hill: University of North Carolina Press, 2005), 23–56 and elsewhere.

3. For one of many instructive readings of the "new rules of *consent*" written and maintained with the active participation of U.S. intellectuals during the postwar moment, see Andrew Ross, "Containing Culture in the Cold War," in *No Respect: Intellectuals and Popular Culture* (New York: Routledge, 1989), 42–64, emphasis in original (42). Ross writes, "If the restorative properties of the new liberal pluralism were to take hold, terms like 'class' and 'mass,' so redolent of that vestigial marxist culture, would have to be quarantined, if not entirely lobotomized from the national mind" (43). It is precisely the influence of this "vestigial marxist culture" that I trace in Ginsberg's poems from the 1950s, which represent Marxist and socialist cultures as actively "quarantined" and even literally "lobotomized"—in the case of Naomi Ginsberg—yet still a source of aesthetic and political agency.

4. For accounts of these and other events in relation to Ginsberg's life and art, see Michael Schumacher, *Dharma Lion: A Critical Biography of Allen Ginsberg* (New York: St. Martin's, 1992).

5. Three essays inspired me to begin thinking about generational rhetorics and the intersecting, synchronic, diachronic, and spatial complexity of social identity: Elizabeth Freeman, "Packing History, Count(er)ing Generations," *New Literary History* 31.4 (2000): 727–44; Marlon Ross, "Camping the Dirty Dozens: The Queer Resources of Black Nationalist Invective," *Callaloo* 23.1 (2000): 290–312; and Robyn Wiegman, "Feminism's Apocalyptic Futures," *New Literary History* 31.4 (2000): 805–25. Though I have a slightly different interpretation of melancholy in general and Benjaminian melancholy in particular, my understanding of Benjamin's writings as an alternative and nonprogressive mode of historical narration has benefited enormously from Wendy Brown's *Politics Out of History* (Princeton: Princeton University Press, 2001). Heather Love's *Feeling Backward: Loss and the Politics of Queer History* (Cambridge: Harvard University Press, 2007) offers a melancholic, Benjaminian reading of queer history that also asks us to revisit common assumptions about linear, generational progress in art and politics.

6. Walter Benjamin, *Illuminations*, ed. Hannah Arendt, trans. Harry Zohn (New York: Schocken Books, 1968), 257–58. For a compelling theory of melancholy as both a mode of historical engagement and an affect that might ground social transformation, see Jonathan Flatley, "Moscow and Melancholia," *Social Text* 19.1 (2001): 75–102.

7. Allen Ginsberg, *Collected Poems 1947–1980* (New York: Harper and Row, 1984), 148 (hereafter cited in text as *CP*).

8. Schumacher, *Dharma Lion*, 9. See Schumacher, *Dharma Lion*, 1–12, for further information about Naomi and Louis's political backgrounds and commitments.

9. Schumacher, *Dharma Lion*, 7.

10. Schumacher, *Dharma Lion*, 23, 115, 120, 129, 279–80.

11. Carl Solomon, "I Was a Communist Youth," in *The Floating Bear: A Newsletter:*

Numbers 1–37, 1961–1969, ed. Diane di Prima and LeRoi Jones (La Jolla: Laurence McGilvery, 1973), 129.

12. See, for instance, Joyce Johnson's *Minor Characters* (Boston: Houghton Mifflin, 1983), 26–34. See also descriptions of Dolly Weinberg, Amiri Baraka's first girlfriend in the Village, in *The Autobiography of LeRoi Jones* (New York: Freundlich Books, 1984), 141–44, and in Hettie Jones's *How I Became Hettie Jones* (New York: Penguin Books, 1990), 29.

13. C. Wright Mills, *White Collar: The American Middle Classes* (New York: Oxford University Press, 1951), xv–xx.

14. Herbert Marcuse, *One-Dimensional Man: Studies in the Ideology of Advanced Industrial Society* (1964; Boston: Beacon Press, 1991), xlii, xliv.

15. Denning, *The Cultural Front*, 462.

16. See Benjamin's "Left Wing Melancholy," trans. Ben Brewster, in *The Weimar Republic Sourcebook*, ed. Anton Kaes, Martin Jay, and Edward Dimendberg (Berkeley: University of California Press, 1994), 304–06. See also Brown's *Politics Out of History*, 168–72, and her frequently cited "Resisting Left Melancholy," *boundary 2* 26 (Fall 1999): 19–27.

17. Stanley Aronowitz, *False Promises: The Shaping of American Working Class Consciousness* (1973; Durham: Duke University Press, 1992), 336.

18. Aronowitz, *False Promises*, 328, 330.

19. See Gitlin, *The Sixties*, 66.

20. Perloff, "A Lion in Our Living Room," 199.

21. Allen Ginsberg with Allen Young, *Gay Sunshine Interview* (Bolinas: Grey Fox Press, 1974), 42.

22. Ginsberg and his brother, Eugene, were legally responsible for their mother once their parents divorced. On the institutionalizations of Carl Solomon and Naomi Ginsberg, see Schumacher, *Dharma Lion*, 87–90, 196, 202.

23. Benjamin, *Illuminations*, 255.

24. On the Cold War as a "consensus formation" still operative in U.S. and global contexts, see Donald E. Pease, "Hiroshima, the Vietnam Veterans War Memorial, and the Gulf War: Post-National Spectacles," in *Cultures of U.S. Imperialism*, ed. Amy Kaplan and Donald E. Pease (Durham: Duke University Press, 1993), 557–80.

25. See Nancy Fraser, "Heterosexism, Misrecognition, and Capitalism: A Response to Judith Butler," *New Left Review* 228 (March/April 1998): 140–49, as well as her *Justice Interruptus: Critical Reflections on the "Postsocialist" Condition* (New York: Routledge, 1997). For a useful account of the complicated relationships between Old Left, New Left, new social movements, and identity politics in Britain and the United States, see Grant Farred, "Endgame Identity: Mapping the New Left Roots of Identity Politics," *New Literary History* 31.4 (2000): 627–48.

Epilogue

1. Andrew Hoberek, *The Twilight of the Middle Class: Post–World War II American Fiction and White-Collar Work* (Princeton: Princeton University Press, 2005), 126.

2. Hoberek, *The Twilight of the Middle Class*, 126.

3. Christopher Nealon, *The Matter of Capital: Poetry and Crisis in the American Century* (Cambridge: Harvard University Press, 2011), 73–106.

4. Jasper Bernes, *The Work of Art in the Age of Deindustrialization* (Stanford: Stanford University Press, 2017), 25, 83.

5. W. H. Auden, *Selected Poems*, ed. Edward Mendelson (New York: Vintage, 2007), 82.

6. On O'Hara's love poems to Warren, see Brad Gooch, *City Poet: The Life and Times of Frank O'Hara* (1993; New York: HarperPerennial, 1994), 329 and following, and Joe LeSueur, *Digressions on Some Poems by Frank O'Hara* (New York: Farrar, Straus and Giroux, 2003), 223–32.

7. On O'Hara's "willingness to lay himself on the line so that each line seems to exhaust what is happening in his present and to position himself on the verge of another investment that may go off on a tangent," see Charles Altieri, "Surrealism as a Living Modernism: What the New York Poets Learned from Two Generations of New York Painting," in *The Cambridge Companion to American Poetry since 1945*, ed. Jennifer Ashton (New York: Cambridge University Press, 2013), 56.

8. See Muñoz's reading of O'Hara's "Having a Coke with You," another love lyric for Warren, in José Esteban Muñoz, *Cruising Utopia: The Then and There of Queer Futurity* (New York: New York University Press, 2009), 5–7. See also Brian Glavey's gloss on Muñoz's reading and extended meditation on the popularity of O'Hara's poem, "Having a Coke with You Is Even More Fun Than Ideology Critique," *PMLA* 134.5 (2019): 996–1011.

9. Michael Davidson, *Guys Like Us: Citing Masculinity in Cold War Poetics* (Chicago: University of Chicago Press, 2004), 69.

WORKS CITED

Abrahams, Peter. "The Blacks." *An African Treasury*. Ed. Langston Hughes. New York: Crown Publishers, 1960. 42–55.

Allen, Donald, ed. *The New American Poetry, 1945–1960*. Berkeley: University of California Press, 1960.

Allen, Donald, and George F. Butterick, eds. *The Postmoderns: The New American Poetry Revised*. New York: Grove Press, 1982.

Altieri, Charles. *The Particulars of Rapture: An Aesthetics of the Affects*. Ithaca: Cornell University Press, 2003.

———. "Surrealism as a Living Modernism: What the New York Poets Learned from Two Generations of New York Painting." *The Cambridge Companion to American Poetry since 1945*. Ed. Jennifer Ashton. New York: Cambridge University Press, 2013. 47–65.

Arendt, Hannah. *The Origins of Totalitarianism*. 1951; New York: Harcourt Brace, 1966.

Aronowitz, Stanley. *False Promises: The Shaping of American Working Class Consciousness*. 1973; Durham: Duke University Press, 1992.

———. "When the New Left Was New." *The 60s Without Apology*. Ed. Sohnya Sayres, Anders Stephanson, Stanley Aronowitz, and Fredric Jameson. Minneapolis: University of Minnesota Press, 1984. 11–43.

Ashbery, John. "Introduction." *The Collected Poems of Frank O'Hara*. Ed. Donald Allen. 1971; Berkeley: University of California Press, 1995. viii–xi.

———. *Reported Sightings: Art Chronicles 1957–1987*. New York: Knopf, 1989.

———. "Writers and Issues: Frank O'Hara's Question." *Selected Prose*. Ed. Eugene Richie. Ann Arbor: University of Michigan Press, 2004. 80–83.

Auden, W. H. *Selected Poems*. Ed. Edward Mendelson. New York: Vintage, 2007.

Baldwin, James. "The Black Boy Looks at the White Boy." *Collected Essays*. New York: Library of America, 1998. 269–90.

Baraka, Amiri. *The Autobiography of LeRoi Jones*. New York: Freundlich Books, 1984.

——— [LeRoi Jones]. *Black Magic: Collected Poetry, 1961–1967*. Indianapolis: Bobbs-Merrill, 1969.

——— [LeRoi Jones]. *Black Music*. 1968; New York: Da Capo Press, 1998.

——— [LeRoi Jones]. *Blues People: Negro Music in White America*. New York: Morrow, 1963.

——— [LeRoi Jones]. *The Dead Lecturer*. New York: Grove, 1964.

——— [LeRoi Jones]. *Home: Social Essays*. New York: William Morrow, 1966.

———— [LeRoi Jones]. "How You Sound??" *The New American Poetry, 1945–1960*. Ed. Donald Allen. Berkeley: University of California Press, 1960. 424–25.

———— [LeRoi Jones]. *The LeRoi Jones/Amiri Baraka Reader*. Ed. William J. Harris. New York: Thunder's Mouth Press, 1991.

———— [LeRoi Jones]. "Milneburg Joys (or, Against 'Hipness' as Such)." *Kulchur* 3 (1961): 41.

———— [LeRoi Jones], ed. *The Moderns: An Anthology of New Writing in America*. New York: Corinth Books, 1963.

———— [LeRoi Jones]. *Preface to a Twenty Volume Suicide Note*. New York: Totem/ Corinth, 1961.

———— [LeRoi Jones]. Reading at Asilomar Negro Writers Conference in Pacific Grove, California, 1964. http://writing.upenn.edu/pennsound/x/Baraka.php.

———— [LeRoi Jones]. *Transbluesency: The Selected Poetry of Amiri Baraka/LeRoi Jones (1961–1995)*. New York: Marsilio, 1995.

Baraka, Amiri [LeRoi Jones] and Larry Neal, eds. *Black Fire: An Anthology of Afro-American Writing*. New York: William Morrow, 1968.

Baudelaire, Charles. "The Painter of Modern Life." *Baudelaire: Selected Writings on Art and Literature*. Trans. P. E. Charvet. 1972; New York: Penguin, 1992.

Benjamin, Walter. *Illuminations*. Ed. Hannah Arendt. Trans. Harry Zohn. New York: Schocken Books, 1968.

————. "Left Wing Melancholy." Trans. Ben Brewster. *The Weimar Republic Sourcebook*. Ed. Anton Kaes, Martin Jay, and Edward Dimendberg. Berkeley: University of California Press, 1994. 304–06.

————. *Reflections*. Ed. Peter Demetz. New York: Schocken, 1978.

————. *Selected Writings, 4: 1938–1940*. Cambridge: Belknap Press, 2006.

————. "Theses on the Philosophy of History." *Illuminations*. Ed. Hannah Arendt. Trans. Harry Zohn. New York: Schocken Books, 1968. 253–64.

Bennett, Chad. *Word of Mouth: Gossip and American Poetry*. Baltimore: Johns Hopkins University Press, 2018.

Berlant, Lauren. *Cruel Optimism*. Durham: Duke University Press, 2011.

Bernes, Jasper. *The Work of Art in the Age of Deindustrialization*. Stanford: Stanford University Press, 2017.

Bernstein, Charles. *Content's Dream: Essays 1975–1984*. 1986; Evanston: Northwestern University Press, 2001.

Breslin, James E. B. *From Modern to Contemporary: American Poetry, 1945–1960*. Chicago: University of Chicago Press, 1984.

Brick, Howard. *Age of Contradiction: American Thought and Culture in the 1960s*. 1998; Ithaca: Cornell University Press, 2000.

Brogan, T. V. F. "Volta." *The New Princeton Encyclopedia of Poetry and Poetics*. Ed. Alex Preminger and T. V. F. Brogan. Princeton: Princeton University Press, 1993.

Brooks, Cleanth. *The Well-Wrought Urn: Studies in the Structure of Poetry*. New York: Harcourt, Brace, 1947.

Brown, Wendy. *Politics Out of History*. Princeton: Princeton University Press, 2001.

———. "Resisting Left Melancholy." *boundary 2* 26 (Fall 1999): 19–27.

Broyard, Anatole. "Portrait of the Hipster." *Partisan Review* 15.6 (1948): 721–27.

Caro, Robert A. *The Power Broker: Robert Moses and the Fall of New York.* 1974; New York: Vintage Books, 1975.

Clay, Steven, and Rodney Phillips. *A Secret Location on the Lower East Side: Adventures in Writing, 1960–1980.* New York: The New York Public Library and Granary Books, 1998.

Clune, Michael. *American Literature and the Free Market, 1945–2000.* New York: Cambridge University Press, 2010.

Crews, Judson. Undated letter from the Judson Crews papers, Harry Ransom Center, University of Texas at Austin.

Culler, Jonathan. *Theory of the Lyric.* Cambridge: Harvard University Press, 2015.

Damon, Maria. *The Dark End of the Street: Margins in American Vanguard Poetry.* Minneapolis: University of Minnesota Press, 1993.

———. "Revelations of Compassionate Love; or, the Hurts of Women: Janine Pommy Vega's 'Poems to Fernando.'" *Girls Who Wore Black: Women Writing the Beat Generation.* Ed. Ronna C. Johnson and Nancy M. Grace. New Brunswick: Rutgers University Press, 2002. 205–26.

———. "Victors of Catastrophe: Beat Occlusions." *Beat Culture and the New America: 1950–1965.* Ed. Lisa Phillips. New York: Whitney Museum/Flammarion, 1995. 141–49.

Davidson, Michael. *Guys Like Us: Citing Masculinity in Cold War Poetics.* Chicago: University of Chicago Press, 2004.

———. *The San Francisco Renaissance: Poetics and Community at Mid-century.* New York: Cambridge University Press, 1989.

DeKoven, Marianne. *Utopia Limited: The Sixties and the Emergence of the Postmodern.* Durham: Duke University Press, 2004.

DeLillo, Don. *White Noise.* 1985; New York: Penguin, 1986.

Denning, Michael. *The Cultural Front: The Laboring of American Culture in the Twentieth Century.* New York: Verso, 1996.

———. *Culture in the Age of Three Worlds.* New York: Verso, 2004.

Diggory, Terence, and Stephen Paul Miller, eds. *The Scenes of My Selves: New Work on New York School Poets.* Orono: National Poetry Foundation, 2001.

Dinerstein, Joel. *The Origins of Cool in Postwar America.* Chicago: University of Chicago Press, 2017.

Di Prima, Diane. *Dinners and Nightmares.* New York: Corinth Books, 1961.

———. *Dinners and Nightmares.* Expanded ed. 1998; San Francisco: Last Gasp, 2003.

———. "Introduction." *The Floating Bear: A Newsletter, Numbers 1–37, 1961–1969.* Ed. Diane di Prima and LeRoi Jones. La Jolla, California: Laurence McGilvery, 1973. vii–xviii.

———. *Memoirs of a Beatnik.* 1969; New York: Penguin Books, 1998.

———. *Recollections of My Life as a Woman: The New York Years.* New York: Viking, 2001.

————. *Revolutionary Letters.* 1971; San Francisco: Last Gasp, 2007.

————. *Selected Poems: 1956–1976.* Plainfield: North Atlantic Books, 1977.

DuPlessis, Rachel Blau. *Purple Passages: Pound, Eliot, Zukofsky, Olson, Creeley, and the Ends of Patriarchal Poetry.* Iowa City: University of Iowa Press, 2012.

"Editorial." *Kulchur* 3 (1961): 2.

Eliot, T. S. *Selected Prose of T. S. Eliot.* Ed. Frank Kermode. New York: Harcourt Brace, 1975.

Emerson, Maude. "James Schuyler's 'Freely Espousing.'" *Jacket2* 30 June 2012. http://jacket2.org/article/james-schuylers-freely-espousing.

Epstein, Andrew. *Attention Equals Life: The Pursuit of the Everyday in Contemporary Poetry and Culture.* New York: Oxford University Press, 2016.

————. *Beautiful Enemies: Friendship and Postwar American Poetry.* New York: Oxford University Press, 2006.

————. "'Building a nest out of torn up letters': James Schuyler, Trash, and the Poetics of Collage." *Jacket2* 30 June 2012. http://jacket2.org/article/building-nest-out-torn-letters.

Farred, Grant. "Endgame Identity: Mapping the New Left Roots of Identity Politics." *New Literary History* 31.4 (2000): 627–48.

Felski, Rita. *The Limits of Critique.* Chicago: University of Chicago Press, 2015.

Filreis, Al, with Herman Beavers, Alan Loney, and Mecca Sullivan. *PoemTalk.* Episode 20. Podcast. 30 July 2009. http://poemtalkatkwh.blogspot.com/2009/07/baraka.html.

Flatley, Jonathan. *Affective Mapping: Melancholia and the Politics of Modernism.* Cambridge: Harvard University Press, 2008.

————. *Like Andy Warhol.* Chicago: University of Chicago Press, 2017.

————. "Moscow and Melancholia." *Social Text* 19.1 (2001): 75–102.

Fraiman, Susan. *Cool Men and the Second Sex.* New York: Columbia University Press, 2003.

Frank, Thomas. *The Conquest of Cool: Business Culture, Counterculture, and the Rise of Hip Consumerism.* Chicago: University of Chicago Press, 1997.

Fraser, Nancy. "Heterosexism, Misrecognition, and Capitalism: A Response to Judith Butler." *New Left Review* 228 (March/April 1998): 140–49.

————. *Justice Interruptus: Critical Reflections on the "Postsocialist" Condition.* New York: Routledge, 1997.

Freeman, Elizabeth. "Packing History, Count(er)ing Generations." *New Literary History* 31.4 (2000): 727–44.

Friedan, Betty. *The Feminine Mystique.* 1963; New York: Laurel, 1984.

Friedlander, Benjamin. "Strange Fruit: O'Hara, Race and the Color of Time." *The Scenes of My Selves: New Work on New York School Poets.* Ed. Terence Diggory and Stephen Paul Miller. Orono: National Poetry Foundation, 2001. 123–42.

Funkhouser, Christopher. "LeRoi Jones, Larry Neal, and *The Cricket*: Jazz and Poets' Black Fire." *African American Review* 37.2–3 (Summer/Fall 2003): 237–44.

Ginsberg, Allen. *Collected Poems, 1947–1980.* New York: Harper and Row, 1984.

————. *"Howl" and Other Poems.* 1956; San Francisco: City Lights, 1993.

————. *Journals: Early Fifties Early Sixties*. Ed. Gordon Ball. New York: Grove Press, 1977.

————. *Journals: Mid-Fifties, 1954–1958*. Ed. Gordon Ball. 1995; New York: Harper-Collins, 1996.

————. Allen Ginsberg Papers, Harry Ransom Center, University of Texas at Austin.

Ginsberg, Allen, with Allen Young. *Gay Sunshine Interview*. Bolinas: Grey Fox Press, 1974.

Gitlin, Todd. *The Sixties: Years of Hope, Days of Rage*. New York: Bantam, 1987.

Glavey, Brian. "Having a Coke with You Is Even More Fun Than Ideology Critique." *PMLA* 134.5 (2019): 996–1011.

————. *The Wallflower Avant-Garde: Modernism, Sexuality, and Queer Ekphrasis*. New York: Oxford University Press, 2016.

Goble, Mark. "'Our Country's Black and White Past': Film and the Figures of History in O'Hara." *American Literature* 71.1 (March 1999): 57–92.

"God-King of Tibet." *New York Times* 4 Apr. 1959: 2.

Golding, Alan. *From Outlaw to Classic: Canons in American Poetry*. Madison: University of Wisconsin Press, 1995.

————. "*The New American Poetry* Revisited, Again." *Contemporary Literature* 39.2 (Summer 1998): 180–211.

Gooch, Brad. *City Poet: The Life and Times of Frank O'Hara*. 1993; New York: HarperPerennial, 1994.

Gray, Timothy. *Urban Pastoral: Natural Currents in the New York School*. Iowa City: University of Iowa Press, 2010.

Grossberg, Lawrence. "Mapping Popular Culture." *We Gotta Get Out of This Place: Popular Conservatism and Postmodern Culture*. New York: Routledge, 1992. 69–87.

Guilbaut, Serge. *How New York Stole the Idea of Modern Art: Abstract Expressionism, Freedom, and the Cold War*. Trans. Arthur Goldhammer. Chicago: University of Chicago Press, 1983.

Hansen, Miriam Bratu. "Benjamin and Cinema: Not a One-Way Street." *Critical Inquiry* 25.2 (Winter 1999): 306–43.

Harper, Phillip Brian. "Nationalism and Social Division in Black Arts Poetry of the 1960s." *Identities*. Ed. Kwame Anthony Appiah and Henry Louis Gates Jr. Chicago: University of Chicago Press, 1995. 220–41.

Harris, William J. "Introduction." *The LeRoi Jones/Amiri Baraka Reader*. Ed. William J. Harris. New York: Thunder's Mouth Press, 1991. xvii–xxx.

Hayot, Eric. *On Literary Worlds*. New York: Oxford University Press, 2012.

Hebdige, Dick. *Subculture: The Meaning of Style*. 1979; New York: Routledge, 2001.

Herd, David. *Enthusiast! Essays on Modern American Literature*. New York: Manchester University Press, 2007.

Herring, Terrell Scott. "Frank O'Hara's Open Closet." *PMLA* 117.3 (2002): 414–27.

Hoberek, Andrew. *The Twilight of the Middle Class: Post–World War II American Fiction and White-Collar Work*. Princeton: Princeton University Press, 2005.

Hornick, Lita. *The Green Fuse*. New York: Giorno Poetry Systems, 1989.

————. "*Kulchur*: A Memoir." *The Little Magazine in America: A Modern Documentary History*. Ed. Elliot Anderson and Mary Kinzie. Stamford: Pushcart Press, 1978. 281–85.

"Intercom." *Merriam-Webster's Collegiate Dictionary*, 11th ed. Springfield: Merriam-Webster, 2003. 652.

Izenberg, Oren. *Being Numerous: Poetry and the Ground of Social Life*. Princeton: Princeton University Press, 2011.

Jameson, Fredric. "Cognitive Mapping." *The Jameson Reader*. Ed. Michael Hardt and Kathi Weeks. Oxford: Blackwell, 2000. 277–87.

————. "Periodizing the 60s." *Ideologies of Theory: Essays 1971–1986*. Vol. 2, *The Syntax of History*. Minneapolis: University of Minnesota Press, 1988. 178–208.

————. *Postmodernism, or, The Cultural Logic of Late Capitalism*. Durham: Duke University Press, 1991.

————. *A Singular Modernity: Essays on the Ontology of the Present*. New York: Verso, 2002.

Jay, Martin. *Songs of Experience: Modern American and European Variations on a Universal Theme*. Berkeley: University of California Press, 2005.

Johnson, Joyce. *Minor Characters*. Boston: Houghton Mifflin, 1983.

Johnson, Ronna C. "'And then she went': Beat Departures and Feminine Transgressions in Joyce Johnson's *Come and Join the Dance*." *Girls Who Wore Black: Women Writing the Beat Generation*. Ed. Ronna C. Johnson and Nancy M. Grace. New Brunswick: Rutgers University Press, 2002. 69–95.

————. "Three Generations of Beat Poetics." *The Cambridge Companion to American Poetry since 1945*. Ed. Jennifer Ashton. New York: Cambridge University Press, 2013. 80–93.

Johnson, Ronna C., and Nancy M. Grace. *Girls Who Wore Black: Women Writing the Beat Generation*. New Brunswick: Rutgers University Press, 2002.

Jones, Hettie. *How I Became Hettie Jones*. New York: Penguin Books, 1990.

Kane, Daniel. *All Poets Welcome: The Lower East Side Poetry Scene in the 1960s*. Berkeley: University of California Press, 2003.

Keller, Lynn. "Becoming 'a Compleat Travel Agency': Barbara Guest's Negotiations with the Fifties Feminine Mystique." *The Scenes of My Selves: New Work on New York School Poets*. Ed. Terence Diggory and Stephen Paul Miller. Orono: National Poetry Foundation, 2001. 215–27.

————. "'Just one of / the girls:— / normal in the extreme': Experimentalists-To-Be Starting Out in the 1960s." *differences* 12.2 (2001): 47–69.

Killian, Kevin. "Spicer and the Mattachine." *After Spicer: Critical Essays*. Ed. John Emil Vincent. Middletown: Wesleyan University Press, 2011. 16–35.

King, Richard H. *Civil Rights and the Idea of Freedom*. New York: Oxford University Press, 1992.

Komanyakaa, Yusef. "Troubling the Water." *The Best American Poetry, 1995*. Ed. Richard Howard. New York: Simon and Schuster, 1995. 129–31.

Konstantinou, Lee. *Cool Characters: Irony and American Fiction*. Cambridge: Harvard University Press, 2016.

Kostelanetz, Richard. "How to Be a Difficult Poet." *New York Times Magazine* 23 May 1976: 18–22.

Latour, Bruno. *Reassembling the Social: An Introduction to Actor-Network-Theory*. Oxford: Oxford University Press, 2005.

Lee, Benjamin. "Spontaneity and Improvisation in Postwar Experimental Poetry." *The Routledge Companion to Experimental Literature*. Ed. Joe Bray, Alison Gibbons, and Brian McHale. New York: Routledge, 2012. 75–88.

Lehman, David. *The Last Avant-Garde: The Making of the New York School of Poets*. New York: Doubleday, 1998.

LeSueur, Joe. *Digressions on Some Poems by Frank O'Hara*. New York: Farrar, Straus and Giroux, 2003.

Libby, Anthony. "Diane di Prima: 'Nothing Is Lost; It Shines In Our Eyes.'" *Girls Who Wore Black: Women Writing the Beat Generation*. Ed. Ronna C. Johnson and Nancy M. Grace. New Brunswick: Rutgers University Press, 2002. 45–68.

Longenbach, James. *Modernist Poetics of History: Pound, Eliot, and the Sense of the Past*. Princeton: Princeton University Press, 1987.

Lott, Eric. *Love and Theft: Blackface Minstrelsy and the American Working Class*. New York: Oxford University Press, 1993.

Love, Heather K. *Feeling Backward: Loss and the Politics of Queer History*. Cambridge: Harvard University Press, 2007.

Lynch, Kevin. *The Image of the City*. 1960; Cambridge: MIT Press, 1992.

Mackey, Nathaniel. *Discrepant Engagement: Dissonance, Cross-Culturality, and Experimental Writing*. New York: Cambridge University Press, 1993.

Mailer, Norman. *Advertisements for Myself*. New York: G.P. Putnam's Sons, 1959.

———. *An American Dream*. New York: Henry Holt and Company, 1964.

Marcuse, Herbert. "The Affirmative Character of Culture." *Negations: Essays in Critical Theory*. Trans. Jeremy J. Shapiro. Boston: Beacon Press, 1968. 88–133.

———. *One-Dimensional Man: Studies in the Ideology of Advanced Industrial Society*. 1964; Boston: Beacon Press, 1991.

May, Elaine Tyler. *Homeward Bound: American Families in the Cold War Era*. New York: Basic Books, 1988.

McRobbie, Angela. *Feminism and Youth Culture*. 1991; New York: Routledge, 2000.

McVay, Gordon. *Esenin: A Life*. Ann Arbor: Ardis, 1976.

Melzer, David, ed. *San Francisco Beat: Talking with the Poets*. San Francisco: City Lights, 2001.

Miles, Barry. *Ginsberg: A Biography*. London: Virgin Publishing, 2000.

Mills, C. Wright. *The Power Elite*. 1956; New York: Oxford University Press, 1980.

———. *Power, Politics, and People: The Collected Essays of C. Wright Mills*. 1963; New York: Oxford University Press, 1972.

———. *The Sociological Imagination*. New York: Oxford University Press, 1959.

———. *White Collar: The American Middle Classes.* New York: Oxford University Press, 1951.

Morris, Adalaide. *How to Live/What to Do: H.D.'s Cultural Poetics.* Urbana: University of Illinois Press, 2003.

Moten, Fred. *In the Break: The Aesthetics of the Black Radical Tradition.* Minneapolis: University of Minnesota Press, 2003.

Muñoz, José Esteban. *Cruising Utopia: The Then and There of Queer Futurity.* New York: New York University Press, 2009.

Nadel, Alan. *Containment Culture: American Narratives, Postmodernism, and the Atomic Age.* Durham: Duke University Press, 1995.

Nealon, Christopher. *Foundlings: Lesbian and Gay Historical Emotion before Stonewall.* Durham: Duke University Press, 2001.

———. *The Matter of Capital: Poetry and Crisis in the American Century.* Cambridge: Harvard University Press, 2011.

Nelson, Cary. *Repression and Recovery: Modern American Poetry and the Politics of Cultural Memory, 1910–1945.* Madison: University of Wisconsin Press, 1989.

———. *Revolutionary Memory: Recovering the Poetry of the American Left.* New York: Routledge, 2001.

Nelson, Maggie. *Women, the New York School, and Other True Abstractions.* Iowa City: University of Iowa Press, 2007.

Neu, Renée S. "With Frank at MoMA." *Homage to Frank O'Hara.* Ed. Bill Berkson and Joe LeSueur. Bolinas: Big Sky, 1988. 91–92.

Ngai, Sianne. *Ugly Feelings.* Cambridge: Harvard University Press, 2005.

Nielsen, Aldon Lynn. *Black Chant: Languages of African-American Postmodernism.* New York: Cambridge University Press, 1997.

———. *Integral Music: Languages of African American Innovation.* Tuscaloosa: University of Alabama Press, 2004.

———. *Reading Race: White American Poets and the Racial Discourse in the Twentieth Century.* Athens: University of Georgia Press, 1988.

O'Hara, Frank. *The Collected Poems of Frank O'Hara.* Ed. Donald Allen. 1971; Berkeley: University of California Press, 1995.

———. *Lunch Poems.* San Francisco: City Lights Books, 1964.

Pease, Donald E. "Hiroshima, the Vietnam Veterans War Memorial, and the Gulf War: Post-National Spectacles." *Cultures of U.S. Imperialism.* Ed. Amy Kaplan and Donald E. Pease. Durham: Duke University Press, 1993. 557–80.

Perkins, David. *A History of Modern Poetry: Modernism and After.* Cambridge: Harvard University Press, 1987.

Perl, Jed. *New Art City: Manhattan at Mid-Century.* 2005; New York: Vintage Books, 2007.

Perloff, Marjorie. *Frank O'Hara: Poet among Painters.* 1977; Chicago: University of Chicago Press, 1998.

———. "A Lion in Our Living Room: Reading Allen Ginsberg in the Eighties."

Poetic License: Essays on Modernist and Postmodernist Lyric. Evanston: Northwestern University Press, 1990. 199–230.

———. "'A Step Away from Them': Poetry 1956." *Poetry On & Off the Page: Essays for Emergent Occasions.* Evanston: Northwestern University Press, 1998. 83–115.

———. *21st-Century Modernism: The "New" Poetics.* Malden: Blackwell, 2002.

———. "Whose New American Poetry? Anthologizing in the Nineties." *Diacritics* 26.3–4 (1996): 104–23.

Pound, Ezra. *Guide to Kulchur.* New York: New Directions, 1938.

Pynchon, Thomas. *The Crying of Lot 49.* 1965; New York: Harper & Row, 1990.

Rasmussen, Waldo. "Frank O'Hara in the Museum." *Homage to Frank O'Hara.* Ed. Bill Berkson and Joe LeSueur. Bolinas: Big Sky, 1988. 84–90.

Riesman, David, with Reuel Denny and Nathan Glazer. *The Lonely Crowd: A Study of the Changing American Character.* New Haven: Yale University Press, 1950.

Rifkin, Libbie. *Career Moves: Olson, Creeley, Zukofsky, Berrigan, and the American Avant-Garde.* Madison: University of Wisconsin Press, 2000.

Rosenbaum, Susan. "O'Hara, Flâneur of New York." *The Scene of My Selves: New Work on New York School Poets.* Ed. Terence Diggory and Stephen Paul Miller. Orono: National Poetry Foundation, 2001. 143–73.

Ross, Andrew. "The Death of Lady Day." *Frank O'Hara: To Be True to a City.* Ed. Jim Elledge. Ann Arbor: University of Michigan Press, 1990. 380–91.

———. *No Respect: Intellectuals and Popular Culture.* New York: Routledge, 1989.

Ross, Marlon. "Camping the Dirty Dozens: The Queer Resources of Black Nationalist Invective." *Callaloo* 23.1 (2000): 290–312.

Saul, Scott. *Freedom Is, Freedom Ain't: Jazz and the Making of the Sixties.* Cambridge: Harvard University Press, 2003.

Schumacher, Michael. *Dharma Lion: A Critical Biography of Allen Ginsberg.* New York: St. Martin's, 1992.

Schuyler, James. *Collected Poems.* New York: Farrar, Straus, and Giroux, 1993.

———. "Frank O'Hara: Poet among Painters (excerpts)." *Homage to Frank O'Hara.* Ed. Bill Berkson and Joe LeSueur. Bolinas: Big Sky, 1988. 82–83.

Sedgwick, Eve Kosofsky. "Queer and Now." *Wild Orchids and Trotsky.* Ed. Mark Edmundson. New York: Penguin, 1993. 237–66.

———. *Touching Feeling: Affect, Pedagogy, Performativity.* Durham: Duke University Press, 2003.

Shaw, Lytle. *Frank O'Hara: The Poetics of Coterie.* Iowa City: University of Iowa Press, 2006.

Shoptaw, John. *On the Outside Looking Out: John Ashbery's Poetry.* Cambridge: Harvard University Press, 1995.

Smethurst, James. *The Black Arts Movement: Literary Nationalism in the 1960s and 1970s.* Chapel Hill: University of North Carolina Press, 2005.

Smith, Hazel. *Hyperscapes in the Poetry of Frank O'Hara: Difference/Homosexuality/Topography.* Liverpool: Liverpool University Press, 2000.

Sollors, Werner. *Amiri Baraka/LeRoi Jones: The Quest for a "Populist Modernism."* New York: Columbia University Press, 1978.

Solomon, Carl. "I Was a Communist Youth." *The Floating Bear: A Newsletter: Numbers 1–37, 1961–1969.* Ed. Diane di Prima and LeRoi Jones. La Jolla: Laurence McGilvery, 1973. 129.

Sontag, Susan. "Notes on Camp." *Against Interpretation and Other Essays.* 1966; New York: Picador, 2001. 275–92.

Sorrentino, Gilbert. "*Neon, Kulchur,* Etc." *The Little Magazine in America: A Modern Documentary History.* Ed. Elliot Anderson and Mary Kinzie. Stamford: Pushcart Press, 1978. 298–316.

Spahr, Juliana. *DuBois's Telegram: Literary Resistance and State Containment.* Cambridge: Harvard University Press, 2018.

Thomas, Lorenzo. *Extraordinary Measures: Afrocentric Modernism and Twentieth-Century American Poetry.* Tuscaloosa: University of Alabama Press, 2000.

"Tibet—ABC of a Remote Land." *New York Times* 29 Mar. 1959: E4.

Tietchen, Todd F. *The Cubalogues: Beat Writers in Revolutionary Havana.* Gainesville: University Press of Florida, 2010.

"Trouble in Tibet." *New York Times* 22 Mar. 1959: E8.

Vincent, John Emil. *John Ashbery and You.* Athens: University of Georgia Press, 2008.

Watten, Barrett. "What I See in *How I Became Hettie Jones.*" *Girls Who Wore Black: Women Writing the Beat Generation.* Ed. Ronna C. Johnson and Nancy M. Grace. New Brunswick: Rutgers University Press, 2002. 96–118.

White, Hayden. *The Content of the Form: Narrative Discourse and Historical Representation.* Baltimore: Johns Hopkins University Press, 1987.

Whyte, William H. *The Organization Man.* New York: Simon and Schuster, 1956.

Wiegman, Robyn. "Feminism's Apocalyptic Futures." *New Literary History* 31.4 (2000): 805–25.

Williams, Raymond. *Drama from Ibsen to Brecht.* New York: Oxford University Press, 1968.

———. *Marxism and Literature.* Oxford: Oxford University Press, 1977.

INDEX

Epstein, Andrew, 45
Esenin, Sergei, 25–28, 30, 118n12
Evergreen Review, 49, 55
everyday, poetry of, 2, 8–12, 45, 108–9; in di
  Prima, 68–71, 73, 78, 84–85
exile: as way of theorizing, 27
experimentalism: as risk, 2, 19–20, 119n24. *See
  also* New American Poetry (experimentalist
  poetry)

fascism, 93
Feather, Leonard, 42, 43
flâneur figure, 14, 115n44
Flatley, Jonathan, 3, 6–7, 14, 24, 51, 113n25
The Floating Bear magazine, 17, 43, 48–49,
  51–53, 91
"For James Dean" (O'Hara), 74
fragmented lineation, 64
Fraiman, Susan, 72
Frank, Thomas, 71
Fraser, Nancy, 104
free verse, 71, 87, 112n9
freedom, 17–19, 38, 69, 92, 95
"Freely Espousing" (Schuyler), 11–12
French Revolution, 23, 26
Friedan, Betty, 46, 123n16
future: pull of, 3, 5–6, 59, 85–86, 87–90, 97,
  100, 109

generational rhetorics, 89, 93–94, 100–3,
  131n5; catalogue as generational parable,
  93, 102
Genet, Jean, 11, 38, 39
Ghana, 2, 38, 39, 63
Ginsberg, Allen, 1, 3, 4, 46, 87–104; use of
  anaphora, 101–2; class consciousness in
  poems of, 97, 99, 104; communist ideals
  of, 13, 93, 98–99, 101, 103; Cuban visit,
  55; elegy in, 88, 96; relation to emergence,
  87–88; *Gay Sunshine* interview, 89; genera-
  tional rhetorics, 89, 131n5; institutionaliza-
  tion of, 16–17, 102–3; longing for Old Left
  past, 87–88, 90–96, 100–4, 130n2; obscen-
  ity charges, 17, 115n49; pivots in, 93–94,
  97–98, 100–1; poetics of industry, 96–98;
  political engagement in, 87–100, 103–4;
  political identifications of, 90–94, 103–4;
  present in, 87–89, 94, 97–98, 102–3; prole-

tariat, longing for, 95–99; repetition in, 89,
  100; *Works:* "America," 90, 95; "The Brick-
  layer's Lunch Hour," 95; *"Howl" and Other
  Poems,* 87–88, 91–100; "In back of the real,"
  21, 95–99, 101; "In the Baggage Room at
  Greyhound," 95; *Journals: Mid-Fifties,* 87;
  "Kaddish," 91; "A Poem on America," 95,
  97; "Sunflower Sutra," 95, 99; "A Super-
  market in California," 95. *See also* "Howl"
  (Ginsberg)
Ginsberg, Louis, 90–91
Ginsberg, Naomi, 90–91, 131n3, 132n22; in
  "Howl," 102–3
global perspectives, 2–3, 9–11, 15, 17–19, 23–
  24, 37, 46–47, 61–62, 72
"The God-King of Tibet" (*New York Times*),
  37
Golding, Alan, 50
Greenberg, Clement, 18, 19, 116n61
Grossberg, Lawrence, 113n25
Guest, Barbara, 10
Guide to Kulchur (Pound), 53
Guilbaut, Serge, 111n5

Harper, Phillip Brian, 126n50
Hartigan, Grace, 3, 10
"Having a Coke with You" (O'Hara), 30, 71
H. D., 10
Hebdige, Dick, 83
hipness: African American invention of, 76–
  77; versions of, 76–79, 84
hipsterism, 11, 67–68; advertising and, 70–72,
  77, 85; as collective experience, 81; criti-
  cisms of, 70–71; detachment of, 68, 70,
  75–80; di Prima's critique of, 68, 74–75, 80;
  as everyday practice, 68–71, 73, 78, 84–85;
  Mailer's view, 73, 76–79; as marketing fea-
  ture, 85; in narrative tone and technique,
  83; parodies of, 70, 72; passive resistance as
  stance, 80, 82; popular figures of, 73–74;
  reinvention of by women, 68–69, 76; rela-
  tion to violence, 79–82; slang phrases, 70,
  74, 77; stereotypes of, 74–75; as structure
  of feeling, 68, 73, 77, 84–85; as subculture,
  68–69, 73, 83–86; toughness as mask for
  vulnerability, 82. *See also* bohemians
historical context, 112n7; belonging, 32,
  36–37, 83, 107; larger historical frame, 7–8,

Lunch Poems (O'Hara), 30–31

Lynch, Kevin, 24

lyric, 2–4, 106; across time, 10; Baraka's use of, 41, 61; di Prima's use of, 68; O'Hara's use of, 29–30, 71, 119n23; politicization of, 14, 109; postmodern, 3. *See also* poetry

Mackey, Nathaniel, 47–48, 60

madness: as trope for social resistance, 103

magazines: jazz, 54; little, 47–50; mimeographed, 52. See also *Kulchur*

Mailer, Norman, 68, 73, 76–79; "The White Negro," 76–77, 81

Manhattan, 9, 12, 15–16, 32–36, 39, 61, 105

Marcuse, Herbert, 18, 19, 46, 70, 93, 116n61

Marxism, 97, 105, 106, 115n41, 123n9, 131n3

mass culture, 38, 46, 69, 99

Matter magazine, 63

McCarthyism, 16, 19–21, 120n31, 130n38

McLucas, LeRoy, 54, 56–59, *58*

McVay, Gordon, 118n12

mediation, 7–8, 24–25, 107–10

melancholy, 83, 96, 131n5; "antidepressive," 113n26; in di Prima, 78, 83–84; in Ginsberg, 88–94, 96, 98–99; left wing, 98–99; in O'Hara, 26–28, 35, 107–8; in Solomon, 92–93

"Memoir of Sergei O. . . ." (O'Hara), 23, 25–28, 33

Memoirs of a Beatnik (di Prima), 74–75

memory, 4, 9, 27, 38–40, 45, 95, 99. *See also* past

Metronome, 43

middle class: complacency of, 2, 18, 46–47; containment culture and, 16; postmodernism turn and, 19, 105, 116n63; precarity of, 3, 105–6, 116n63

military-industrial development, 3

Mills, C. Wright, 8, 17–18, 19, 34, 69, 93

Mix, Tom, 45

modernism, 1, 3, 9, 13, 19, 116n61

The Moderns (ed. Baraka), 79

"More or Less Love Poems" (di Prima), 6, 10–11, 13, 75, 79

Morris, Adalaide, 10

Moten, Fred, 41

Mozart, Wolfgang Amadeus, 63

multimedia techniques, 2, 41

Muñoz, José Esteban, 30, 109, 127n15

Museum of Modern Art (MoMA), 29, 118–19n18

"Music" (O'Hara), 30–33, 35

Nadel, Alan, 16

Naked Ear magazine, 51

The Nation, 107

Nealon, Christopher, 25, 106, 111n3

negative affect, 60, 64, 126n54

Neon magazine, 52

The New American Poetry (ed. Allen), 1, 2, 50, 51, 71, 88–89, 127n17

New American Poetry (experimentalist poetry): criticisms of, 1–2, 70–71; open form, 3, 68, 88; spontaneous, process-oriented approaches, 4, 7–8, 14, 61, 68, 71, 75, 104, 112n9; tensions within communities, 56. *See also* experimentalism; pivots

New Critics, 1, 8, 13, 49, 87, 88. *See also* academic world

New Left, 18, 46, 54, 87, 93, 103–4

New York City, 19, 23, 47, 85. *See also* Manhattan

New York Poets Theatre, 16

New York Post, 39

New York School poets, 9–10, 19, 41, 52, 71, 88

The New Yorker, 50–51

Ngai, Sianne, 6, 7, 14, 113n25

Nichols, Barbara, 26, 27

"Nightmares" (di Prima), 78

Nkrumah, Kwame, 63

nuclear war, fears of, 11, 16

O'Hara, Frank, 3, 23–40; advertising language in, 29–30, 71, 106, 127n13; affective engagement, shifts in, 4–5, 23–25, 30–31; affective mapping in, 25–28, 37–38; alternative historiographies in, 33, 37–38; associative rhetoric in, 34; on beauty and clarification, 112–13n15; cognitive mapping in, 24–26, 37–38; collective experience in, 4, 32–33, 39–40; elegiac tradition in, 4, 26, 38–40; emergent historicism in, 23–28, 30–31, 35, 38; failures of mood and attunement in, 31–32; geographical references in, 15, 26–27, 33–35; on Ginsberg, 100; hu-

mor, use of, 26, 33; "I do this I do that" (autobiographical and occasional) poems, 4, 28, 38, 61, 118n15; *Kulchur* and, 52, 53; at Museum of Modern Art, 29, 118–19n18; use of pivot, 8–9, 23, 26–29, 35; poetics of emergence in, 23, 30, 33, 35, 45, 47; political engagement in, 23, 32, 35–40, 114–15n41; present in, 24, 28, 30, 33, 39; queerness and sexual politics of, 29–30; revolution in works of, 23, 26–28, 30, 33, 38–39, 115n41; shame in, 25, 30, 32–33, 36; structures of feeling in, 24–26, 32–34, 40; *Works:* "Art Chronicles" (in *Kulchur*), 53; *Collected Poems*, 33; "The Day Lady Died," 26, 28, 31–32, 38–40, 122n46; "For James Dean," 74; "Having a Coke with You," 30, 71; "In Memory of My Feelings," 3–5, 10; "Joe's Jacket," 5; *Lunch Poems*, 30–31; "Memoir of Sergei O. . . .," 23, 25–28, 33; "Music," 30–33, 35; "Naphtha," 23; "Personal Poem," 28, 31; "Poem (Khrushchev is coming on the right day!)," 23, 36; "Poem (Lana Turner has collapsed!)," 28, 31; "Present," 107–10; "Rhapsody," 6, 8, 20, 23, 33–36; "A Step Away from Them," 26
Old Left: agency of, 93–94, 104; Ginsberg's references to, 87–88, 90–96, 100, 104, 130n2; in Solomon's writing, 91–93; work/art dialectic, 95
Olson, Charles, 48–49, 50, 112n9
"On Some Motifs in Baudelaire" (Benjamin), 1, 4
One-Dimensional Man (Marcuse), 93
one-dimensional thinking, 46
open form, 3, 68, 88–89, 112n9
The Organization Man (Whyte), 69
Origin, 50
The Origins of Cool in Postwar America (Dinerstein), 69

painting: influence on New York poets, 9–10
panic, 3, 10
Partisan Review, 16, 50, 53
past, 3–6, 82; Old Left, 87–88; reconfiguration of in present, 9–10, 13, 62–63, 75, 87–90, 93–94. *See also* memory
Perloff, Marjorie, 1–2, 28, 30, 100, 117n2
"Personal Poem" (O'Hara), 28, 31

Phelps, Donald, 52
Pilgrim State Hospital, 102
pivots, 8–14; in Baraka, 44–45, 60–61, 125n47; between depression and optimism, 17, 19–20; celestial viewpoints, 8–9, 107–9; in Ginsberg, 93–94, 97–98, 100–101; global perspectives, 9–11; hypocrisy and coercion of American culture, 21; in O'Hara, 8–9, 23, 26–29, 35; synchronic, 20–21; utopianist, 10–11; volta/turn, 9, 26. *See also* affect; history; poetics of emergence
"Poem (Khrushchev is coming on the right day!)" (O'Hara), 23, 36
"A Poem on America" (Ginsberg), 95, 97
"A Poem Some People Will Have to Understand" (Baraka), 59
poetics of emergence, 6–7, 21, 114–15n41; in di Prima's poetry, 68–69, 72–73, 77, 86; in Ginsberg's poetry, 87–88; in O'Hara's poetry, 23, 30, 33, 35, 45, 47
poetry: of everyday, 2, 8–12, 45, 68, 108–9; management of threat through, 4; as mode of explicit confrontation, 45–46. *See also* lyric
"The Poet" (di Prima), 79–80
"political apoliticism," 111n5
political idealism, 97
political insurgencies, 1960s, 21
"Political Poem" (Baraka), 46, 59
politics, 71–73; in Baraka's work, 41, 43–50, 54–57, 59–64, 71, 115n41; of class, 2, 36–37, 64, 99, 105; cultural, 10–11, 21, 44–45, 48, 62; in di Prima's work, 75, 85–86, 115n41; in Ginsberg's work, 87–100, 103–4; movement toward, 114–15n41; in O'Hara's work, 23, 32, 35–40, 114–15n41; sexual, 11, 13, 28, 83, 85–86. *See also* history; poetics of emergence
popular culture: transformed into mass culture, 46
Popular Front, 93, 99, 101
populist elitism, 75
Port Huron Statement, 100
"A Portrait of the Hipster" (Broyard), 70
postcolonial independence movements, 2–3, 39
postindustrial society, 18, 46, 99, 107
postmodern lyric, 3

Jorie Graham: Essays on the Poetry
edited by Thomas Gardner
University of Wisconsin Press, 2005

Gary Snyder and the Pacific Rim: Creating Countercultural Community
by Timothy Gray

Urban Pastoral: Natural Currents in the New York School
by Timothy Gray

Poetics and Praxis 'After' Objectivism
edited by W. Scott Howard and Broc Rossell

Ecopoetics: Essays in the Field
edited by Angela Hume and Gillian Osborne

Racial Things, Racial Forms: Objecthood in Avant-Garde Asian American Poetry
by Joseph Jonghyun Jeon

We Saw the Light: Conversations between the New American Cinema and Poetry
by Daniel Kane

Ghostly Figures: Memory and Belatedness in Postwar American Poetry
by Ann Keniston

Poetics of Emergence: Affect and History in Postwar Experimental Poetry
by Benjamin Lee

Contested Records: The Turn to Documents in Contemporary North American Poetry
by Michael Leong

History, Memory, and the Literary Left: Modern American Poetry, 1935–1968
by John Lowney

Paracritical Hinge: Essays, Talks, Notes, Interviews
by Nathaniel Mackey

Behind the Lines: War Resistance Poetry on the American Homefront since 1941
by Philip Metres

Poetry Matters: Neoliberalism, Affect, and the Posthuman in Twenty-First Century North American Feminist Poetics
by Heather Milne

Hold-Outs: The Los Angeles Poetry Renaissance, 1948–1992
by Bill Mohr

In Visible Movement: Nuyorican Poetry from the Sixties to Slam
by Urayoán Noel

Reading Project: A Collaborative Analysis of William Poundstone's Project for Tachistoscope {Bottomless Pit}
by Jessica Pressman, Mark C. Marino, and Jeremy Douglass

Frank O'Hara: The Poetics of Coterie
by Lytle Shaw

Renegade Poetics: Black Aesthetics and Formal Innovation in African American Poetry
by Evie Shockley

Questions of Poetics: Language Writing and Consequences
by Barrett Watten

Radical Vernacular: Lorine Niedecker and the Poetics of Place
edited by Elizabeth Willis